The Natural History of Britain and Ireland

Foreword by
Bruce Campbell

Text by
Heather Angel
Eric Duffey
John Miles
M. A. Ogilvie
Eric Simms
W. G. Teagle

The Natural History of Britain and Ireland

**Photographs by
HEATHER ANGEL**

PEERAGE BOOKS

First published in Great Britain in 1981 by
Michael Joseph Limited

This edition published in 1986 by
Peerage Books
59 Grosvenor Street
London W1

This book was designed and produced by
George Rainbird Limited
40 Park Street, London W1Y 4DE

ISBN 1 85052 064 X

Printed in Hong Kong

Frontispiece
Flowering water-crowfoot fringes the
River Bandon at Inishannon.

The illustrations opposite are details taken
from the opening photograph to each chapter
as follows:

Coastlands and islands
Intertidal seaweeds exposed by the receding
tide drape themselves over rocks on a north
Devon shore.

Freshwater wetlands
In still water, pink water ferns and green duckweeds float above filamentous green algae.

Lowland grasslands and heaths
Pink flowers of the Cornish heath bring bright
splashes of colour to the coastal heath of the
Lizard in August.

Uplands
A colourful mosaic of upland moorland
vegetation in Scotland includes red bog moss,
heather and bilberry.

Woodlands and hedgerows
Freshly fallen leaves from beech and oak trees
float on water before they are broken down
and eaten.

Towns and suburbs
Mosses and lichens make a colourful contrast
to a red brick wall bordering a town car park.

Contents

Acknowledgments

Assembling such a broad-based collection of photographs within a year would have been an impossible task without the help and assistance of numerous people. Heather Angel would like to thank everyone who so generously gave their time to answer many queries and to show her locations. She would like to thank the Nature Conservancy Council, the Forestry Commission, the National Trust and the Crown Estate Office of The Great Park, Windsor, for granting her access to certain sites. The Regional Officers and Assistant Regional Officers of the Nature Conservancy Council were particularly helpful with information concerning NCC sites. Additional information was supplied by the Norfolk Naturalists Trust, the Ecological Parks Trust and English China Clays Ltd. Many wardens and foresters advised and assisted her with photography on location. The photograph of the corn cockle was taken by kind permission of the Butser Ancient Farm Research Project Trust, Hampshire, and the Reindeer Company Ltd, Cambridge, kindly assisted with photography of the Cairngorm herd.

Information about Irish sites and subjects was not readily accessible, and so special thanks for assistance here go to: Prof. Brian Bary, Dr David Bellamy, Dr David Cabot, J. Curtis, J. J. Farrelly, Dr Roger Goodwillie, Oscar Merne, Prof. J. J. Moore, Jo Moran and Prof. David Webb.

Heather Angel would specifically like to thank the following individuals who helped with information about British sites and subjects: Alison Bolton, Gordon Booth, Robin Bovey, Colin Brown, Colin Campbell, Niall Campbell, J. Carter, Dr June Chatfield, Michael Clark, John Cresswell, Edwin Cross, Kim Debenham, Dr Frances Dipper, Ron Eastman, David Edwards, Bill Elliot, Peter Fordham, Neville Foxon, Dennis Furnell, Dr Larch Garrad, David Gowans, Lt-Col. J. P. Grant, Fiona Guinness, Jack Hammond, David Hunt, Peter Jones, Roy King, Claire Knee, Stewart Linsall, Roger Lovegrove, Peter Marren, John Mitchell, Martin Musgrove, Prof. David Nichols, Frank Pigg, Peter Reynolds, Michael Richardson, D. J. Slinn, P. G. F. Steele, Bob Sutton, Bert Taylor, Chris Taylor, John Theaker, Bobby Tulloch, Chris Tydeman, John Tyler, Tony Waddell, R. Whitta, Laurie Whittle, Trevor Williams, Steve Woods and Malcolm Wright.

Several people made bird photography at the nest possible: Alan Goodger, Richard Littleton, Iain Malin, Paul Morrison, Brian Rodgers, Vic Scott and Chris Tracey all spent considerable time in locating nests and erecting hides.

In addition, Heather Angel would especially like to thank Express Design Service for processing her films so speedily, Dorothy Herlihy for typing innumerable picture and location lists as well as picture captions, Mary Oates for her geographical advice and general help, Padraig Herlihy for his courier service, Peter Hobson for technical advice and assistance, Mary Stafford Smith for help all round at the eleventh hour, and Martin Angel for his constant involvement and help.

John Miles would like to thank Dr M. P. Harris.

W. G. Teagle would like to thank the following: Dinah Brown, C. Douglas Deane, P. G. Lansdowne and Terence Murphy.

The editors at Rainbird would like to thank the following for their help and guidance in connection with the maps: An Fóras Taluntais, Dublin; Department of Agriculture and Fisheries, Edinburgh; Department of the Environment (Map Library); Embassy of the Republic of Ireland; Emlyn Evans; Forestry Commission (particularly Mr Keith Wilson); Nature Conservancy Council, London and Edinburgh (particularly Mr Malcolm Rush); and Ordnance Survey of Ireland (particularly Mr Bernard Lewis). They would also like to thank the Clarendon Press and John Bartholomew & Son Ltd for providing information which helped them to produce the 'Coastlands and Islands' map, and the 'Freshwater Wetlands' and 'Towns and Suburbs' maps respectively.

Foreword

This is not the first book to be written about the natural history of Britain and Ireland, nor will it be the last. Even in a group of islands so closely observed for so many years, there are discoveries still to be made about the past. Also, the status of plants and animals is constantly changing, often due to man's activities but also to natural causes.

The early 1980s are as good a time as any to take stock; concern for our wildlife has never been greater and the better informed we are about all parts of Britain and Ireland, the more effective we shall be in relating the claims of the natural world to the demands of development.

This book is not directly about conservation. Its aim is to give a picture of the natural scene, treated as six different habitats. Each habitat is described in an introductory essay and the field guide sections at the end of each essay contain a selection of photographs of the characteristic flora and fauna of that habitat.

These groupings are bound to be arbitrary since nature does not work within the confines of paper, with tidy beginnings and endings. It seems reasonable, however, to start with Heather Angel's survey of coastlands and islands. She brings out the enormous differences which exist between the different coastal habitats which range from sandy beaches and weed-draped shores of a sea loch through to rocky coastlands and cliffs. Proceeding by way of an estuary, we enter the freshwater wetlands; a term used to comprehend everything from a fen to an oligotrophic lake. These are Malcolm Ogilvie's province. A specialist in wildfowl, he is also concerned with the basic factors which give freshwaters their different characters.

Wetlands often shade into lowland grasslands and then into heath. The latter should be one of our most cherished possessions since it is confined to northwest Europe and has been under attack and erosion for so long. Eric Duffey has made long-term studies of different types of grasslands and heaths and here describes these threatened habitats. Heathland shades into moorland, the dominant cover of the highland zone, which John Miles describes with enthusiasm, since it contains our nearest approaches to natural situations on land.

Eric Simms has probably walked through more woodlands than any other naturalist and has brought out their range of habitats from conifer 'thickets' to ancient oak woods. Since trees are used to embellish the urban landscape they lead on to a survey of the wildlife found in towns and suburbs, a fascinating subject which W. G. Teagle has made his own and in which there is an increasing interest.

Finally, I must pay a tribute to Heather Angel who has taken a vast majority of her photographs specially for this book over a year of hectic travel round Britain and Ireland. The results speak for themselves. They are a presentation of our much-loved countryside and its wildlife as we can see them today, if we are prepared to make the effort.

Bruce Campbell

The photographer's year

During the year I covered 48,000 kilometres by car, plane, boat, and train, visiting many locations for the first time. Before I could start taking photographs, however, an extensive location and species picture list had to be researched and compiled. This was essential in order to see the geographical spread of the sites so that a rough itinerary could be planned. Throughout the year, this list provided a firm base for photography, but it was constantly being added to as authors researched their particular areas and I saw additional sites and species.

Once I had selected the areas for the habitat shots, local contacts gave me invaluable practical advice on the optimum time to visit, points of access and necessary permits, as well as suggesting viewpoints for photography. When such help was unavailable, I scanned 1 : 50,000 Ordnance Survey maps for high viewpoints adjacent to low-level sites. If no suitable viewpoints existed I cast my eye around for a variety of alternative vantage points, which ranged from deer-stalkers' high seats and pill boxes to a car roof rack. On several occasions I used the car as a hide for photographing birds feeding away from the nest.

The main problem was that of timing. Only a limited number of subjects could be taken in the winter, so the majority had to be taken in the spring and summer of 1980. By the time this book is published in late spring 1981, last year's summer will have paled into insignificance; but right from the start, the weather was the major adverse factor which played havoc with tight schedules.

Ireland in November 1979 was superb. Beautiful autumn colours in the Killarney oak woods, with, surprisingly, only one day of rain. There was early snow on the Comeragh mountains and an afternoon's photography on the 800-metre summit of Kippure, south of Dublin, was so cold that the exposure meters lied and many of the ice and frost pictures were underexposed. However, this boded well for some exciting winter photography in the Cairngorms in January, until it turned out to be an exceptionally mild winter. Interminable days of rain obliterated the mountains. Then, a massive snowfall one night was followed by a clear, sunny day when it was a race against time to capture the snow-laden trees.

After the dismal winter, the start of the long, hot, dry spring seemed a welcome bonus. The oaks began to leaf out, but the drought continued, the acid-yellow spring growth suddenly shrivelled and turned brown; shallow-rooting plants visibly wilted. We returned to Ireland in late May. Driving to the west coast the weather was clear and bright; but the next day the drought broke and the almost continuous rain meant that even the simplest plant close-up, which normally would take a few minutes, took hours to photograph. The greater butterwort, a speciality of southwest Ireland where it is locally abundant, was a high priority subject. Finding the plant was no problem, but ankle-deep in water, in pouring rain and a stiff wind, meant endless hours of shielding the cameras with umbrellas in order to take a few one-second exposures.

Aside from weather, other unforeseen problems arose. Within minutes of starting to photograph a pair of pied wagtails which had nested in the brickwork of a bridge over the Basingstoke Canal, an Army unit arrived to make a reconnaissance of the very same bridge. A tactful word with the officer-in-charge, however, saved the situation: the men worked on the opposite side of the bridge which allowed the birds to carry on feeding and me to get my pictures.

Locating specific subjects could be very time consuming. An original telephone enquiry could lead to a dozen or more calls. From bitter experience I soon learnt that non-photographers are extremely optimistic about working distances, especially bird-watchers using powerful binoculars. It was essential to cross-question a highly confident contact so as to pre-empt any obvious snags. On the other hand, a tentative, throw-away comment could turn out to be a winner. Even habitat shots were not always straight-forward and there were several locations which I had to visit more than once. For three days I sat viewing the low cloud blanketing the beach at Borth in Wales, before the sun broke through to highlight the submerged forest. Occasionally though, luck was on my side: when visiting Blakeney, in Norfolk, for salt marsh photographs, finding a mass of painted lady butterflies feeding on sea lavender was an unexpected bonus.

I always use two camera systems since this allows for flexibility of format as well as providing insurance against a processing fault in a single stock of film. In the field I used six lenses ranging from 50mm to 350mm with the Hasselblad system, and ten lenses which ranged from 20mm to 400mm with the Nikon F2 system. In order to show birds in relation to their surrounding habitat, many of the bird photographs have been deliberately taken not using the longest focal length lens available. For the same reason several photographs of flowers and fungi were taken using a wide-angle lens to include the habitat as a backcloth.

Right from the outset I decided against using elaborate photographic techniques, so that I could concentrate completely on the subject in the viewfinder. The only picture which I did not compose was the woodmouse which took its own photograph by breaking a pair of photo trip beams after I had gone to bed. I consider lighting to be all important whether it be natural or flash.

A field notebook was essential, not only for recording detailed exposures or individual frames, but for noting time of day, aspect, dominant flora and other information; all of which proved invaluable when I came to captioning the photographs, checking information and identifying specimens. I was therefore dismayed to find the notebook was missing on return from my last visit to Cwm Idwal. A fortnight later, it miraculously came thudding through my letterbox. After two weeks' exposure to rain and wind the pages were falling apart but the notes were still quite legible.

The final collection of pictures is the outcome of a year's endeavour mixed alternately with frustration and elation as success followed failure. To attempt to illustrate the many facets of the natural history of Britain and Ireland would have been an ambitious task in a lifetime, let alone a mere fourteen-month span. So varied are these islands scenically, seasonally and in the rapid alternation of weather patterns that if the same task was repeated, even by the same person, the pictorial representation would have quite a different flavour. This wealth of variety is a heritage and a responsi-bility. If these pictures encourage us all through greater awareness to be more observant, then it has been a year well spent.

Heather Angel

Coastlands and islands

Coastlands and islands

- cliffs over 7.5 metres
- cliffs over 30 metres
- sand dunes
- salt marsh
- shingle

The changing coastline

The coastline of mainland England and Wales alone is estimated to be some 4400 kilometres in length, and the addition of the indented Scottish and Irish coastlines more than doubles this figure. The coastal scenery, as we see it today, has been shaped by the interaction of the sea with the land, by fluctuating sea levels – notably before and after the ice ages – and by erosion and deposition. It varies from spectacular rocky headlands, to boulder beaches, rock platforms, long shingle spits, sheltered sandy bays and flat muddy saltings. In the west of Britain and Ireland, the older, harder rocks dominate the rugged coastline, whereas along the less exposed coastal areas of southeastern England, large expanses of mud flats, salt marshes and sand dunes are a more common feature.

Rocky shore profiles relate closely to the geology. They may appear durable and permanent, but any faults are weak lines for pounding seas to attack and erode, to be later weathered by frost and sun. Atlantic breakers exert pressures of up to thirty tonnes per square metre during a storm. Sea stacks, arches, caves, blow holes and geos are striking features shaped by such forces. Although coastal scenery is sculptured by the sea and weather, it is the colour of the rock itself which characterizes certain regions: the Old Red Sandstone of Devon, South Wales and the Moray Firth, the chalk cliffs of Dover or the grey Lewisian gneiss of the Outer Hebrides.

On the southwestern coasts, the rock folds are at right angles to the coastline, so that the rocky headlands extend westwards in to the sea. Peninsulas separated by long rias, or drowned river valleys, are a feature of southwest Ireland. The sinking coast of Devon and Cornwall is indented with smaller rias, such as along the Tamar, Fal and Camel. In these sheltered drowned valleys, the trees grow down to tidal waters and are pruned by the high tides. Numerous sea lochs peppered with islands, typical of the West Highland coast and the Outer Hebrides, also indicate a drowned coastline, and most of the Shetland voes have originated in this way. Along parts of the Scottish coast, the sea lochs and valleys tend to run northeast–southwest, parallel with the main fault lines.

Raised beaches and submerged forests are additional coastal features which show that sea levels fluctuate. Raised beaches, which are most widespread in north Scotland, appeared as the land rose after the ice sheets melted. Where the sea level has risen relative to the shore, submerged forests are now visible only at low tide off southeast and southwest Britain as for example at Bexhill in Sussex, at Bridgwater Bay in Somerset, at Borth along the mid-Wales coast, and at Llanaber, which is the coastal part of the Snowdonia National Park.

Coastlines are ever changing. Southwest gales can over night transform a sandy cove into a shingle shore. On exposed coasts, regular gales prune all trees and shrubs into bizarre, lop-sided shapes. On sheltered rocky shores, the brown wracks festoon the rocks throughout the year, so, unlike deciduous woodland, the seasonal changes are more subtle. There are spring migrations of many invertebrate animals up the shore to spawn and others, such as prawns and shrimps, move into offshore waters in winter.

Fragmentation of rock by weathering and erosion contributes towards the building up of deposition beaches. But, not all 'sandy' beaches are pure quartz fragments; tiny pieces of shells may also accumulate as gravel. There are beaches of pure shells, notably at Mochras, south of Morfa Harlech; and 'coral' beaches, composed of fragments of coralline algae which live below low tide mark, occur in Mannin Bay in Connemara. Also in Connemara are white 'sand' beaches built up from minute shells of deep sea animals called Foraminifera.

The shape of Britain's coastline is a product of the interaction between the structure of its rocks and its exposure to the erosive power of the waves. Here at Kynance Cove in Cornwall *(above),* the powerful action of the winter storm waves can be seen. The rocks seem immutable, but after several hundred years of pounding by the sea, this view will appear substantially changed.

Once the sea breached the hard outer Jurassic limestone ramparts, differential marine erosion attacked the softer Wealden clays inside to form the circular bay of Lulworth Cove in Dorset *(left)*. The cliffs on each side of the Cove have retained the limestone ramparts. In the foreground, the rampart has been breached in three places to form the Stair Hole.

Shingle beaches

The longshore drift of sand and shingle along coastlines is caused by wave action. Shingle ridges build up at right angles to the wave direction. If waves break on a beach at an angle, the pebbles are also deposited at the same angle but the undertow drags them perpendicularly back down the shore. The direction of movement depends on the coastal contours and prevailing winds. Groynes built out at right angles to the beach help to check longshore drift. On the south coast, the shingle moves from west to east; while in east Norfolk and Suffolk the drift is from north to south. At Dungeness, the huge shingle expanse has been built up as a series of successive storm beaches.

The development of the large, shingle spit at Orfordness can be traced on maps made in the sixteenth century. It extends down the coast for nineteen kilometres from Aldeburgh and directs the flow of the rivers Alde and Butley many kilometres southwards before they enter the sea near Shingle Street, Orfordness. The adjoining island of Havergate is now the major breeding ground for avocets *Recurvirostra avosetta* which returned to breed here and at Minsmere in 1947 after an absence from Britain of almost a century. Avocets winter in Devon along the Tamar estuary.

After Dungeness, Orford Beach and Shingle Street carry the most extensive shingle flora in Britain. Most shingle deposits in Britain and Europe have no flowering plants at all partly because the spaces between the pebbles tend to be large and so water quickly drains away. But some carry a rich lichen flora. Exposed shingle beaches are also constantly pounded by the sea, and it is only when the pebbles are no longer moved around by the sea that these beaches become stabilized and then have a chance of being colonized.

Exposed at low tide, shingle cusps near Lyme Regis extend down at right angles to the shore. The unstable nature of this beach makes it inhospitable to all animals apart from microscopic organisms known as interstitial fauna, which live in a surface film of water surrounding the shingle.

The attractive oysterplant *Mertensia maritima* grows on the top of shingle and boulder beaches. This fleshy perennial is in flower from June to August; at first blue, the flowers later turn pink. The name oysterplant is derived from the distinctive taste of the fleshy leaves. Now rare in England, it is very local in Scotland and parts of northern Ireland.

The 29-kilometre long shingle spit of Chesil Beach forms a bar enclosing a freshwater lagoon known as the Fleet. Plants grow only on the stable beach crest and on the landward side of the bar because it is here that organic material can collect. Along the margin of the Fleet is a band of shrubby sea blite *Suaeda fruticosa*. At Blakeney Point in Norfolk, its seeds are carried by spring tides along the leeside of the shingle bank where they get stranded as the tide recedes. The plants, therefore, tend to grow in a series of bands which correspond to successive high tide levels. Shingle plants do not suffer from drought, for water can always be found several centimetres below the surface.

Large coastal lagoons which have formed behind a shingle bar such as Slapton Ley in Devon, and the Fleet in Dorset, are rare. Smaller lagoons, which are more frequent, include the Hebridean machair lochs, permanent dune slack ponds and pans in salt marshes. The flora of coastal lagoons depends on the salinity of the water.

Birds which nest on shingle bars include the little tern *Sterna albifrons*, the sandwich tern *S. sandvicensis* and the common tern *S. hirundo*, the oystercatcher *Haematopus ostralegus* and the ringed plover *Charadrius hiaticula*. Indeed, oystercatchers will nest in big shingle as will the common gull *Larus canus*.

Sand dunes and their flora

Sandy beaches typically develop at right angles to the direction of the prevailing wind and waves. On the north coast of Devon, Saunton Sands are backed by the extensive sand dune system of Braunton Burrows. The system shows the full succession from young dunes right through to mature dunes covered with a scrub of hawthorn *Crataegus* and blackthorn *Prunus*. Dry sand is blown inland and so builds up the dunes which are initially unstable, but begin to stabilize once pioneering plants, such as marram grass *Ammophila arenaria*, take root. Marram grass is restricted to young dunes but sea couch grass *Agropyron junceiforme*, which will tolerate short immersion in sea water, can extend down to the highest tide levels.

Typical dune plants have leaf adaptations which help to reduce water loss by evaporation: sea holly *Eryngium maritimum* has spiny leaves with a tough cuticle, rest harrow *Ononis repens* has very hairy leaves, while marram grass has leaves which roll up in drought and unroll when it rains. Further inland appear flowering plants, mosses, lichens and even fungi, which are not all restricted to living on dunes. The succession from pure marram on the seaward edge, through heath-with-marram, to birch wood can be seen in the series of dune ridges at Studland in Dorset. These dunes have cut off the Little Sea, a lake which was last flooded by the sea in the eighteenth century.

The troughs between dunes which are moist either from the water-table, which is near the surface, or from occasional flooding by the sea, are known as dune slacks. Here, localized marsh and fen plants can grow, the species varying with the quantity of calcium carbonate in the dune sand. The calcareous dunes of Braunton Burrows, Whiteford in the Gower and Newborough Warren in Anglesey have much richer floras than other non-calcareous dunes. A lime-rich or calcicolous grassland peculiar to the northern Scottish Highlands and the Outer Hebrides is the gentle undulating coastal machair which is formed from shell sand wind-blown from the dunes and the shore. It has shallow slopes with no long dune grasses.

Natural woodland does not develop on coastal dunes, but several species of pines – notably Corsican pine *Pinus nigra* var. *maritima* – have been planted extensively to help fix dunes on Culbin Sands in the Moray Firth and at Tentsmuir in Fife. The system at Culbin is the largest in Britain, while the lime-poor system at Tentsmuir has developed extensively during the last 40 years where plants, such as crowberry *Empetrum nigrum*, are abundant. Strong winds can erode the sides of stabilized dunes to form blow-outs. Repeated trampling extends the blow-outs, hindering natural stabilization of the dunes. At Oxwich in the Gower, the erection of fences and the planting of pine-branch barricades have been used to prevent erosion, and marram grass has been planted to help build up the dunes.

Many sand dunes are now used as golf links, which protects them from development. But, more important than the grass sward are the roughs which are left untouched; these act as valuable reservoirs for many plants. In Kent, lizard orchids *Himantoglossum hircinum* grow amongst marram grass; while at Berrow, clumps of marsh helleborine *Epipactis palustris* thrive in wet slacks.

Newborough Warren in Anglesey *(below right)* has the sixth largest dune system in Britain, half of which has been planted with conifers by the Forestry Commission, the remaining half surviving as a National Nature Reserve. In the wetter parts of these flats grow an interesting flora including grass of Parnassus *Parnassia palustris*, common butterwort *Pinguicula vulgaris* and round-leaved wintergreen *Pyrola rotundifolia (below left)*, seen here growing among creeping willow *Salix repens*. The dunes have not always been present at Newborough. Stormy weather during the fourteenth century carried sand inshore burying coastal farms. To help arrest the spread of the dunes into farmland, a law was passed during the reign of Queen Elizabeth I, which made it illegal to cut marram grass, seen growing in the foreground.

The painted lady is an immigrant butterfly which flies across from the Continent to Britain each year, since it cannot survive our winters. It is, therefore, often seen at the coast as here, at Blakeney in Norfolk, where it is feeding on rock sea lavender. Apart from the occasional clump of yellow horned poppy, this sea lavender was one of the first food plants available for the migrants after they had reached land.

Sand dune fauna

The grayling *Hipparchia semele* and the common blue *Polyommatus icarus* are two butterflies which frequent sand dunes. The painted lady *Vanessa cardui* and the red admiral *V. atalanta* are both migrants which annually cross the Channel to feed and breed in Britain. They are not specially attracted to sand dunes, and will feed on whatever plants are flowering when they reach landfall. These may be sea lavenders *Limonium* adjacent to the sea, or red valerian *Centranthus ruber* on coastal walls and buildings. Several species of spiders and snails occur on dunes. The latter are most conspicuous when they emerge to feed after rain. During drought, the sandhill snail *Theba pisana* remains attached to the stems of dune plants where it aestivates until the weather breaks.

Dune slacks in Merseyside are an important breeding site for the natterjack toad *Bufo calamita*, which has lost 80 per cent of its British breeding sites this century. This toad is restricted to sand dunes and heathlands, both of which have been extensively exploited for building and afforestation, and is one of the animals protected under the 1975 Wild Creatures and Wild Plants Act.

Birds which nest on sand dunes include little, Sandwich and common terns oystercatchers, ringed plovers, meadow pipits *Anthus pratensis*, skylarks *Alauda arvensis* and lapwings *Vanellus vanellus*. Cuckoos *Cuculus canorus* will lay their eggs in meadow pipit nests and, less commonly, stock doves *Columba oenas* will occupy rabbit holes. Before myxomatosis, rabbits thrived on sand dunes, but their numbers are now much reduced. Low-angled early morning or late evening light will reveal animal tracks and signs left in bare sand by wood mice *Apodemus sylvaticus*, foxes *Vulpes vulpes* and, in Dorset, the protected sand lizard *Lacerta agilis*.

Estuaries

Silt carried downstream by a river accumulates to form extensive tidal mud flats typical of estuaries. All round the coast, there are estuaries which are internationally important sites for overwintering waders and wildfowl, notably the Severn, the Cheshire Dee, Morecambe Bay, the Solway, the Wash flats and the North Bull near Dublin.

Seaweeds never flourish in estuaries and may be totally lacking. The annual, green *Enteromorpha* occurs spreading across the surface of stable mud flats; and some brown wracks will grow on flats if they can attach to rocks or to pier supports. Both *Enteromorpha* and the two species of eel grass *Zostera nana* and *Z. hornemanniana* are important foods for over-wintering brent geese *Branta bernicla*. When seen under water, the green, strap-shaped leaves of eel grass resemble under-water meadows.

The large concentrations of invertebrates which occur on the flats are winter food for wading birds from both Britain and Europe. As the tide ebbs, the birds can begin to feed. Short-legged waders such as dunlin *Calidris alpina* and knot *C. canutus* feed at the water's edge, while the longer-legged curlews *Numenius arquata* and redshank *Tringa totanus* wade out to feed. The food taken by each species is determined by the depth to which the tip of the bill reaches. Knots and dunlin, with bill lengths of between 30 and 38 millimetres and 25 and 34 millimetres respectively, both feed on small crustaceans, such as *Corophium volutator*, and worms; while the 120-millimetre-long curlew bill penetrates deep down for lugworms *Arenicola marina* and bivalve molluscs in their burrows.

The tidal flats of Morecambe Bay support the largest concentration of overwintering waders in Britain. Counts between 1957 and 1972 gave a mean

A stream beside Arch Brook Bridge is one of many which feed the Teign Estuary. The Teign, like the Tamar and Dart which also run out on to the south Devon coast, is a drowned river valley. Beyond the stream mouth stretch the estuarine mud flats. The Teign has both spring and autumn salmon runs. Eels also move up and down the Teign and beneath rocks in the stream young eels or elvers can be seen sheltering in spring and summer.

A flock of wild barnacle geese from Spitsbergen grazing on the merse in Caerlaverock National Nature Reserve in the Solway Firth. Merse is the name for a northern type of salt marsh which is pioneered by sea manna grass and which is grazed by sheep and cattle. So that the movements of individual birds can be studied, a proportion are marked with brightly coloured rings. Yellow picric acid is also used to mark the tail and this can be seen on one bird in the centre of the flock.

annual total of 235,000 waders. The Wash, with a total of over 18,000 waders is the second most important area in Britain. In addition, the Wash also supports a large flock of brent geese, pink-footed geese *Anser brachyrhynchus* and several duck, with wigeon *Anas penelope* and shelduck *Tadorna tadorna* outnumbering mallard *Anas platyrhynchos* and teal *A. crecca*. Unlike waders, geese use intertidal mud flats and sand banks for roosting at night and they move inland to feed on saltings and grassy fields. The total Spitsbergen population of barnacle geese *Branta leucopsis* overwinter in the Solway Firth where they can be observed feeding on the merse. The larger East Greenland population overwinters on the island of Islay, on the Inner Hebrides, and in the Wexford Slobs, Eire. Greenland white-fronted geese *Anser albifrons* also overwinter on Islay. All the pinkfeet which breed in Iceland and East Greenland and all the Iceland greylag geese *Anser anser* overwinter in Britain, mostly in Scotland. They arrive in October and leave for Iceland in April. At Slimbridge, the headquarters of The Wildfowl Trust, on the margins of the Severn Estuary, European white-fronts, Bewick's swans *Cygnus columbianus*, mallard and wigeon are the most numerous of the winter wildfowl.

Estuarine animals have to tolerate wide fluctuations in the salinity during the tidal cycle and during the seasonal cycle of spate and drought of the river's outflow. Sea water has a salinity of 35 parts per thousand, and there are only a few truly estuarine species living in salinities below 30 parts per thousand, but they occur in very dense concentrations. The six-millimetre-long snail *Hydrobia ulvae* which is an important food item of small-billed waders, occurs at densities up to 42,000 per square metre in the Clyde estuary. The crustacean *Corophium volutator* has been recorded in the Dovey Estuary at densities of 63,000 per square metre.

Some marine animals penetrate estuaries from the seaward end and some freshwater animals move down from the rivers. The shore crab *Carcinus maenas*, the edible mussel *Mytilus edulis*, the lugworm, the edible cockle

Cerastoderma edule, the peppery furrow shell *Scrobicularia plana* and the Baltic tellin *Macoma balthica* are all marine animals which occur in estuaries. The sludge worm *Tubifex*, normally a freshwater animal, can be so abundant in the Thames that the mud flats appear quite red. Each worm lives head downwards in a tube, with its tail projecting out and beating back and forth to drive a water current down towards the head. *Tubifex* can survive low oxygen levels and pollution so it can take full advantage of the reduced competition for food. Pintail *Anas acuta* and mallard both feed on *Tubifex* worms in the inner Thames, either by up-ending in shallow water or by walking over the exposed mud.

Fish such as the flounder *Platichthys flesus*, the grey mullet *Crenimugil labrosus* and the common goby *Pomatoschistus microps*, move up to feed in estuaries; while the European eel *Anguilla anguilla* and the Atlantic salmon *Salmo salar* both make spectacular migrations through estuaries. Eels spend most of their life in freshwater, feeding up river. During this stage they are known as yellow eels. When the male eels reach 400 millimetres, at 7 to 12 years and the females 600 millimetres, at 9 to 10 years, they move down towards the sea in late summer, usually on moonless nights after heavy rain. As they migrate, their bodies undergo changes: their bellies turn silver, their nostrils and eyes enlarge, their lateral lines become more conspicuous and their gut degenerates so they do not feed. These silver eels have never been seen spawning, but from the large numbers of their flattened Leptocephalus larvae caught in the Sargasso Sea, it is believed they spawn there. The Leptocephalus larvae are carried in the North Atlantic Drift current towards Europe. After two and a half to three years, they reach British shores and have metamorphosed into transparent glass eels or elvers. Large numbers move up the west coast estuaries in particular, and they are caught in special, boat-shaped nets in the Severn Estuary. The breeding and feeding migrations made by the Atlantic salmon are in reverse: the fish move up-river to spawn and down into the sea to feed off the Greenland coast.

Salt marshes

Along the margins of sheltered parts of estuaries, salt marshes develop. Initially, one or two plant species stabilize the mud to form the lower marsh. Most salt-marsh plants are perennials, but marsh samphire *Salicornia europaea* and sea blite *Suaeda maritima* are annuals which pioneer the unstable muddy sand along the seaward edge of marshes where they may be submerged for over 50 hours a month. Sea manna grass *Puccinellia maritima* is another early colonizer of mud flats. The most successful colonizer of bare mud is cord grass *Spartina* x *anglica*, a vigorous, fertile hybrid derived from the original sterile hybrid *S.* x *townsendii*, which is a cross between an American species *S. alternifolia* and a native species *S. maritima*, and first appeared in Southampton Water in 1870. Cord grass has great hybrid vigour, spreading rapidly by means of stolons and is now extensively planted for land reclamation.

Silt starts to accumulate around the stems and leaves of these early pioneer plants. As the deposits build up, the plants become exposed to the air for longer periods between successive tides, so other plants can invade. Natural reclamation is a slow process. To accelerate it, man plants pioneer species, drains land and erects sea walls to prevent erosion. However, more silt will be deposited giving higher quality land if the process of reclamation is not speeded up too much.

In the Wash, reclamation dates back to Roman times; since then Norfolk has gained 3240 hectares and the South Holland area of Lincolnshire 1499

hectares. Large areas in Morecambe Bay and the Solway Firth have also been reclaimed. The land on which sheep now graze on Romney Marsh was reclaimed from the sea over a period of several thousand years. Sand banks initially formed offshore in prehistoric times, marshy areas gradually developed on their landward side, then these marshes drained as the sea level dropped from about the sixth century.

On each side of Wexford Harbour in southeast Ireland, about 10,125 hectares of mud flats were reclaimed in the middle of the last century, to form the North and South Slobs. (Slob lands are alluvial flats reclaimed from water.) Resembling Dutch polders, the flat land is divided into fields separated by drainage channels. The North Slob is now grazed and cultivated. For six months of the year, half of the world's population of 12,000 Greenland white-fronted geese overwinter in the North Slob, together with several hundred Bewick's swans and other species of geese, swan and wildfowl.

A walk from the landward side of a salt marsh towards tidal water will pass through distinct zones of plants reflecting the natural succession as the land dries out. Cord grass is highly efficient at colonizing bare mud, but it

Late on a winter's afternoon, Bewick's swans and white-fronted geese gather in a stubble field on the Wexford Wildfowl Reserve in Ireland. Established in 1969, this Reserve is the overwintering ground for fifty per cent of the world's population of Greenland white-fronted geese for six months of each year. At night, the geese roost on sand banks in Wexford Harbour.

Salt marsh at Blakeney in Norfolk *(below left)* showing salt pans filled with water. Green algal mats can be seen in the pool, while sea lavender flowers colour the marsh surface in July. Growing with the sea lavender is marsh samphire and sea purslane.

Cord grass *(below right)* colonizing the mud flats near Southampton Water where this hybrid form was first recorded. This vigorous perennial reclaims land from the sea more rapidly than other pioneer plants by trapping silt in its thick clumps of stems and leaves.

grows so vigorously that few of the other salt marsh plants can invade. Sea aster *Aster tripolium*, sea lavender and thrift *Armeria maritima* colour the middle marsh in July in places where sea blite and samphire have pioneered the way. Thrift is a highly successful maritime plant; it tolerates grazing on saltings and grows well on cliff tops and rocks. On the shores of sheltered Scottish sea lochs and Irish loughs, it grows down to the upper limit of the brown wracks.

The meandering creeks of the salt marshes in the south of Britain are bordered by sea purslane *Halimione portulacoides*, a greyish-white shrub which may spill over the banks and invade the flats on either side. Salt pans develop where small drainage channels are blocked. These refill with sea water during high spring tides, but the saline water may then either be diluted by rain or concentrated by evaporation. Thus the highly variable salt concentration prevents the growth of plants in the pans. In prolonged dry weather, the water evaporates completely· and the sand cracks into typical polygonal stress patterns.

Cliffs

The best place for viewing cliff plants and birds is often from a boat rather than from the cliff top. This also applies to coastal waterfalls along the north Cornwall coast. The common flora of sea cliff ledges includes thrift, sea campion *Silene vulgaris* subsp. *maritima*, rock samphire *Crithmum maritimum* and sea plantain *Plantago maritima* as well as many lichens. More limited in distribution are roseroot *Rhodiola (Sedum) rosea*, which grows on the impressive Cliffs of Moher in Co. Clare as well as on Scottish cliffs,

The impressive cliffs of Moher in Co. Clare drop 197 metres sheer into the Atlantic and extend for eight kilometres. The base of the cliffs is shale, above which are flagstones, capped with a thick, yellow sandstone. On the cliff walls grow typical maritime plants such as thrift, sea plantain and sea campion. Various birds, including kittiwakes, razorbills, guillemots, fulmars and shags, nest on the steep walls of the cliffs.

and the hottentot fig *Carpobrotus edulis* – introduced from South Africa – and locally abundant on Cornish and Devon cliffs. Where a reasonable soil cover builds up on cliffs, a grassy sward develops, and coastal plants may intermingle with carpets of bluebells *Endymion non-scriptus* and pockets of red campion *Silene dioica*.

On exposed coasts, where the prevailing winds whip the sea spray up on to the cliff tops, the maritime lichens extend far up cliff faces. On Dale Peninsula in Dyfed, the supralittoral lichens occur in four distinct zones – each one containing an indicator species – up to 20 metres or more above Chart Datum, which is the level based on the Lowest Astronomical Tide and is used to measure the soundings on Admiralty charts. The lower limit of the supralittoral zone is the top of the black *Verrucaria maura* belt, which resembles a thin layer of dried crude oil.

Splash-zone animals may be able to live high up on very exposed cliffs. The nocturnal sea slater *Ligia oceanica* is a terrestrial animal which has penetrated the upper limit of the shore. On St Kilda, it lives 150 metres up in a sea cliff grassland. The sea slater is sensitive to light and will not emerge to feed when the full moon is shining.

Tides

The flow and ebb of the tide up and down the shore occurs twice a day in most parts of Britain. Both the times of low and high water and the range of the tide changes daily. Tide tables list all these changes. Since the moon lies closer to the earth than the sun, the tidal rhythm is primarily linked to the lunar cycle. Each fortnight, at new and full moon, the moon lies more closely in line with the sun and their combined pulls result in the big ranging spring tides (Old English *springan* meaning to rise) which alternate with the low ranging neap tides (Old English *nēpflōd*). At the time of the spring (21 March) and autumn (21 September) equinoxes, the most spectacular spring tides occur. If these tides coincide with a storm surge, severe coastal flooding may occur. The threat of this type of flooding, along the tidal Thames, is increasing because central London is slowly sinking on a bed of clay and the high tide levels are gradually increasing. They have risen by more than 60 centimetres at London Bridge during the last century. The Greater London Council's flood prevention scheme includes a rising sector gate barrier across the Thames–Woolwich reach (due to be completed at the end of 1982) and raised banks down river.

On the open coast, both the rise to high water and the fall to low water take approximately six hours. However, the lunar cycle is somewhat over 24 hours, so the times of low and high water are several minutes later on each successive tide. Also, since the tidal wave takes time to move around Britain, the time of low or high water varies from one locality to another on any one day.

The species diversity of life in the littoral zone, that is from high water of spring tides (HWST) to low water of spring tides (LWST), relates to the type of shore and its range of microhabitats, the tidal range and the degree of exposure. The tidal range is influenced by the shape of the coastline as well as the spring–neap cycle. Thus some parts of Britain experience big ranging tides, and others quite small ranging tides. The height of tides is measured in relation to Chart Datum. The Jersey port of St Helier in the Channel Islands, has a mean spring range of 9·8 metres and the north east rocky shoreline of Jersey is rich both in overall density of animals as well as species. By contrast, Lerwick in the Shetland Islands has a mean spring range of only 1·7 metres. Here, the cool summer sea-level temperatures, equal to the temperatures at an altitude of 300 metres in the central Scottish

The striking landscape above Wolf Caves, on the north coast of Jersey, in the Channel Islands, has coastal scrub extending right down the cliff tops which plunge to the rocky shore below. In April, the brown, dead, bracken fronds stand out among the dark green clumps of gorse and heather. Since this narrow strip of coastal heath is bordered on its landward side by cultivated fields, it is a valuable habitat for nesting birds. Kestrels hunt this terrain.

Highlands, enable some animals which are confined to the sublittoral zone below LWST in England to live in the littoral zone.

The means of high water spring tides and of high water neap tides are referred to as MHWST and MHWNT respectively; and the means of the low water levels as MLWST and MLWNT. Life around MLWST is exposed for only four per cent of the tidal cycle, while higher up the shore, around MLWNT, exposure is five times longer; and still higher at MHWNT, the shore is exposed for as much as 80 per cent of the cycle.

The submerged forest at Borth lies within the Dyfi National Nature Reserve on the mid-Wales coast. The 6000-year-old stumps and boles are exposed at low tide. The wood is infested with piddocks, bivalve molluscs which use their shells to bore a neat circular hole in wood and soft rocks. Honeycomb worms build their colonial reefs on the old stumps.

Origins of marine fauna

The oceans present distinct barriers to the movement of terrestrial species on and off oceanic islands. Oceans themselves have no clear boundaries within them, but five distinct zoogeographic zones can be recognized. These are the tropical, sub-tropical, warm and cold water temperate and polar zones. Britain lies within the cold water temperate or boreal zone. In addition, our shores are washed by warm temperate or Lusitanian waters and by cold Arctic waters.

The English Channel is the southern limit of the boreal zone, and the marine life of the Channel Islands is particularly interesting since it is the northern limit for several Lusitanian species typical of more southern European regions. In this category is the ormer *Haliotis tuberculata* which is a Channel Island delicacy. The distribution of Lusitanian species is limited within a certain sea water temperature range, so the boundaries of this and other zones will fluctuate with changing climate. Lusitanian species with planktonic larvae may be able to feed, grow and develop into

The limestone outcrop which has made the Burren in Co. Clare an internationally famous botanical site extends down on to the shore. Here, the rock surface has been eroded into irregular shapes, assisted by the rock urchins in the shallow pools. The dark purple urchins adorn themselves with shell and rock fragments, held in position above their upper surfaces with suckered tube feet; as they rotate, they grind out small pits in the soft rock. This warm-water species which is common in the Mediterranean, is able to live in Irish waters which are washed by the warm, North Atlantic Drift current. Acorn barnacles, dog whelks and mussels can be seen on the exposed rock.

adults in British waters; but only in exceptionally warm summers are they able to breed off Britain. So, the warm North Atlantic Drift current which flows northwards up the west coast of Britain and Ireland enables the spiny starfish *Marthasterias glacialis* to live in water off the southwest of Britain; the common octopus *Octopus vulgaris* to penetrate the English Channel and the rock sea urchin *Paracentrotus lividus*, well known to divers in the Mediterranean, to live off western Ireland both in the littoral zone and below. The Burren in Co. Clare is renowned by botanists the world over for its arctic–alpine plants which grow on the grassy swards on top of the limestone and in the grykes of the pavement; but the shoreline is equally intriguing. Here the limestone has been weathered into irregular shapes which tear at flimsy footwear. Large, shallow pools at LWST are pitted with hollows each made by a rock sea urchin rotating in the soft limestone.

Strandlines

The North Atlantic Drift sometimes carries tropical beans from the West Indies which get beached in the strandlines on our southwest beaches. In west Wales, mothers used these outsize beans to help cut their babies' teeth. This current may also bring floating planktonic animals such as the violet sea snails *Janthina* which are buoyed up by their bubble raft, the stalked goose barnacles *Lepas*, the stinging Portuguese man-o'-war *Physalia physalis* and various jellyfish.

Around Britain, sandhoppers *Talitrus* are permanent inhabitants of the strandline, living beneath the rotting beached seaweeds. Turnstones *Arenaria interpres* energetically feed on these crustaceans by flipping up the

A sandhopper's eye view of the incoming tide washing the shell strandline further up a sandy beach on Samson, in the Isles of Scilly, in April. Among the limpet shells are yellow, orange and brown flat-topped winkles, rough winkles and cockle shells, as well as portions of egg wrack *Ascophyllum nodosum.*

seaweed or turning over stones. As sandhoppers are nocturnal, when exposed to the light, they move rapidly – by a series of random leaps – under cover. Kelp flies *Coelopa*, which rest on top of beached seaweed and rise up as a cloud when disturbed, are much more conspicuous. They also make mass migrations, for short distances, less than a metre above the shore.

Beached seaweeds are utilized by man as a natural fertilizer; and by sheep and cattle, as an additional food source on the shores around northern Scotland and the offshore islands. The 2000 sheep on North Ronaldsay, the most northerly of the Orkney group, are confined to the foreshore. They are kept off the grass and arable lands by an approximately two-metre-high stone dyke built around the 19-kilometre island perimeter. Here, they feed solely on seaweeds; moving down to browse in the littoral zone during low tides in the summer, but taking advantage of seaweeds piled up at the top of the shore after winter storms.

Rocky shores

The most widespread coastal habitat is the rocky shore; it dominates the west and north coasts. Sheltered shores with a variety of niches such as crevices, pools, rocky overhangs, boulders and gulleys support a large diversity of species, most of which are not obviously visible during low tide exposure. Molluscs and crabs, with hard outer coverings, are more resistant to the drying action of wind and sun than soft-bodied sea anemones, worms and sea slugs; even so, many molluscs and crabs tend to move beneath the moist seaweed blanket or into pools and crevices so they are not exposed on a sunny day. On overcast still days, exposed flat-topped winkles *Littorina littoralis* will stay crawling and feeding on brown wracks; and even limpets will continue to crawl over rocks – especially north facing ones – when they can be heard rasping at the algal film with their toothed radulas (or 'tongues'). Generally, littoral animals cease feeding when exposed to the air. Low tide is a time when filter-feeders are forced to stop feeding because they are not covered by food-carrying water, and even scavengers and predators tend to rest before becoming active again as the tide rises.

Animals in rock pools can continue feeding during low tide, but on warm days as the water warms up there is less available oxygen so they need to conserve their energy. Also, on hot days, the salinity of water in pools is

Loch Eynort in South Uist is a long, sea-water loch which extends westwards from the east coast. The small tidal range exposes a narrow band of brown algae at low tide. Above the algal zone is a conspicuous band of white lichens beneath the green vegetation.

increased by evaporation, whereas a shower of rain will decrease it. Pools low down the shore are subjected to much less dramatic temperature and salinity fluctuations, and so support a much richer assortment of marine life than the high-level pools.

Crevices formed by weathering of rocks provide sheltered hide-outs for both marine and terrestrial animals. Marine bristletails *Petrobius maritimus*, which are primitive wingless insects related to silverfish, live in splash-zone crevices. The slate-blue springtail *Anurida maritima* is another marine insect which survives being submerged during high tide and can be found crawling over rocks and on the surface film of rock pools.

Loch Creran *(left)* is a sea loch on the west coast of Scotland, north of Oban, which follows the diagonal line of the Great Glen to the south. In the foreground, egg wrack *Ascophyllum nodosum* is one of the partly exposed brown wracks. The large bladders, arranged singly down the stem, buoy up the seaweed with the rising tide.

Caves, which are much enlarged versions of crevices, offer protection for rock-clinging animals from buffeting waves. Where the sea carries abundant plankton (the microscopic plants and animals which drift in the surface waters) into a cave, the walls are lined with an abundance of colourful filter-feeding invertebrates such as sponges, hydroids, sea anemones and sea squirts. As adults, these soft-bodied, sessile animals are fixed for life and so their planktonic larvae favour sheltered, shady sites, such as caves or rocky overhangs, on which to settle.

The distribution of rocky-shore animals (as well as seaweeds) is directly related to the amount of exposure they can tolerate. As with plant communities on land, certain species predominate. In the same way as alpine plants are zoned up a mountain, dominant marine species are zoned down the shore. The limits of marine zones are determined by many factors including exposure, climate, type of substrate, time of low water and competition between species. Where there is a small tidal range, as on the west coast of Scotland, the zones are compressed so that they are very clearly visible, with a lower zone of brown wracks, above which is a beige barnacle zone, followed by a black lichen zone and topped by green terrestrial plants.

On exposed coasts, the effective height of the tides is considerably increased by wave action. This means that acorn barnacles can live higher up the shore. They can filter-feed only when submerged because only then can the hairs on their legs trap food carried in the water. *Balanus balanoides* is a common intertidal barnacle which lives for three to five years depending on where it settles on the shore. Barnacles which settle low down on the shore are submerged for more of the tidal cycle and so can feed for a longer period. They grow more quickly and are able to breed after only one year, but they die after three years. Those which settle higher up the shore are exposed for longer and so can spend less time feeding during each tidal cycle. They grow more slowly, taking two years to reach breeding size, but

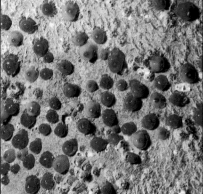

When exposed to the air, beadlet sea anemones *(above)* contract down to unattractive blobs of jelly. When covered by water, the tentacles unfold from the central mouth, ready to capture passing prey. These anemones were living on the inner walls of a cave on Sark.

On the north coast of Scotland, in Sutherland, Smoo Cave *(right)* is a striking feature of the Durness limestone, which dates back to the Cambrian. Ferns and liverworts flourish on the end wall which gets some light thrown on it via holes in the cave roof.

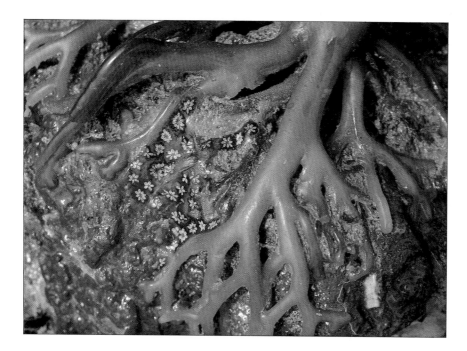

Brown seaweeds are attached to a firm substrate such as rock, by a basal disc known as a holdfast. The oarweed has an elaborate, branching holdfast which provides a place for small crabs, worms, molluscs and even fish to take shelter. Sea squirts, such as this star sea squirt, *Botryllus schlosseri,* sponges and hydroids often grow attached to the outside of holdfasts. In very stormy weather, holdfasts of sublittoral algae get pulled from the rocks and beached on the shore.

live for five years. Although there is less variety of animal species living on exposed rocky coasts as compared with sheltered ones, the densities of the animals are often greater.

Mussels, like barnacles, are filter-feeders whereas limpets and winkles are herbivorous browsers. On exposed shores, dog whelks often congregate in vertical crevices to shelter from rough seas, spreading out during high tide to prey on barnacles and mussels. The seaweeds typical of these exposed coasts, such as tangle *Laminaria digitata* and the edible dabberlocks *Alaria esculenta,* are attached to the rock by strong basal holdfasts.

Rocky shores are less attractive to birds than mud flats or sandy beaches, but there are a few characteristic species. Oystercatchers commonly pick over the shore, feeding on mussels, and purple sandpipers *Calidris maritima* consume crabs, winkles and dog whelks. The only small passerine uniquely adapted to shore life in all seasons is the rock pipit *Anthus spinoletta.* It breeds on sheltered rocky headlands, in sea lochs or on exposed cliffs, but tends to winter on beaches where there is rotting seaweed full of invertebrate life.

The shore at night

Bioluminescence is common among marine organisms. The cold light is produced chemically by the oxidation of a substance called luciferin. Blooms of the microscopic dinoflagellate *Noctiluca miliaris* produce the summer phosphorescence seen on the surface and in waves breaking on the shore at night. The jellyfish *Pelagia noctiluca* which sometimes occurs in southwestern waters, produces a strongly luminescent slime, which will persist on the hands of anyone who touches it.

Inhabitants of rocky shores are much more active during a low tide at night than by day. Limpets no longer have to clamp tightly to rocks to conserve moisture, so they are able to crawl around to feed. Hunting shore crabs *Carcinus maenas* find the active limpets and the green leafworms *Eulalia viridis* easy prey. In rock pools, prawns and fish leave the cover of the seaweeds to feed out in the open. At the top of the shore, sea slaters emerge from their damp daytime hideouts to forage on the small, brown, channelled wrack *Pelvetia canaliculata* and on animal remains.

Flashlight illuminates a sight not often seen by day – a limpet browsing on a rocky shore at night. As it moves forward with outstretched tentacles, the shell is lifted well clear of the rock surface.

This magnificent stretch of white sand can be seen at Dog's Bay Strand in Connemara. The beach is built up from the shells of tiny, deep-sea animals known as Foraminifera instead of quartz grains. As many as 124 species of Foraminifera have been identified on this beach. The Strand is one side of a tombola which connects a granitic island to the mainland.

Sandy beaches

Flat, sandy beaches occur all round Britain wherever particles accumulate in bays or sheltered stretches. They may be backed by shingle ridges and beach cusps. The scale of the map shown on page 12 makes it impossible to show all the small sandy coves nestling between cliffs which occur around the coastline.

Flat expanses of sand exposed at low tide appear barren of life. Indeed, where the beach is constantly pounded by heavy surf, the sand gets churned up by the sea, and little life can survive. Where conditions are more sheltered, detritus accumulates and enriches the sand, and a rich assortment of animals occurs. But since there are no seaweeds, boulders or pools to provide shelter from desiccation, sand-beach fauna burrows down into the sand with the ebbing tide. The fauna is dominated by marine bristle worms or polychaetes, and bivalve molluscs. Although the animals are out of sight, they do leave various clues on the sand surface. The ends of tubes constructed by sedentary polychaetes project above the sand, while many mollusc burrows remain open at the surface. The keyhole openings of

Sea sandwort *Honkenya peploides* and the pink-flowered sea milkwort *Glaux maritima* are both perennial plants which will invade bare sand at the top of the shore. Growing together here with beached bladder wrack and wood they make a natural still life in Brandon Bay, Eire in June. Sea sandwort, which is much more widespread than sea milkwort, can form immature dunes by trapping sand among its fleshy leaves.

razorshell *Ensis* burrows are distinctive, and are quickly pin-pointed if a razorshell squirts out a jet of water as it burrows deeper in response to vibrations from a person walking nearby.

Most animals are either suspension-feeders (fan worms and many bivalves) which trap food particles carried in sea water, or deposit-feeders (some polychaetes, bivalves with long breathing and feeding tubes or siphons, and the heart urchin *Echinocardium cordatum*) which ingest detritus from the beach surface. When submerged, peacock worms *Sabella pavonina* unfold their fan of tentacles from the ends of their tubes, and bivalves, such as razorshells and edible cockles *Cerastoderma edule*, move up just below the sand surface, open their shells and extend their siphons above the sand. Water is drawn in through one siphon, the suspended detritus filtered off by the gills inside, and the water is then ejected out of the second, smaller siphon. Lugworms are deposit-feeders. They sit in their U-shaped burrows swallowing large amounts of muddy sand. They have to feed for five to eight hours each day to glean enough food. The sand mason worm *Lanice conchilega* uses long, fine tentacles, which emerge from the tufted end of its sand-grain tube, to wipe detritus off the tube branches and also to collect it from the beach surface. The density of sand mason worms is so great on some Jersey shores that their exposed tube ends resemble a forest of miniature sand trees.

Despite living buried in the sand, many of the particle-feeders fall prey to the carnivores. The necklace shells *Natica* and the burrowing starfish *Astropecten irregularis* both feed on burrowing bivalves; *Natica* bores a hole through one shell to reach the food, while *Astropecten* consumes bivalves whole, later ejecting the shells. In spring, the pliable, sandy, egg-collars, which are laid by necklace shells, can be found low down on sandy beaches. Other predators include fish which swim up over flats with the rising tide. By day, shrimps *Crangon crangon* bury themselves beneath the sand, but emerge during high water at night to feed on small crustaceans, worms and even small fish. The masked crab *Corystes cassivelaunus* is another nocturnal hunter which feeds indiscriminately on any prey it can grasp with its pincers.

In the southwest, where rocks extend down into the lower part of sandy beaches, honeycomb worms *Sabellaria alveolata* construct their communal sand reefs by glueing together sand grains churned up by the sea. The yellowish reefs are quite hard and may reach up to 60 centimetres across, when they become more susceptible to being broken up by storms.

Exposed at low tide are the tufted ends of sand mason tubes on a Jersey shore. This close-up shows how larger grains are selected for the cylindrical tube and smaller ones for the branching tuft. When covered by sea water, the worm extends long tentacles from the centre of the tufted end, which are used for feeding and picking up sand grains. The grains are then sorted by bilobed lips around the mouth and cemented together with a mucus secretion.

The island archipelago landscape of Clew Bay, Co. Mayo, seen from Croagh Patrick in November, with distant snow-capped mountains. The islands were formed when the sea level rose and partially submerged a drumlin swarm. Fierce Atlantic breakers have completely destroyed the westernmost islands, and continue to attack the seaward ones, so that the steep cliffs plunge into the sea on the west coasts and the gentle slopes remain only on the east sides.

Island origins

The western and northern coastlines of Britain and Ireland are dotted with offshore islands whereas, apart from the Isle of Wight, no large islands lie off the southern or eastern coasts. Most of the rocks along the south and east are soft, and because they weather easily, they do not persist as small islands. However, the hard, igneous rocks of the Farne Islands off the Northumberland coast survive buffeting by the North Sea. The drowning of the west Irish and Scottish coastlines has resulted in the formation of copious islands – notably the Outer Hebrides.

Apart from Rockall, all the islands of Britain and Ireland lie on the Continental Shelf fairly close to the mainland, and their geological affinities with the mainland are readily appreciated on a geological map. The same igneous granitic rocks that form Lands End also make up the Isles of Scilly, 43 kilometres southwest. The Devonian Old Red Sandstone of Caithness extends northwards throughout most of the Orkney group; whereas most of the more distant Shetland group are made of much older metamorphic rocks, chiefly gneisses. The Carboniferous limestone, which is a significant feature of Irish geology, outcrops in the Burren and extends out to form the offshore Aran Islands, where some of the Burren limestone plants occur.

Islands around Britain and Ireland have been formed by the sea cutting through the narrow neck of a peninsula to leave an isolated headland; by the sea level rising and isolating high points as islands; and by the sea level falling to expose sand or shingle banks or rocky reefs. Most of the islands were separated from the mainland by rising sea levels after the last ice age.

Speciation of island animals

When differently sized islands of similar terrain and latitude are compared, it becomes apparent that the larger islands can potentially support more animal species. These islands have a bigger surface area and longer coastline for potential colonization, as well as a wider range of available habitats. There is a direct correlation between the number of species of wild small mammals surviving and the size of the individual islands. Four species of wild small mammals occur in Jersey (117,000 hectares); whereas Guernsey (48,000 hectares) supports three species, and Sark (5000 hectares) and Herm (240 hectares) each have two species of their own. The Channel Islands were never covered by ice, and the water which separates them from the French coast is quite shallow so that within the last few thousand years the islands would have been connected to the Normandy coastline.

But as well as size, the geological history of an island can be an important limiting factor. For example, Ireland and the Isle of Man were both cut off from mainland Britain by rising sea levels before many mammals had moved up from the southern mainland after the last ice age, and each possess only a few native small mammals, which include the pygmy shrew *Sorex minutus* and the hedgehog *Erinaceus europaeus*. Apart from bats which can fly over water, other land mammals have been introduced both accidentally and deliberately by man.

The isolation of a small breeding population reduces the potential gene flow within the population. But the likelihood is that predators will be fewer, or even totally absent, and there will be far less competition for food or living space. The mechanisms whereby natural selection operated are weakened, so, as the individuals adapt to the local environment, the conditions are right for the population genetically to drift away from its parent stock. Initially, differences are slight, but eventually the stock may be recognized as a distinct subspecies. Once the differences become large enough for the island animals to be genetically or behaviourally incompatible with the parent stock, they become a new species.

On many islands, distinct subspecies of small mammals exist. The Scilly shrew *Crocidura suaveolens cassiteridum* is a subspecies of the European lesser white-toothed shrew. Another subspecies *C.s suaveolens* occurs in Jersey and Sark in the Channel Islands. The Orkney and Guernsey voles are both subspecies of the European vole *Microtus arvalis* which does not occur in Britain; whereas the Skomer vole *Clethrionomys glareolus skomerensis* is one of the four island races of the mainland bank vole. Several subspecies of the wood mouse *Apodemus sylvaticus* occur on islands: *A.s. thuleo* on Foula, *A.s. granti* on Yell, *A.s. fridariensis* on Fair Isle, *A.s. hirtensis* on St Kilda and *A.s. hamiltoni* on Rum. The wood mice on Yell show more affinities with Norwegian wood mice than Scottish ones, and it seems that the Yell population originated from Norway, and later colonized other islands in the Shetland group and the west coast islands when boats frequently traded up and down the coast. Probably accidentally, man has been the agent of spread.

The Shetland wren *Troglodytes troglodytes zetlandicus* and the St Kilda wren *T.t. hirtensis* are examples of birds which have been isolated from the mainland breeding stock long enough to have evolved into distinct races. Shrubs and trees began to invade St Kilda some 7000 years ago and wrens probably colonized the island shortly afterwards; since then local variations in the size, the song, the plumage, as well as the habits developed. St Kilda is one of the more remote outlying groups of islands and stacks which lie off the coast of Scotland.

Compared with the mainland, islands, by nature of their size and reduction in habitats, support fewer species of plants and animals. The number of species of regularly breeding birds decreases with distance from the mainland. In the Cairngorms (25,000 hectares) there are 69 species; on the Isle of Rum (11,000 hectares, 24 kilometres off the mainland) the total is 40 species of land birds and 14 species of sea birds, and on St Kilda (875 hectares and 72 kilometres west of North Uist) it has dropped to 25 species of which 17 are sea-bird species. Rum is an island National Nature Reserve to which access is controlled. Much research has been done on the vegetation and fauna of this island; notably a lengthy study on the ecology and behaviour of the red deer *Cervus elaphus* population, involving marking individuals with coloured collars and ear tags.

Red deer graze at Kilmory on the Isle of Rum in July. Beyond the sea are the Skye Cuillins which are snow-capped in winter. The biology and ecology of these deer have been extensively studied over a period of many years on this island National Nature Reserve. The stags lose the velvet covering on their antlers in August, so they become hardened ready for inter-male rivalry during the autumnal rut. The antlers are cast after the rut and new ones begin to grow almost immediately.

Rum is one of the Inner Hebridean islands. To the north lies Skye, the largest of the Inner Hebrides, with spectacular mountains which offer much more of interest to the geologist than to the naturalist. Interesting alpine plants grow on the mountains, but the sea cliffs do not attract large numbers of nesting sea birds. To the south, the main islands are Mull, Jura and Islay. Like Skye, Mull has spectacular scenery and attracts breeding golden eagles *Aquila chrysaetos*.

Island climate and vegetation

The climate of islands is reflected in the flora. The Isles of Scilly lie on latitude 49°N and have a warm oceanic climate with the mildest winters in Britain where frosts are a rarity. There is only a 9·2 Centigrade difference between the average temperature for August (16·5°C) and February (7·3°C). As on the extreme west of Ireland, Scilly has an average of over 350 days a year with the air temperature exceeding 5°C. Subtropical plants from the Canaries and New Zealand thrive in the Tresco gardens and the commercial spring bulbs flower well before those on the mainland. But, in common with many islands, the Isles of Scilly are frequently subjected to strong winds. Gales occur throughout the year, albeit more frequently in winter. The bulb fields are protected from wind by tall wind-breaks especially of the New Zealand plant karo *Pittosporum crassifolium*, which is now a naturalized alien.

The dwarf pansy *Viola kitaibeliana* is a Mediterranean plant which occurs on the west coast of France, the Isles of Scilly and the Channel Islands, but not on mainland Britain. Natural introduction of plant species to islands takes place by the dispersal of seeds and fruits by air and water, as well as by transportation on birds' feet or undigested in their crops. The mild Scilly and Channel Island winters have encouraged the deliberate introduction of many colourful exotics. Once established, they add colour and variety to the local flora. However, the aggressive competitive vigour of some aliens can make their introduction an ecological disaster. The three-cornered leek, *Allium triquetrum*, which is now a feature of Scilly walls, was probably first introduced as a garden plant at the end of the last century. All attempts to eradicate it have failed. Within the last century, some 700 new species of naturalized plants have been recorded in the Channel Islands alone.

Regular exposure to gales makes it difficult for trees to survive and grow on islands, except where they have been carefully planted and nurtured by man. The shelter belts planted at Kergord in the Weisdale valley on the Shetland mainland are the most extensive plantings in the islands where gales (when the wind exceeds 61 kilometres per hour for more than one hour) occur on an average of 58 days in a year. It is not only trees that suffer from exposure to gales; gorse *Ulex europaeus*, *U. gallii* and heather *Calluna vulgaris* grow on the lee side of boulders on Tresco.

Sea birds

Gulls, more than any other sea birds, dominate the coast. There are few places where the piercing, wailing call of the herring gull *Larus argentatus* cannot be heard in summer since it breeds all round the coast of Britain and Ireland except for an almost continuous stretch from south Yorkshire to the Thames estuary. In winter, many move into towns to feed on refuse tips. The largest of the breeding gulls in Britain, the great black-backed *L. marinus*, will scavenge as well. It also preys on the eggs and young of other birds, especially Manx shearwaters *Puffinus puffinus* and puffins *Fratercula arctica* if they are nesting neighbours. Unlike herring and lesser black-

The three-cornered leek is very much a feature of the walls and bulb fields in the Isles of Scilly when it flowers in April. This naturalized alien is a native of the west Mediterranean. Introduced as a garden plant at the beginning of the century, it has spread explosively throughout the islands. In the Scillies, it is known locally as white bluebell. It also occurs in the Channel Islands, southwest England, south Wales and south Ireland where it is generally on the increase.

One of the most distinctive of all sea birds, the puffin stands with a beakful of sand eels on Skomer. Puffins feed by diving from the sea surface, using their wings to move through the water and usually returning to their burrows with the catch, early in the morning or late in the afternoon.

backed gulls *L. fuscus*, great black-backed gulls have only rarely bred inland in Britain. The common gull *L. canus*, which is far outnumbered by both herring and black-headed gulls *L. ridibundus*, is very much a northern species nesting inland on moors and beside water, as well as on the coast. Like the herring gull, it will drop bivalve molluscs from the air to break open the shells. The gull which breeds most successfully inland is the black-headed gull, which loses its dark brown head in winter. During the last century, this gull was severely threatened by shooting and egg collection but between 1938 and 1973 the population almost trebled.

Offshore sea stacks are used by many other nesting sea birds in preference to mainland cliff tops because there is less disturbance. Guillemots *Uria aalge* and razorbills *Alca torda* favour stacks as well as steep rocky over-hanging cliffs. Nesting guillemots may pack so tightly together on top of a stack, that any sudden disturbance may cause the birds to dislodge their eggs over the side. Cliff ledges are used for nesting by kittiwakes *Rissa tridactyla*, shags *Phalacrocorax aristotelis* and fulmars *Fulmarus glacialis*.

Empty rabbit burrows may be taken over by nesting puffins and Manx shearwaters. Towards the end of the day puffins may be seen returning to their burrows, with a row of sand eels *Ammodytes* clamped in their brilliantly coloured bills, waddling across a pink carpet of thrift flowers. If the surface vegetation is eroded by trampling, the roofs of nest burrows can become very friable and may collapse. On Skomer, off Dyfed, access to cliff top sites has had to be restricted because of this danger.

Except in bright moonlight, Manx shearwaters leave their burrows at night to feed at sea on small fish. Late in the day they assemble in huge rafts on the sea offshore. At night fall, they return to relieve their mates, emitting eerie, screeching calls to announce their presence. Shearwaters usually nest on small islands, and if the soil is soft they are able to excavate their own burrows. On the Isle of Rum, south of Skye, over 100,000 pairs nest three kilometres inland at an altitude of over 650 metres.

Off the west Dyfed coast lie several, famous, sea bird islands. Skokholm, Skomer, Ramsey and St Margaret's Islands are relatively close to the main-land, whereas the low, basaltic rock of Grassholm is 22 kilometres offshore. Rabbits were introduced to Skokholm and Skomer in the winter of 1387–8 and formed important warrens on both islands in the Middle Ages. They are still there today. On Skokholm, where the Old Red Sandstone rocks make an attractive setting for both birds and vegetation, there have been extensive studies of the large Manx shearwater colony of 35,000 pairs which nest in the old rabbit holes; 600 pairs of storm petrels *Hydrobates pelagicus* also nest there. Many birds pass through Skokholm on migration; in October large numbers of finches and thrushes predominate. Skomer, the largest and most accessible of the near islands, has a huge breeding colony of Manx shearwaters (50,000–60,000 pairs) and, in common with Skokholm, large numbers of guillemots, razorbills and puffins. Ramsey has high densities of breeding choughs *Pyrrhocorax pyrrhocorax*, ravens *Corvus corax* and common buzzards *Buteo buteo*, as well as sea birds. A large colony of cormorants *Phalacrocorax carbo* breeds on St Margaret's. Several sea birds nest on Grassholm, but it is most famous for its gannet *Sula bassana* colony (15,000 pairs) which is one of the seventeen occupied gannetries in Britain and Ireland. In all, they carry over 140,000 pairs which is over 70 per cent of the world population, with St Kilda (59,000) carrying more than 40 per cent. Other island gannetries occur off Alderney in the Channel Islands, on the Bass Rock in East Lothian, Ailsa Craig in Ayrshire, Hermaness and Noss in Shetland, Sula Sgeir (an isolated stack, where the young gannets are collected by inhabitants of Ness on the Isle of Lewis) and Sule Stack in

Orkney. Bempton Cliffs in Yorkshire support the sole mainland colony of gannets in Britain. The largest gannetry in Ireland is on Little Skellig in Co. Kerry with much smaller colonies on Bull Rock in Co. Cork and Great Saltee in Co. Wexford. Great Saltee is the larger of a pair of important Irish sea-bird islands. The Saltees also support many inland breeding birds and provide an important landfall for passage migrants. It is remarkable that 218 of the 375 species of birds on the Irish list have been recorded on these two islands which only cover an area of just over 125 hectares.

Fair Isle, the most southern island of the Shetland group, a mere five kilometres long and two and a half kilometres wide, attracts large numbers of birds. More than 320 species, which represents well over half of the British list, have been recorded. These include many passage migrants which use the island as a landfall on their journeys to and from their breeding grounds. The migration routes for birds that breed in Iceland, Greenland and the Faeroes as well as those that breed in the Arctic, Scandinavia and Russia, meet at Fair Isle. In the spring, they pass quickly through on their way to their northern breeding grounds, whereas in the autumn they rest for longer before moving on. As well as these regular migrants, irregular bird visitors descend on Fair Isle when unfavourable weather in the north drives them south. Fair Isle, with the Isles of Scilly and other outlying islands, are welcome landfalls for rare migrants which get blown off course.

In June, every available ledge is occupied by breeding sea birds on Great Saltee island, off southeast Ireland. At the southern end of the island, a portion of dissected boulder clay cliff painted with the white guano from nesting gannets, guillemots and kittiwakes, makes a distinct mosaic. The kittiwake nests are quite conspicuous to the right of the picture, and the gannet nests are also visible on the left, but the tightly packed guillemots do not build nests.

The Farne Islands group comprises 28 rocky islands but it is on only three – Inner Farne, Brownsman and Staple – that large numbers of kittiwakes, puffins, shags and guillemots nest. Four species of terns: common, arctic *Sterna paradisea*, Sandwich and roseate *Sterna dougallii*, nest only on Brownsman and Inner Farne, as well as eiders *Somateria mollissima*. The Farnes are one of the most southern breeding sites in Britain and Ireland for this duck, which is widespread around the Scottish mainland and offshore islands. At the end of March, rafts of eiders assemble there inshore before nesting along the coasts and up to several kilometres inland. After the ducklings hatch in June, they swim around in the sea, closely supervised as they feed under water among the brown wracks.

Marine mammals

Sharing some of the sea-water lochs and voes with eiders, are the otters *Lutra lutra* which are almost exclusively marine mammals in northern Scotland. Around Fetlar in Shetland, they feed mainly on fish, but also on crabs and duck. In estuaries, they feed on migrating eel and salmon and they have been caught in crab and lobster pots. Two or three young are reared in a shelter, known as a holt, behind boulders or, where they live inland, behind tree roots lining river banks.

Seals, dolphins and whales are exclusively marine mammals. Both common and grey seals breed around Britain and Ireland, whereas dolphins and whales are casual visitors. Common seals *Phoca vitulina* breed in the Wash, Shetland, Orkney, the east and west Scottish coasts, including the Inner and Outer Hebrides, and northern Ireland. The single pup which is born in mid-summer can swim and dive at birth. Grey seal *Halichoerus grypus* pups are generally born later in the year in the autumn, but occasionally earlier. The main grey seal breeding grounds in Britain are along the Dyfed coast and outlying islands, the Isles of Scilly, the Farne Islands, the Inner and Outer Hebrides, North Rona and Orkney and, in Ireland, on Clare Island, Great Saltee and Lambay Island. Ramsey has the largest Welsh breeding colony of Atlantic grey seals.

Seals exemplify some of the problems of marine conservation. Recently, climatic conditions have favoured their survival and the populations of grey seals have greatly increased, much to the annoyance of inshore fishermen who view them as a serious threat to their livelihoods. The plan to cull the populations met with a public outcry. However, the outcry is muted when the country's economic health requires the building of a huge oil terminal at Sullom Voe, the transportation of dangerously lethal chemicals, or maybe the construction of a tidal barrage across the Severn Estuary or Morecambe Bay. The outcry against whaling is deafening, but who is concerned for barnacles, limpets and seaweeds? Yet such marine life threatened by oil pollution, toxic substances within industrial effluents, heat from power stations, untreated sewage and the development of the coastline for ports, leisure and industry, may in the long term be more important in maintaining the general balance of our ecosystem.

Feeding on sandy beaches

Apart from the carnivorous animals, the fauna of sandy beaches gleans its food either by straining particles from the sea water, or by feeding on detritus or bacterial growth in the sand itself. Detritus feeders not only include worms and bivalve molluscs which live buried in the beach, but also sandhoppers which feed on seaweed beached in the strandline. Detached seaweeds, from rocky areas, and other debris are left stranded by the receding tide at the high water mark on all beaches. However, it is on flat sandy beaches, wherever these strandlines are continuous and conspicuous, that birds can be seen foraging systematically along the line. As the tidal range decreases from springs to neaps, successive strandlines are left on the shore. Large, attached seaweeds are absent from sandy beaches except where there are rocks or breakwaters, but microscopic plants are present either as plankton suspended in the water or as green-brown films on the sand surface. Like seaweeds, these microscopic algae are primary producers on which the herbivores graze. In turn, these herbivorous animals fall prey to carnivores.

The best surfing beaches, where the waves constantly crash down, are almost devoid of worms and molluscs since the light detritus particles do not settle out with the heavier sand grains. In more sheltered bays where detritus accumulates in greater quantities the density of the beach fauna correspondingly increases. Fish such as dab, sole, turbot, sand eels, sand goby and young flat fish swim into sandy bays to feed at high tide. Birds, however, fly in to feed as the tide falls. They feed on small crustaceans, polychaetes and molluscs. Both are attracted in by the abundance of potential food. The size of the sand grains is an important factor affecting the colonization of many burrowing animals, especially for those worms which select a particular grain size for the construction of their tubes.

1

1 On Tresco in the Isles of Scilly, turnstones *Arenaria interpres* forage back and forth along the strandline at the top of the shore. The short, stout bill is used to flick up seaweed or turn over shells, stones or wood in the search for sandhoppers and other food.

2

2 This marine terebellid worm *Polymnia* lives in a flimsy tube made from mud and bits of gravel which it builds on the undersides of rocks and boulders resting on muddy sand. It emerges from the open end of the tube to feed by extending long tentacles over the beach surface to pick up detritus. Also visible is the pair of red, branching gills.

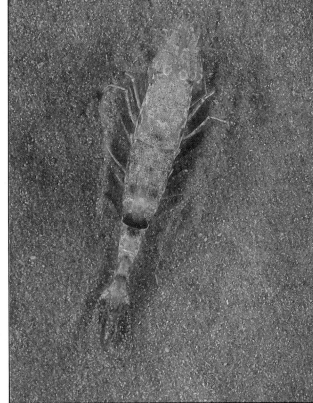

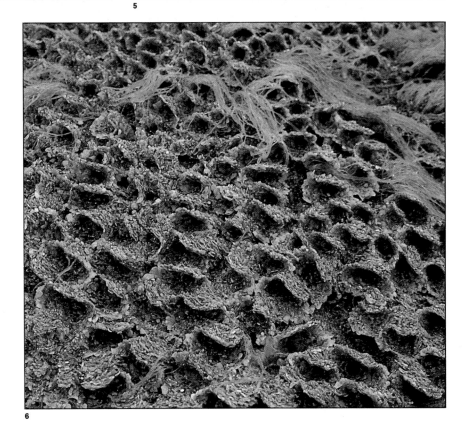

3 On sandy beaches in the southwest, carabid beetles *Eurynebria complanata* live in the strandline beneath beached wood or plastic objects. Sandhoppers are grasped by the strong pair of jaws.

4 The carnivorous necklace shell *Natica alderi* is holding a flattened banded wedge shell *Donax vittatus,* prior to boring a neat hole through one valve and eating the inner flesh.

5 The mottled coloration of a live shrimp *Crangon crangon* blends in well with the sand in which it lives buried by day. At night, shrimps emerge to feed on organic detritus, crustaceans, worms or even small fish.

6 Reefs made by the communal honeycomb worm *Sabellaria alveolata* occur on rocky outcrops low down on sandy beaches. A reef, which can reach a width of 60 cm, is formed by each individual worm building a tube from sand grains and shell fragments. When the sea submerges the reef, the worms can emerge from their tubes to feed.

Inhabitants of rocky pools

Rock pools develop in rocky shores wherever water remains trapped in vertical crevices or shallow depressions after the tide recedes. Life in these miniature, natural aquaria can none the less be harsh, since shallow pools high up the shore experience sudden temperature and salinity changes.

On a sunny day, copious gas bubbles will be seen in pools with seaweeds, especially green ones. These arise as the seaweeds utilize energy from sunlight, carbon dioxide and water to form sugars and give off oxygen. This oxygen is then used by both seaweeds and animals for respiration. The size of pools varies greatly, but it is the small, shallow ones lined with pink, calcareous algae which are most attractive. Associated with these pools are beadlet sea anemones, topshells, small hermit crabs in winkle shells, mussels, and in the spring and summer months, edible prawns.

Also sheltering in weedy pools live tiny chameleon prawns which change their colour from green to red or brown to blend in with the surrounding seaweeds. At night, they revert to a translucent blue colour. But not all shore animals will tolerate living in pools. Acorn barnacles on rocks adjacent to pools peter out just above the water level. The inhabitants of the large, deeper pools low down the shore are often sublittoral species which will not survive being exposed to the air. When large, brown oarweeds grow in these pools their expansive fronds obscure much of the pool interior. Gullies on rocky shores, which retain water long after the tide has fallen, are like enlarged versions of the low level pools and are particularly rich sites. Many creatures which are unable to survive on the exposed shore inhabit these sheltered niches.

1

1 Branching straps of thongweed *Himanthalia elongata* spread out over the surface of a rock pool. Also growing in this pool are small, pinkish, coralline seaweeds *Corallina,* and large brown oarweeds *Laminaria.*

2 When exposed to the sun, brown wracks, such as this spiral wrack *Fucus spiralis,* dry out and turn blackish. A pool keeps the swollen, reproductive ends moist.

3 The sea hare *Aplysia punctata* ejects a deep purple dye as a deterrent to predators. Entirely herbivorous, it browses on seaweeds and eel grass on the lower shore.

2

3

4 The candy-striped flatworm *Prostheceraeus vittatus* is one of the more spectacular British marine flatworms. It moves forward with out-stretched tentacles by undulating the sides of its flattened body. On Jersey, this worm lives beneath boulders in deep gullies.

5 The shanny *Blennius pholius* is cleverly camouflaged by irregular patches of light and dark colours which create an indistinct shape that confuses predators. The shanny uses broad, flattened teeth for biting barnacles off rocks, and it also feeds on crustaceans and fish.

6 Empty whelk shells are often utilized by hermit crabs *Pagurus bernhardus* as a protective home. On top of this shell are several old barnacles, while hydroids grow attached to the underside. A hermit crab grows by moulting its hard outer carapace and expanding into a new softer one beneath. It then has to find a larger shell for its home.

7 The spiny squat lobster *Galathea strigosa* extends up from the sublittoral on to the lower parts of rocky shores. Like the smaller and more widespread *G. squamifera* it has a minute pair of hind legs tucked beneath the body.

4

6

5

7

Breeding in the sea

The ways in which marine animals reproduce are diverse, but each reproductive effort involves an energy output. Many marine invertebrates produce freely floating planktonic larvae either directly or via an egg stage. Such a larval stage aids dispersal of a species from one part of the coastline to the next. These larvae feed in the plankton, especially on the microscopic plant cells or phytoplankton. Breeding often occurs in the spring so as to coincide with the spring plankton bloom. Some species are hermaphrodites, containing both ovaries and testes, and can cross-fertilize each other. The gregarious habit of acorn barnacles is essential if the adults are to have a mate, since once they have settled, they remain fixed for life. Adult barnacles secrete a chemical attractant which is detected by the settling larvae.

Species with planktonic larvae tend to produce large numbers of offspring to compensate for the high wastage in the first few days of life. Dogfish and skate, however, lay large, yolky eggs, which provide food for the embryo to grow to a comparatively large size when it hatches, and thereby increase the chance of survival. Reproductive success is insured by synchronous spawning in lugworms; they back up towards the top of their burrows, liberating their gametes which are fertilized externally in shallow pools on the beach surface. In summer, spiny spider crabs aggregate under water in large, breeding piles. The soft, recently moulted female crabs cluster in the centre, with the large mature male crabs outside. Several molluscs are able to change their sex. Oysters which begin their lives as males, change sex throughout their lives, whereas slipper limpets pass through a hermaphrodite stage as they change from males to females.

Several species of fish care for their offspring for some time after they are laid. These include the butterfish, which coils its body around the egg cluster beneath rocks, the male blenny which broods eggs laid by the female in a rock crevice and the male worm pipefish which carries the eggs cemented to the underside of his body.

1 Sea slugs, or nudibranchs, are marine molluscs which lack all trace of a shell. The pink spawn ribbons of a pair of *Precuthona peachi* have been laid on top of a winkle shell inhabited by a hermit crab. Growing attached to this shell is the whitish hydroid *Hydractinea echinata* on which *Precuthona* feeds.

2 Chains of slipper limpets *Crepidula fornicata* are shown exposed at low tide on a Sussex shore. The youngest and smallest limpets are males, which change their sex as they grow. The largest limpets at the bottom of the chain are females which brood egg capsules beneath their foot until they hatch into planktonic larvae.

3

4

3 Flask-shaped egg capsules laid by netted dog whelks *Nassarius reticulatus* in spring and summer, on eel grass leaves. Several hundred eggs are laid within each capsule.

4 Ball-shaped egg clusters of several hundred capsules are laid by the common whelk *Buccinum undatum* attached to a shell or to the underside of rocky overhangs. One whelk lays up to 2000 capsules and sometimes outsized clusters form when several whelks lay their capsules together.

5 Unlike the nudibranchs, the sea spiders have separate sexes and the male fertilizes the eggs as they emerge from the genital pores on each leg of the female. A male sea spider *Nymphon gracile* carries the brown fertilized egg masses on a pair of small legs or ovigers.

6 A live planktonic larva of the crab *Liocarcinus (Macropipus) marmoreus* was brought up in an autumn plankton haul off Scotland. In relation to the body size (the carapace of this specimen was one millimetre wide) the eyes are disproportionately large.

5

6

Cliffs and sea birds

Cliffs occur all round Britain and Ireland, but there are no long stretches on the east coast between the Humber and the Thames estuaries. The most spectacular cliffs occur on the islands off north Scotland. The lushness of cliff vegetation relates to the climate as well as the depth of soil. On steep cliffs, with few ledges, soil cannot easily collect and if cliffs are constantly fragmenting, there will be little chance of plants establishing themselves. Cliffs which fall to the sea by a series of ledges, however, will tend to be well vegetated since they offer numerous sites to colonizing species.

Lichens are among the first plants to colonize cliffs, often on exposed, sunny rocks; whereas ferns, such as sea spleenwort, seek shady overhangs or clefts. In southwest Britain, throughout the summer months, the seaward face of cliffs are attractive natural rock gardens as a succession of plants such as thrift, sea campion, English stonecrop, rock sea lavender, cliff spurrey and sea samphire come into flower. Added to these species, in the north of Britain, are roseroot, mountain avens and Scots lovage.

Where sea-bird colonies develop on cliffs, their excrement will enrich cliff soils, releasing nitrogen and phosphorous. The soil on cliff tops may be more stable, but they are also windy and so the submaritime heath which develops is typically wind pruned. Gorse often features on cliff tops, with bluebells, spring squills and primroses on the more sheltered, landward slopes. Here, the flora relates to the rock type. Cliff nesting birds do not have the same requirements and so they are not all competing for the same available sites. For example, kittiwakes select narrow ledges to build a large, cup-shaped nest from plant debris and mud, fulmars seek a broad ledge for incubating their eggs on bare rock, and puffins and Manx shearwaters nest in burrows underground.

1

1 A variety of lichen species form a colourful mosaic on red sandstone rocks in South Wales above the high tide mark out of reach of the waves. Two growth forms can be seen: encrusting species such as the orange *Xanthoria* grow flush with the rock, while tufted forms like sea ivory *Ramalina siliquosa* are attached just by their bases.

2

2 In early June many cliff tops are ablaze with flowers. On the Lizard, in Cornwall, the mild climate combined with the rich soils provided by the eroding serpentine rock, create ideal conditions for a variety of plants. Here, the large, cerise flowers of the introduced hottentot fig *Carpobrotus edulis* overshadow the native sea campion *Silene maritima*, thrift *Armeria maritima*, wild carrot *Daucus carota* and kidney vetch *Anthyllis vulneraria*.

3

4

5

3 A fulmar *Fulmarus glacialis* utilizes a broad, rocky ledge for nesting on the Inner Farne in June. On the upper bill the conspicuous tubular nostrils can be seen. Also visible in this picture are orange lichens encrusting rocks and sea campion growing out from rock crevices.

4 Neighbouring gannets *Sula bassana* fighting on Grassholm off Dyfed in June. The nests of these colonial birds are seldom more than a metre apart and so neighbouring squabbles often occur.

5 Kittiwakes *Rissa tridactyla* nest on narrow ledges of precipitous cliffs. This nest on the Inner Farne in June shows an adult shielding two chicks from direct sunlight.

6 Breeding guillemots *Uria aalge* cluster tightly together on top of a stack on Staple, one of the Farne Islands. Larger than razorbills, they waddle, rather than walk, on land. But they are efficient surface swimmers and they use their wings for moving under water. Nesting in the foreground are shags and kittiwakes.

6

Sea birds *(continued)*

1 Herring gulls *Larus argentatus* scavenging on waste fish thrown overboard from a fishing boat in Lerwick Harbour, Shetland.

2 An adult shag *Phalacrocorax aristotelis* stretches a wing beside its chick on Great Saltee Island, in Ireland, early in June. Shags are exclusively marine birds which resemble cormorants, but they are smaller and do not have a white face patch.

3 Razorbills *Alca torda* rest on a rocky promontory on Great Saltee Island, where they breed. These sea birds return to their colonies at the beginning of the year, preferring to nest individually or in small groups.

4 Intent on fishing, a grey heron *Ardea cinerea* stands in the shallows at the edge of a tide race flowing beneath a bridge in Co. Mayo. Small fish are swallowed whole, while larger ones are stabbed with the strong, pointed bill before being taken to land where the flesh is plucked from the body.

5 Female eider *Somateria mollissima* with young, feeding in tidal waters of Weisdale Voe, Shetland, in early July. Clutches of up to ten eggs may be laid, but there is a high mortality rate during the first week of life.

5

6 Oystercatchers *Haematopus ostralegus* lifting off from a ridge on the banks of the Dyfi Estuary as the tide rises.

6

Freshwater wetlands

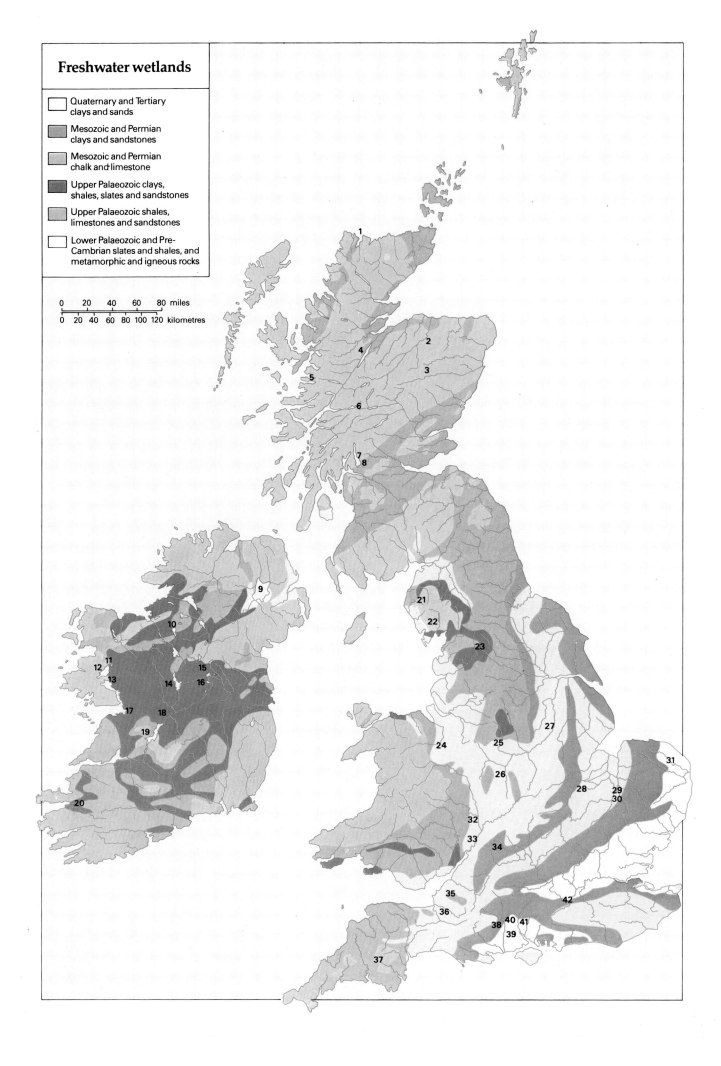

Freshwater wetlands

- Quaternary and Tertiary clays and sands
- Mesozoic and Permian clays and sandstones
- Mesozoic and Permian chalk and limestone
- Upper Palaeozoic clays, shales, slates and sandstones
- Upper Palaeozoic shales, limestones and sandstones
- Lower Palaeozoic and Pre-Cambrian slates and shales, and metamorphic and igneous rocks

0   20   40   60   80 miles
0 20 40 60 80 100 120 kilometres

Rocks of the Mesozoic, that is over 65 million years old, usually lack the useful minerals that can be leached out by rain, and the far older sedimentary rocks of the Palaeozoic era no longer contain any useful minerals. These rocks tend to be acidic as do the waters overlying them. Water flowing over limestone rocks tends to be alkaline, but the degree of alkalinity is dependant upon the solubility of that particular type of limestone. This map shows the distribution of these rocks and the locations marked are those referred to in this chapter.

The variety of wetlands

The life that is dependent upon freshwater is abundant and varied. Indeed, at its richest, a freshwater wetland will support a greater quantity as well as diversity of plants and animals than any other habitat. Conversely, some freshwaters are so nearly sterile as to resemble life-less deserts. Contrast, for example, the sheer exuberance of life in a lake in southern England with a Scottish Highland loch or a pool in an Irish peat bog.

A drop of water from that English lake is alive with microscopic life, both plant and animal. More easily visible to the naked eye are innumerable swimming creatures: pond-skaters on the surface, water-boatmen, stickle-backs and tadpoles swimming about, while crawling over the muddy bottom are larvae of caddisflies, beetles and dragonflies. The shores and shallows of the lake are thick with plants on which snails and leeches crawl. Birds abound, whether a brood of young grebes being fed with small fish by their parents, or martins hawking insects from low over the water.

The most barren lakes of, particularly, northern Scotland and Ireland are on the peat, their water stained brown. There is very little life in them. Microscopic plankton is scarce, while several groups of animals, for example the molluscs, leeches and water mites, so conspicuous in the lowland lake, are virtually absent. Plant growth is often limited to mosses, some rushes and a few floating-leaved species such as water-lilies. Bird life is restricted to species seeking the security that the water gives, perhaps, like the gulls, looking for nesting sites on tussocks of rush, but not for food.

This great variation in what can or cannot live in and around an area of freshwater is largely controlled by the fertility of that water; what nutrients it contains and in what quantities. In turn, the quality of the water is dictated by the underlying rocks and soils. Rivers and streams carry dissolved chemicals from the rocks whence they emerge and over which they run. Lakes and ponds may be filled by the same running waters, or may receive nutrients from the run-off of agricultural land or slowly from the decay of the life they already contain. Although the number of chemical compounds that can be found in freshwater is very large, the major nutrients are essentially two: nitrogen and phosphorus. These can exist in various forms, including phosphates, nitrites, nitrates and ammonia.

In order to convey more than a superficial impression of the variety of freshwater wetlands, it is necessary to find some basis of classification; and one that can be applied to whatever form the wetland takes, be it still or running water, large or small. Chemical analysis based on nitrogen and phosphorus is too complicated and their concentrations can vary widely through a year. The pH of the water, a measure of the ratio of dissolved hydrogen to hydroxyl ions, has been used in the past but is now known to be unreliable, especially in the summer. The most widely used criterion is the alkalinity, measured as the quantity of dissolved calcium carbonate. There is a good correlation, indeed a direct relationship, with the concentrations of dissolved nutrients, and also with the pH, but without the variability through the seasons that these show.

When the alkalinity is high, nutrients are present in large quantities; the water is fertile and both plants and animals proliferate. As the alkalinity decreases and the water becomes more acid, so the range and quantity of life declines also. Other factors, such as depth of water, size of the lake and speed of flow in a river, can moderate or enhance this basic factor without changing the essential character of the water.

The nutritional rating of a freshwater is often referred to as its trophic status. On this have been built the names used to describe the different types of water. The two commonest freshwater types are eutrophic (for

A profusion of plants including heather, crow-berry, birch and rowan, grow on the rocks surrounding the headwaters of a highland stream *(far left)* but the water flows too fast for any sediment to collect for water plants to root in. Furthermore, the water is flowing directly from acidic rocks and is therefore oligotrophic, containing little in the way of nutrients. As a river reaches the lowlands, however, it slows and broadens and becomes more fertile as it flows through richer soils. The River Severn between Newtown and Welshpool *(left)* is becoming mesotrophic, with emergent plants such as the white-flowered water-crowfoots and hemlock water dropwort. But at this stage, the river lacks stands of vegetation along its banks which it acquires as it slows and becomes eutrophic.

alkaline waters, from the Greek *eu* meaning good) and oligotrophic (for acid waters, from the Greek *oligos* meaning little). Not all waters fit happily into just two categories and three other states have been identified and named. These are marl, where the alkalinity is greater than in eutrophic waters; mesotrophic, for a smallish group of waters which share some of the characteristics of oligotrophic and eutrophic and have an alkalinity that falls between the two; and dystrophic, for waters even more acid than oligotrophic. Other major features of each type of water will emerge in due course.

The geology of the British Isles dictates to a large extent the distribution of the different types of freshwater. The main areas of acidic rocks are in the uplands of Wales, northern England and Scotland, and in the north and extreme west of Ireland. Alkaline freshwaters are found in the lowlands of England, which broadly means the south and east, where the rivers and streams get most of their water from the chalk and limestone of the region, and the lakes are enriched by agricultural fertilizers. In Ireland, there are extensive river and lake systems on limestone, though blanket bog has widely overlaid the more fertile bedrock.

Topography also affects the type of freshwater. Most of the acidic rocks in the British Isles form the upland areas, and the water bodies are likely to be both large and deep, as, for example, the lakes of the Lake District and the lochs of the Scottish Highlands. Both these physical attributes limit the fauna and flora which will grow in such lakes, as will be seen in more detail later. At the opposite end of the scale, the majority of lowland lakes are relatively small and shallow, thus adding to the potential richness that the fertility of the water already allows.

Thus, one does not need to carry around a chemistry set in order to assess the water type of a particular lake or river. Firstly, one's whereabouts in the country will give a very good clue. Secondly, a brief examination of the plant and animal life will indicate in almost all cases whether the water is eutrophic, oligotrophic, or some other status.

Just to add to the interest, not all waters are of the same type throughout. Some of the larger lakes of northern England and Scotland, while predominantly oligotrophic as might be deduced from their size and situation, have more alkaline areas, particularly where rivers enter them and some shallows occur. A good example of this is Loch Lomond in Scotland. The loch is oligotrophic at its northern end where it is fairly narrow and very deep. This end is fed by numerous small streams but, as they are all coming off acidic rocks, they add no useful nutrients to the water. At the southern end, the loch broadens out and becomes more shallow, and, most importantly, it is fed by the River Endrick. This river flows through agricultural land and brings into the loch a good deal of dissolved nutrient. As a result, this end of the loch is at least mesotrophic, and tending to eutrophic round the river mouth. Here, a considerable area of silt has been deposited on which vegetation has built up, contrasting well with the stony shores of the northern half.

A great many rivers change their type as they flow down to the sea. The Severn, Britain's longest river, has its beginnings in the acid rocks of central Wales. It is oligotrophic at its source and has, therefore, little in the way of vegetation or invertebrates. Both, of course, are additionally inhibited by the speed of the water flow. As the river descends into the agricultural valleys of eastern Wales and out into the Shropshire plain, so the nutrients begin to enter the water, and it gradually alters through mesotrophic to eutrophic. It remains eutrophic, though subject to man's pollution, until it becomes tidal north of Gloucester.

Derwent Water *(left)* is typical of the lakes of the Lake District and other upland regions, with its steep hillsides of metamorphic rocks plunging into deep water.

Eutrophic wetlands: open waters, chalk streams and fenlands

A eutrophic water, whether still or flowing, can be first and most easily identified by the amount and variety of the vegetation growing along its shores. In still water, there is a natural succession of plant forms; an area of open shallow water is gradually invaded by submerged and emergent plants and, in time, this area fills in with swampy reeds and rushes, and then becomes virtually dry land with large trees. Such a complete succession is not very common as man frequently interferes by allowing grazing to the edge of the water, or by draining the area of swamp or wet scrub if it becomes too large. The vegetation of a stream or river is necessarily different. The speed of the water dictates which plants can anchor themselves under water, and, even more than for still waters, there are few stretches left undisturbed by man where a natural succession can develop.

But it is in the water that the primary components of the eutrophic fauna and flora occur. Here can flourish, thanks to the rich supply of nutrients, a really abundant phytoplankton. In fact, the growth of algae may be so great that in the deeper lakes the light is prevented from penetrating to the bottom. And it is algae, too, that produce the late summer 'blooms'. These occur where excessive amounts of nutrient, usually run-off of fertilizers from farmland, but sometimes sewage, pollute the water. The algae grow so profusely that they use up most or even all of the available dissolved oxygen. Die-offs of fish and other animals may occur as a result.

When in balance, though, the algae form the first link in the complex food chains which allow so many different species to live within a eutrophic lake. Feeding on the algae are the zooplankton, among which perhaps the most obvious are the various species of cyclops, including *Cyclops vicinus* and *C. hyalinus*, and water-fleas, *Daphnia pulex*, *D. cucullata*, and *Simocephalus vetulus*. Both groups are tiny crustaceans, one to three millimetres long, with jointed limbs and antennae. Cyclops have a single dark eye in the centre of their heads, hence their name. Water-fleas have a rounded body and move through the water in a series of flea-like jerks or 'hops'. Both can occur in such swarms that they become readily visible to the naked eye, and the water takes on the appearance of a nutritious soup – a view clearly shared by the many animals which feed upon it. Even a casual look into the shallow waters at the edge of a pond or lake will reveal the larger invertebrates most of which feed on the plankton: pond-skaters, beetles, leeches, snails, water-bugs, water-boatmen and many others. Dragonflies, mayflies and midges dance and hover over the water while, down below, their carnivorous nymphs live out the first stages of their complex lives.

This variety of life, of prey and predators as well as many vegetarians, depends for shelter and often for food on the plants growing in the water. There are far more animals living among the plants of a river or lake than away from them. In turn, the plants root themselves in the rich, organic mud fertilized by the nutrients in the water. The interdependence of a eutrophic water is thus complete.

Some plants dispense with roots altogether. Duckweed *Lemna* is the most familiar example; its tiny, round, pale green leaves form extensive mats which sometimes give sheltered bays or ditches a complete green covering. Others of this type include frog-bit *Hydrocharis morsus-ranae* and water-soldier *Stratiotes aloides* as well as *Wolffia arrhiza* which has the distinction of being Britain's smallest flowering plant though, ironically, it has never been known actually to flower in this country.

Such rootless plants also exist where the water is too deep for light to penetrate to the bottom so that bottom-rooting plants cannot become

A small pond in winter at Greywell, Hampshire *(above)*, still shows the abundance of vegetation which flourished in summer, including the seeding heads of reedmace. In summer, such a pond would be alive with animal life including swarms of water-fleas *(left)*.

established. Nutrient is taken in directly from the water by fine rootlets hanging down beneath the leaves. The mats of leaves drift with the wind, often taking with them small snails and other animals. The free-floating, aquatic plants are virtually restricted to the nutrient-rich eutrophic waters in Britain and Ireland, and their presence, therefore, is an excellent indicator of alkaline conditions.

Where the bottom shallows sufficiently for plants to be able to root, there first come completely submerged species whose stems and leaves rarely reach the surface. Several species of pondweed including fennel-leaved *Potamogeton pectinatus* and shining *P. lucens* live in these conditions. Their rather pale and fragile leaves and stems are entirely buoyed up by the water. They have no need for strengthening cells and if taken out of the water will break up unless handled very carefully. Some plants, like spiked water-milfoil *Myriophyllum spicatum*, also have their leaves entirely under water, but send up a flower spike to reach the air.

Another submerged water plant is the introduced Canadian pondweed *Elodea canadensis*. First brought to this country from North America in the last century, it spread very rapidly across Britain and Ireland because, like others of its family, it propagates vegetatively. It flowers only rarely and sets seed even less often. Instead, small buds form in the axils of the leaves during the summer, swell with food reserves, and then drop off in the autumn and winter. Since each bud can grow into a new plant, its initial colonization of a new water can be very dramatic, and canals and slow-moving rivers have been virtually blocked by its luxuriant growth. A state

of equilibrium is reached after a few years, though, and now the weed co-exists with most other water plants, and the fears that it was ousting native species by crowding them out have been allayed. This rapid multiplication followed by sharp decline is probably linked to the take up and subsequent exhaustion of some mineral nutrient or nutrients. It flourishes best in eutrophic water but is successful enough to occur in less alkaline conditions.

Further species of pondweed, including broad-leaved *Potamogeton natans* and fen *P. coloratus*, send their leaves up to the air to lie flat along the water surface. Sometimes their leaves form considerable mats, along with those of the widespread white and yellow water-lilies *Nymphaea alba* and *Nuphar lutea*, both of which can occur in mesotrophic and even oligotrophic waters. Several species of emergent plants are, however, more or less restricted to eutrophic waters, and among the most prominent are reed sweet-grass *Glyceria maxima*, two or three sedges including cyperus sedge *Carex pseudocyperus* and greater pond-sedge *C. riparia*, and the delightful flowering rush *Butomus umbellatus*. All these species can form dense stands of vegetation, a metre or more in height, running back from the shallow water on to dry land.

Those zones in a eutrophic lake which contain the bottom-rooted submerged and emergent plants often hold the greatest variety and abundance of invertebrate life to be found in any water in the country, except, perhaps, in a chalk stream. This is a direct effect of the great diversity of habitats occurring there. There are homes for invertebrates in the muddy substrate, among the roots of the plants, among and on the stems and leaves under water, and even, because of the sheltering effect of the emergent leaves, on or in the surface film. The plants above the water give shelter not only to insects and other invertebrates but to small mammals and birds.

Flatworms and leeches are two groups very typical of eutrophic waters. Indeed, all 12 species of triclad flatworms are found in this type of water. This is also true of the large number of molluscs, though some may be confined to running rather than standing water because their delicate feeding mechanisms easily clog up with silt. As well as the freshwater limpets and freshwater winkles there are two different types of water-snail – those with roughly conical shells such as *Lymnaea*, and those whose shells are flattened from side to side such as *Planorbis*. All the snails are plant-feeders, grazing on algae growing as a thin film both on the bottom and on plants, or sometimes eating the plants themselves.

Several groups of flying insects, including mayflies, stoneflies and dragonflies, have larvae which live as carnivores under water. Among these are the mayflies *Ephemera danica* and *Eloeon simile*, the stonefly *Chloroperla torrentium*, and the dragonflies *Aeshna cyanea* and *A. grandis*. Most of these also need vegetation on which to lay their eggs. The nymphs themselves climb up the stems of plants out of the water when they are ready to emerge as adults. While some species of the dragonflies, for example, occur in oligotrophic waters, there are many, including *Anax imperator*, which are restricted to the more fertile lakes and rivers.

Other conspicuous groups of invertebrates abound in eutrophic waters. Whirligig-beetles *Gyrinus*, diving-beetles *Dytiscus* and water-beetles, *Hydroporus* and *Haliplus*. Many kinds of water-bugs crawl along the water surface or beneath it. These include the water-scorpion *Ranatra linearis* (also called the water stick-insect), pond-skaters *Gerris*, and several species of lesser water-boatmen *Sigara* and *Corixa*, which sometimes become extraordinarily abundant. Their main food is algae, and so they flourish in all nutrient-rich waters, including the smallest ponds and ditches.

One can find marsh marigolds *Caltha palustris* in a wide variety of wetlands from small eutrophic lowland ponds to boggy moorlands. They flourish in shady conditions such as beneath these willows.

Shallow, gravel-bedded Dockens Water in the New Forest, when the blackthorn is in flower *(left)*, is a spawning site for brook lampreys *Lampetra planeri (above)* in April. Females clamp themselves on to the stones while each male sucks on to a female's head and twines his body round hers.

This myriad invertebrate life provides food for amphibians, fish and birds, the first two also providing meals in some cases for the last. While the crested newt *Triturus cristatus*, the common frog *Rana temporaria* and the common toad *Bufo bufo* may be found in waters of almost any type they, and the other species of newts and frogs, are most common in alkaline conditions. Carp *Cyprinus carpio*, tench *Tinca tinca*, rudd *Scardinius erythrophthalmus* and roach *Rutilus rutilus* are among the most widespread and common fish. The rich algal growth in the water means that unlike the brown and rainbow trout *Salmo trutta* and *S. gairdneri* which find their food by sight, these fish have to rely upon their sense of smell. Whereas the trout spawns in clean gravel, these other species do so in weed beds and thus find all their needs satisfied in eutrophic waters.

The bird life of eutrophic waters can be divided into two groups. The largest group, at least in terms of the number of species, gets much of its food from the life and plants in the water, may breed in the vegetation, and may additionally gain sanctuary from being able to sit out in the middle of the lake or hide in the surrounding fringe of plants. The second group uses the water only as a place of sanctuary, and feeds away from it.

In the first group, the most completely aquatic species are probably the great crested grebe *Podiceps cristatus* and the little grebe *Tachybaptus ruficollis*. Both hardly ever leave the water except to climb out on to their floating nests of water weed which are anchored to stems of other water plants. All their food, mainly small fish and the larger invertebrates, comes from the water.

Many different species of ducks also breed and feed mainly within the confines of freshwater. The shoveler *Anas clypeata* sifts small invertebrates and seeds from the surface layers of the water, and two diving ducks, the tufted duck *Aythya fuligula* and the pochard *A. ferina*, find their food under water. These two are often seen in large mixed flocks on, for example, the various reservoirs and gravel pits in the London area, and following the general rule that two species do not occupy exactly the same ecological niche, the tufted duck tends to eat invertebrates, including small molluscs and crustaceans, while the pochard depends more heavily on plant food, especially stoneworts *Chara*. At times of abundance of either plant or animal food, both species can become omnivorous. Clearly, the food needed to

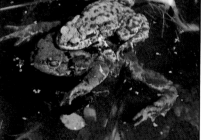

Common frogs *(top)* and toads always return to the water to spawn. When a male finds a female he climbs on top of her; grasping her firmly with his forelimbs, he fertilizes the spawn externally as it is laid. Common toads *(above)* spawn later than frogs and lay their eggs in a long rope instead of a mass which becomes entwined round plants under water. An egg rope can here be seen draped over the large, female toad.

Lough Corrib is one of the largest eutrophic lakes in the British Isles and is rich in emergent vegetation. Parts of it contain so much calcium carbonate that there are deposits of marl. Beneath the surface, stoneworts grow in abundance and provide food for great numbers of diving ducks.

support large flocks of such ducks, and their numbers can run into hundreds or even thousands in the winter months, can only come from really productive waters.

Two of the largest concentrations of pochard in the British Isles, over 20,000 birds in each case, occur on Lough Neagh in Northern Ireland and Lough Corrib in Eire. The former, with an area of over 250 square kilometres, is the largest inland water in the British Isles and is both shallow and highly eutrophic. Its fertility comes not only from the underlying soil but also from the run-off of the agricultural land which surrounds it. Counts in excess of 40,000 diving ducks have been made here; the majority of these were pochard, but there were also some tufted duck and goldeneyes *Bucephala clangula*. Lough Corrib, which is 180 square kilometres in area, lies among the limestone pavements of Galway. It is, in part, a marl lake, which will be discussed later. Of particular note is the prolific growth of stoneworts in the summer, and it is on these that the pochard feed. They arrive early in the autumn, reach peak numbers in September, and move away as winter approaches, probably because they have exhausted even this abundant food supply.

The extensive submerged and emergent plant stands of eutrophic waters attract such exclusive vegetarians as coot *Fulica atra* and swans. Coot dive for some of their food, but at other times pluck leaves from the water surface and graze on the banks. All three swans – mute *Cygnus olor*, whooper *C. cygnus* and Bewick's swans *C. columbianus* – use their long necks to reach deeper-growing plants but will also feed on surrounding farmland.

Apart from these truly aquatic species of birds, there are many other kinds which are normally to be found associated with lowland lakes, rivers and canals. Some, like the kingfisher *Alcedo atthis* and dipper *Cinclus cinclus*, are wholly dependent upon open water for finding their food, and their nests are placed in close proximity to it. Others, like the sedge warbler *Acrocephalus schoenobaenus* and reed bunting *Emberiza schoeniclus*, can be found in the thick vegetation beside a lake or river but are equally at home in an overgrown ditch. The heron *Ardea cinerea* is another species which can often be seen stalking fish in shallow water, but can live equally well on invertebrates and reptiles found in ditches or damp meadows. Finally, the swarms of hatching midges attract swallows *Hirundo rustica*, martins and swifts *Apus apus*. Of these, only the sand martin *Riparia riparia* normally nests by water, the others can be many kilometres away but find the richness of the food supply worth travelling for.

The habit of using an area of open water as a safe roost, while feeding away from it, is well developed among waterfowl. Many ducks, such as mallard *Anas platyrhynchos*, teal *A. crecca* and pintail *A. acuta*, roost during the day and go out to feed at night. This is forced on them, at least in part, by the disturbance and shooting that they would suffer if they reversed the process. In contrast, geese, particularly in Britain the pink-footed *Anser brachyrhynchus* and greylag *A. anser*, roost at night and feed on surrounding farmland during the day. It is the distribution of the feeding area which dictates which waters can be used for roosting; most ducks and geese rarely fly more than 10 kilometres, though pinkfeet can fly as far as 30 kilometres. Thus, it is principally eutrophic lowland waters that are used. Furthermore, the water must be reasonably small and sheltered, which again rules out many oligotrophic waters.

Large numbers of gulls roost at night also on lakes and reservoirs and feed away from them during the day. Like the waterfowl, they bring back considerable quantities of nutrient which they deposit into the water via their droppings. Some lakes are becoming noticeably more eutrophic through this process.

The British Isles have few aquatic mammals, and, of those we do have, only the introduced coypu *Myocastor coypus*, found mainly in the Norfolk Broads and the Fens, is confined to eutrophic waters. While the water vole *Arvicola terrestris* is commonest in this type it is also found in less fertile waters. The water shrew *Neomys fodiens* is more catholic in its tastes and largely prefers running water. The otter *Lutra lutra* may once have had preferences for eutrophic waters but man has done his best to oust it from the lowlands. This delightful animal is now to be found most frequently in upland streams, or on the coast.

This discussion of eutrophic waters and their plant and animal life has concentrated on the typical lowland lakes of the British Isles. Most of what has been described also applies to the slow-moving waters of lowland eutrophic rivers. Some of these rivers overspill their banks in the winter, though man does his best to prevent this, and flood the adjacent meadows.

The vegetarian water vole *(below left)* has the blunt nose and large front teeth typical of a rodent. It shares with the squirrel the ability to sit on its haunches while holding its food in its paws. Half its size, at about nine centimetres, the water shrew *(below right)* eats invertebrates, tadpoles and even small fish catching them in the very sharp teeth of its pointed jaws.

The River Shannon in Ireland still does this extensively, as does the River Avon in Hampshire. In a few places, the floods are created deliberately; at the Ouse Washes in the Fens, an extensive area of grassland is used to store excess water from the rivers and so prevent the flooding of more valuable arable land. The seeds and invertebrates that get washed out of the vegetation as the floodwater rises provide food for large flocks of waterfowl, including shoveler, mallard, pintail and teal.

The fast-running streams and small rivers that emanate from the chalk and limestone areas of the British Isles, such as the Test and Itchen in Hampshire, the Dove in Derbyshire, and some of the streams of the limestone region of western Ireland, have certain characteristics of their own. For a start, most of them are managed fairly intensively. Weed-cutting and dredging help to maintain the flow, reduce the risk of flooding, and keep the stream in perfect condition for trout.

Such streams have very clear water, most of it coming from underground springs. Under-water plants flourish exceedingly well and, if permitted, can form thick clumps covering the bottom and growing to the surface. Various species of narrow-leaved water-crowfoots *Ranunculus aquatilis*, *R. circinatus* and *R. fluitans*, and the pondweeds *Potamogeton perfoliatus* and *P. pusillus* are the most frequent, often together with Canadian pondweed. They grade into dense stands of emergent plants growing along the banks, among which watercress *Rorippa nasturtium-aquatica*, meadowsweet *Filipendula ulmaria* and purple loosestrife *Lythrum salicaria* are usually prominent. If this luxuriant growth of vegetation is permitted to remain in place it is the home of the most diverse and abundant communities of invertebrates to be found in any running water in the British Isles. The larvae of many small insects, especially certain kinds of mayflies, *Ecdyonurus insignis*, *Centrophilum luteolum* and *Baëtis atrebatinus*, are inhabitants of weeds, while the freshwater shrimp *Gammarus pulex* is often the single most numerous invertebrate present.

A specialist animal of fast-running eutrophic streams is the crayfish *Austropotamobius pallipes*. This is a freshwater relative of the lobster and crab, and looks a little like a small lobster. The adults are dark brown and grow up to 10 centimetres long, plus the large foreleg pincers. They usually live in holes in the banks or under large stones. They were formerly much

The female crayfish carries the fertilized eggs which adhere to the underside of her abdomen. She keeps them from the time of mating, in October or November, until they hatch, the following May or June.

A very fine example of a clear, chalk stream, with flourishing clumps of submerged and emergent vegetation, is the River Itchen in Hampshire, here seen in August. In the left foreground is a large clump of starwort and behind it, a smaller clump of water-crowfoot. Along the banks are reedmace and willows.

more common throughout the country and were taken for food by man. They are still abundant in some parts, especially in the least-polluted waters.

Temporary floods generally take their character from the river whence comes the water, but if they stand for any length of time then the underlying soil can have an effect. Most riverside floods in lowlands are therefore eutrophic. Usually the short-term nature of the water greatly restricts the purely aquatic life which can survive, though some molluscs, including *Lymnaea glabra* and *Planorbis leucostomus*, are resistant to drought. The fairy shrimp *Chirocephalus diaphanus* has eggs which resist desiccation and may appear in quite small puddles. Other winged species can fly in and utilize the temporary water but may be killed off when the water recedes.

In Ireland, a particular type of temporary water is the turlough, of which Rahasane is the largest surviving example. They are really lakes, situated on limestone, which dry out completely, or nearly so, each summer, but fill again in the autumn, or after any heavy rain. The rising water-table brings water bubbling out of swallow-holes in the limestone. At Rahasane, there is usually some permanent water, as well as the river running through it, and here there are dense beds of stonewort, forming an almost pure stand. In the areas which are flooded very frequently, thick growths of reed sweet-grass occur, thinning out to include various grasses and some sedges in the less often flooded parts. Exposed rocks and boulders within the flood zone are usually covered with patches of the distinctive black moss *Cinclidotus fontinaloides*.

There is a further kind of calcareous standing water, found in both lowlands and uplands, called a marl lake. They occur solely in areas of chalk and limestone where the amount of calcium carbonate in the water is very high.

The permanent waters in the heart of the limestone region of the Burren, like Lough Gealain *(right)*, are mainly marl lakes; their water is a clear pale blue. Other waters on the limestone of western Ireland are only temporary, flooding in winter through the limestone. In summer these turloughs *(below)* almost dry out and the previously submerged black moss dies back on the boulders.

When freshwaters freeze *(left)* the birds are forced to leave. Under the ice, however, the fish and invertebrates are not seriously affected. Many are hibernating or dormant in the bottom mud while others remain active.

So high, in fact, that the carbonate is precipitated out of the water and forms a layer, known as marl, on the bottom of the lake. This has an important side effect: most of the available phosphorus in the water is also precipitated out. As this is one of the vital nutrients for the phytoplankton, the latter is usually very poor. However, plants with roots in the bottom sediment of marl can get at the phosphorus.

This combination of poor phytoplankton and rich conditions for submerged plants provides the more obvious distinguishing characteristics of a marl lake. The clarity of the water, which often appears blue, further encourages plant growth to a much greater depth than is possible in the murkier depths of eutrophic waters with their limits on light penetration.

The submerged plants themselves typically include immense beds of stoneworts *Chara aspera* and *C. hispida*, and many of the pondweeds *Potamogeton* of eutrophic waters. Emergent vegetation is not usually very prominent, unless an entering stream produces conditions more akin to eutrophic waters, when reeds and rushes may become established. Many marl lakes have, therefore, relatively bare, exposed shores, or only a narrow fringe of plants.

The shortage of phytoplankton has its effect right up the food chain, and the number of different species of invertebrates in marl lakes is often very restricted. Since the conditions are restrictive, some species may be present in very large numbers through lack of competition. The gradual decomposition of the vegetation provides a muddy layer on the bottom which is inhabited by midge larvae. The thick plant layer provides a home for many molluscs, caddisfly larvae and beetles.

The best-known marl lake in the British Isles is probably Malham Tarn in Yorkshire. A Field Study Centre close by has provided a series of long-term studies on virtually every aspect of the tarn and its surroundings. Other

marl waters are scattered from the Durness lochs, Sutherland, to the extensive group of very fine gravel pits on the Gloucestershire–Wiltshire border known as the Cotswold Water Park. These latter number over 70 individual pits, mostly under 30 hectares, with others in the course of excavation. Colonization by plants of the oldest pits, now over 30 years old, has been quite slow, which is typical of marl waters, and they lack the air of maturity of gravel pits in areas less dominated by limestone. However, the submerged plant growth is already very rich, and some groups of invertebrates, such as the dragonflies, are prominent. Coot and pochard, and other plant-eating birds, are numerous in winter, while there is a long list of other species attracted by the presence of the water in a formerly dry region.

Marl waters also occur in Ireland. Lough Corrib and its associated Loughs Carra and Mask contain some marl areas, but other parts are essentially eutrophic. Thus, one has extensive reed and rush stands growing well out into the shallow water, as well as very bare areas with deposits of marl on the bottom. Other marl waters in Ireland include Lough Derg in Co. Galway, and Loughs Derraveragh and Owel in Co. Westmeath.

Mesotrophic waters

Wholly mesotrophic waters are not very common in the British Isles, though, as already mentioned, several of our rivers have mesotrophic sections lying between their oligotrophic beginnings and their eutrophic lower reaches. The example of Loch Lomond as a large oligotrophic standing water with a mesotrophic area at one end, has already been cited. Mesotrophic lakes are most often found, as might be deduced, at the junction between acid uplands and calcareous lowlands, where neither exert a predominant influence.

One of the largest mesotrophic lakes, certainly in England, is Esthwaite Water in Cumbria. It is the richest of the lakes in the Lake District, which were all originally oligotrophic, some of the enrichment coming from agricultural run-off. Indeed, a number of formerly oligotrophic lakes have become mesotrophic, and, like Esthwaite Water, may be gradually moving towards eutrophic status because of the amount of nutrient reaching them from farmland and from sewage effluent.

The phytoplankton and the higher plants and animals dependent upon it are nothing like as abundant as in eutrophic waters, though well above the levels reached in oligotrophic conditions. Invertebrates restricted to mesotrophic waters are relatively few, as the typical fauna includes elements drawn from the two other trophic states. However, the bottom muds of the deeper mesotrophic lakes often become rather short of oxygen in the summer when mixing with the surface layer does not take place. In these conditions certain chironomid midge larvae can flourish, as do the larvae of the phantom midge *Chaoborus flavicans* which is characteristic of mesotrophic waters.

With a reduced phytoplankton, light can penetrate further than in eutrophic, plankton-rich waters, so that the submerged plants are found in deeper water, though rarely below about six metres. Some plants, like the invertebrates, are more or less restricted to mesotrophic conditions, though many more occur as well in other states. Pillwort *Pilularia globulifera* and spring quillwort *Isoetes echinospora* are more often found in mesotrophic standing waters than in any other kind, as are the waterworts *Elatine hexandra* and *E. hydropiper*. But stoneworts and pondweeds are examples of submerged plants of eutrophic conditions which also grow in mesotrophic waters. Emergent and shoreline vegetation is much less vigorous, though successions do develop as they have in Esthwaite Water.

At one end of Esthwaite Water, a succession of plants has developed in an area which has been protected from grazing. The water is not particularly rich and so the water plants are restricted to common reeds, bulrushes and sedges behind which have developed alders and birches.

The invertebrate life among the submerged and emergent plants is less diverse and abundant than in richer waters, though virtually all the main groups are represented. The vertebrates are similarly affected. For them, the mesotrophic lakes are a transition between eutrophic and oligotrophic conditions. So, rudd, roach and pike *Esox lucius* are present, along with trout. The numbers of dabbling and diving ducks are lower. There are also fewer of those birds, such as coot, mute and whooper swans, that are dependent solely on the vegetation. By contrast, the fish-eating species tend to be more frequent; while the numbers of fish are not necessarily greater than in eutrophic waters, the clearer water means that they are more easily seen and caught.

Oligotrophic and dystrophic waters: lochs, upland streams and peat pools

The majority of the larger natural waters in Britain are oligotrophic. They lie, as already stated, in the western and the northern uplands, and occupy

Loch Maree *(above)* in Ross and Cromarty, is a typical steep-sided and very deep, oligotrophic lake lying in a U-shaped glacial trough.

The Moat Pond at Thursley in Surrey *(left)* is one of the very few acid heathland pools in southern England. Thick rafts of marsh St John's wort *Hypericum elodes* appear round the edges along with rushes typical of acid waters.

valleys and depressions gouged out of the rocks by the glaciers of the last ice age. Lochs Ness and Maree in Scotland are classic examples of these long, narrow and very deep waters. In Ireland, several of the larger waters lie on limestone and are therefore relatively fertile. In some areas, though, as in the headwaters of the River Shannon, the loughs, such as Lough Allen and Lough Ree, are oligotrophic.

Away from the uplands, in the Outer Hebrides for example, there are areas holding many small oligotrophic lakes. There are, however, few oligotrophic waters south of the limit reached by the ice during the last glaciation, a boundary which runs in England from the Severn estuary to the River Blackwater in Essex. They are mostly small and usually associated with patches of acid heathland, for example the Moat Pond on Thursley Heath in Surrey.

All the larger oligotrophic waters are readily distinguished by their bare, stony shores. Only in the most sheltered bays, or where a sediment has built up, perhaps through erosion, do emergent plants gain a foothold and rather scanty growths of reed and sedge occur. The water is generally fairly clear, there being little phytoplankton due to the lack of available nutrient. However, what plankton there is can be found down to considerable depths as light penetration is so good. The plankton shows many similarities with the range found in eutrophic waters, although not all the same species; it is the abundance that is so different. The bottom of the lakes usually has a layer of mud in which live midge larvae, leeches and water mites, as well as the larvae of certain caddisflies and other insects.

The River Feshie in the Cairngorms, seen in the depths of winter, is flanked by the Caledonian forest of old Scots pines.

The existence of submerged plants in oligotrophic lakes depends on the amount of sediment that has built up, and on the degree of shelter. Little can grow even under water on very exposed shores such as occur around large bodies of water. The range of species tolerant of acid waters is also small. Common quillwort *Isoetes lacustris* and the stonewort *Nitella opaca* are often found growing together down to depths of eight metres. In shallow waters, one finds the bog pondweed *Potamogeton polygonifolius*, starworts *Callitriche* and the floating bur-reed *Sparganium angustifolium*.

The presence of these plants allows a fair variety of invertebrates to find a home, including flatworms, a certain number of molluscs, though nothing like as many as in more fertile waters, as well as beetles and water-boatmen. Although the latter group are very widespread and occur in almost every water type, in common with some other invertebrate groups, particular species may be confined to a certain water condition. Thus the water-boatman *Sigara scotti* is the species that is probably most commonly found in oligotrophic waters, and very rarely in anything richer. Mayfly nymphs are often very plentiful. When the adults hatch on the surface of the water and take to the wing, they form an important food for fish, especially trout, which is the characteristic species of oligotrophic conditions.

The sheltering plants, such as they are, also contain many caddisfly larvae, and considerable numbers of midge larvae of several different species. As the transition takes place from submerged to emergent vegetation, the invertebrate life shows rather little change, and there is certainly not the difference to be found that occurs between the zones in a eutrophic water. Some species do become more plentiful, for example the dragonflies and beetles, and where emergent vegetation protects small surface areas then whirligig-beetles, pond-skaters and other surface-dwellers appear.

Such plant and animal communities form only a small part of the total shoreline and shallows area of an oligotrophic water, the typical stony or sandy edge predominating. Even this can support some life, though plants are generally restricted to algae clinging firmly to the substrate, and a few water mosses. Because of the constant wave action on the shore, there is a basic similarity between the conditions found between the stones of a large lake edge and the bottom of a fast-flowing river. Both are provided with a constantly renewed supply of well-oxygenated water, and both are relatively free of suspended matter. These environments are suitable for well-adapted species of invertebrates. The freshwater limpet *Ancylus fluviatilis* is as well adapted for a life in moving water as its marine counterparts, because it is able to cling on to rocks. By contrast, the freshwater shrimp, which also has a familiar relative of the seashore, the sandhopper, hides beneath stones and quickly moves to the shelter of another if disturbed. It occurs in considerable numbers in some streams and rivers. The larvae of many mayflies and stoneflies lurk between the stones waiting for prey, as do a limited number of flatworms and leeches. But there are few plants and animals for the last two groups to feed on.

Not only are most of the rivers and streams in the upland areas oligotrophic in nature, but, as already mentioned, so are the upper reaches of many of the rivers which, later in their course, wind through the lowlands. The existence of a strong and permanent current of water inhibits the growth of any plankton and, in the faster reaches, restricts plant and animal life to what is able to stay firmly attached to rocks or large stones, or perhaps stay hidden beneath them. Only as the flow of water slows can more species get a hold, and the succession down a stream is not very different from that between the most exposed shore and a sheltered bay of an oligotrophic lake. Emergent plants will only grow where there is a sufficient deposit of silt in

The broad, shingle reaches of the River Spey near Newtonmore. Not only is the water oligotrophic, but the river is subject to floods which prevent anything more than sparse colonization by plants.

which to root, and many of the rivers have largely stony beds in their upper reaches. Sometimes these beds extend quite far down their length, as they do in the River Spey, Inverness.

The brown trout is the fish which is most typical of oligotrophic waters, both still and running. It is the invariable species in such clear waters, if fish are present at all. This is its natural habitat, where the water is cool and rich in dissolved oxygen. Trout feed on invertebrates of all kinds as well as small fish and tadpoles. For spawning they must have clean, gravelly areas, which are found more readily in oligotrophic waters than in waters of any other kind.

Man has, of course, interfered with the natural life of the trout, and hatcheries now provide large numbers of fish for stocking eutrophic lakes and reservoirs where they would not normally live, but where they provide a quarry for fishermen. Indeed, the trout hardly breed at all in these waters and continued restocking is necessary to replace what the fishermen remove. Chalk streams are also managed for trout, the weed being cleared and spawning areas kept clean for them.

Salmon *Salmo salar* and sea trout (a migratory form of the brown trout) also occur in oligotrophic rivers, ascending these to spawn, and often passing through the larger lakes to reach the smaller streams. Two waves of fish come up the rivers, in spring and in autumn. Fish of the latter wave usually spend the winter in the river before laying their eggs. The young of both species remain in freshwater for one to five years before making their way down to the sea. They feed on invertebrates from the bottom of the river or stream, and catch small fish when older. The common coarse fish of more fertile waters are generally absent, but sticklebacks *Gasterosteus* and eels *Anguilla anguilla* are found, as in almost any type of water.

Birds are not normally very plentiful on acid waters. A few fish-eating species occur, for example the black-throated diver *Gavia arctica*, red-breasted merganser *Mergus serrator* and goosander *M. merganser*. These last two also breed beside rivers as well as lakes. The dipper, feeding as it

The heavily peat-stained waters of a small stream on Islay contain very little life. This is never more apparent than when streams pour down from the moors in winter floods.

does on under-water invertebrates, and therefore needing clarity of the water in order to see its prey, has a somewhat odd distribution as it finds these conditions in the clear chalk streams with their highly enriched water, as well as along the shores of large oligotrophic lakes.

At the lowest end of the scale of water fertility come dystrophic lakes and pools. Their calcium carbonate level is very low, perhaps only a hundredth that of a marl lake, and their fauna and flora is equally poor. The main distinction from oligotrophic waters, with which they overlap in calcium carbonate levels, is the colour of the water which is stained brown from the peat on which they are situated. The myriad small pools that are scattered across any area of peat bog in Ireland or the uplands of Britain are mainly dystrophic. For example, the pools at Fox Tor Mire, Dartmoor, fall into this category, as do those on the very extensive Rannoch Moor in Scotland.

There are few large dystrophic lakes, but one or two occur in Scotland with their catchment areas entirely on peat. There are also a few dystrophic pools in the English lowlands, where peat has formed over the centuries and then man has come to dig it and created holes which become filled with peat-stained water. Shapwick Heath in Somerset is an example of this, while in Cheshire, the pools of Sweat Mere include dystrophic peat-stained water in the midst of more fertile surroundings. Most other meres in Cheshire, as well as those in neighbouring Shropshire, are eutrophic.

The very shallow pools of the peat bogs are characterized by various emergent plants, including bogbean *Menyanthes trifoliata*, bog-cotton *Eriophorum angustifolium* and bog pondweed. There is little plankton, and certain groups of invertebrates, including the molluscs, are completely absent; conversely others, including water-bugs, beetles and certain dragonflies, seem to flourish.

Pools formed in lowland peat bogs are generally richer in species, often because of colonization from nearby richer waters which are absent in the uplands. However, the limited plankton has a restricting effect on those species reliant on it for food, and therefore reduces the variety of animals further up the food chain. Dragonflies are again common and varied, their carnivorous larvae perhaps relying as much on insects falling into the water as on what is already living there.

Fish are not plentiful in dystrophic waters. While the trout can do well in very acid conditions, it does require clean gravel for spawning and this is not present in peaty pools. Birds, too, are scarce, with just a few species nesting either on or beside the small bog ponds. Mallard, teal and wigeon *Anas penelope* often nest on peat moors, their young feeding, at least to start with, on small insects. Densities are always very low, however. Red-throated

Small, freshwater pools on the peat contain just a few acid-tolerant plants. Bogbean and cotton-grass can be seen growing in this small lochan in Shetland.

divers *Gavia stellata* traditionally nest in the tiniest pools but find all their food elsewhere; the adults fly, often many kilometres, to a larger lake containing fish, or out to sea. Only the black-headed gull *Larus ridibundus* seems at all characteristic of dystrophic waters. Again this is only for nesting; they also find their food further afield. But, where the colonies of nesting gulls are situated, there is gradual enrichment from the birds' droppings, and tiny communities of richer plant and insect life can occur, surrounded by the more sterile peat.

Man and wetlands

This survey has revealed that there are very many different habitats within our freshwaters; these habitats are based on variation in the nutrient content of the water, and on the different zones, from deep water to the shore, within each site. Natural change in these systems is very slow but man's effect has been to speed up the process, or to produce more dramatic alterations. Eutrophication through sewage pollution and the run-off from over-used agricultural fertilizers has, therefore, been an increasingly important factor.

Lough Leane in Co. Kerry is a eutrophic lake because it is situated mainly on limestone. However, discharge of inadequately treated sewage from nearby Killarney is having a very serious effect on the aquatic life of the lake. Unfortunately, the largest amount of polluted water enters the lake in the summer months when the water and its oxygen content are at their lowest levels and so least well able to deal with it.

The Norfolk Broads have shown in recent years some of the effects of high human use. Although there are probably many factors operating here, there has been considerable nutrient enrichment not only from agriculture but also from sewage effluent and from the very high boat traffic. The latter has also churned up the water and prevented weed growth. The net effect has been a drastic reduction in submerged plants, which have disappeared altogether from some of the Broads, such as Rockland and Surlingham, and a consequent reduction in the invertebrate life dependent upon them. The few Broads which retain good growth of under-water plants, such as Calthorpe, are those with little or no boat traffic and with only limited connections with the river systems.

Algae *(below left)* are one of the first stages in a freshwater food chain. When they become dominant though, it is an indication that the balance has been upset by excess nutrients. The red scum *(below right)* is composed of millions of individual *Euglena* each no longer than one-hundredth of a centimetre.

What happens to a river when sewage and other wastes are poured into it. Oxygen is depleted, killing off vegetation growing in the water and along its edges. The foam is caused by detergents.

Algal blooms from over-enrichment now occur quite regularly in some lowland lakes and reservoirs, as they do in Chew Valley reservoir in Avon. These can lead to mass die-offs of fish and other life through the rapid decrease in the amounts of dissolved oxygen in the water. Furthermore, the algal growths can kill off aquatic plants by coating them with such a thick layer that they are effectively smothered. Unless it is controlled, this process leads to the virtual destruction of the delicately balanced natural web of life that is dependent on the water. Certain groups of animals and plants cease to occur, while others, particularly the algae, become dominant, instead of just being one item in a multi-species system.

Our rivers have long been used for the transport of sewage and other waste products, though recent legislation in Britain is leading to the cleaning up of some rivers. A river can only deal with as much effluent as its oxygen content allows. Once this point is over-reached, life in the river will decline, if it has not been already poisoned. A good deal has been made of the return of various fish species to the lower Thames after years of absence, and there is little doubt that, in general, our rivers are cleaner than they used to be. However, this is a long way from reproducing the diversity of life that once existed and could perhaps return if all the natural conditions were to

prevail once more. Some rivers, particularly those like the Trent and the Tame in the Midlands, are still a long way from recovery.

Recreation in all its forms is a serious threat to all types of wetlands. This is not to deny sailors, fishermen, water-skiers, and others, their enjoyment of water but merely to warn that the pressure of these activities on some waters is already too great. Disturbance to birds, the effect of boats on water plants, the dangers from cast-off fishing lines, are all potential and actual serious threats.

The above threats may cause adverse changes, but they rarely destroy the water and its life completely. Drainage, however, removes a wetland for good. The process is a very old one, of course, and the largest areas of natural wetlands, such as the East Anglian Fens, were drained hundreds of years ago; only tiny relicts remain, as at Wicken and Woodwalton Fens. The pace of drainage has been increasing in recent years, and the winter floods along river valleys in southern England and the once-numerous turloughs in Ireland are rapidly becoming features of the past. The Somerset Levels are currently under great threat of drainage as is Rahasane Turlough in Co. Galway. If they disappear, each country will have lost one of the best of its few remaining natural wetlands.

These wetlands are being replaced by valuable and necessary farmland, though it is arguable whether the replacement of flood-enriched grassland by arable is automatically a good thing. The stage has now been reached when conservation bodies are prepared to fight for what is left, simply because there is so little remaining of this important habitat.

Loss through drainage is not confined to large-scale schemes threatening hundreds of hectares. All over Britain and Ireland, country farm and village ponds are being filled in, while better land drainage lowers the water table and turns well-filled, overgrown ditches into ruler-straight cuts, as nearly dug as the dragline can manage, devoid of vegetation and, therefore, of so much other life.

It is very difficult to measure what has been lost through all this destruction. The larger and more obvious species attract attention, but it has to be assumed that all the myriad smaller forms of life suffer in proportion. Many

The Norfolk Broads were created by man in the thirteenth century as a result of extensive peat digging. In some the vegetation, particularly reeds, encroached to leave only narrow channels *(above left)*. In others a very rich diversity of water plants developed. Recent years have brought an increase in boat traffic which together with the pollution from sewage and agriculture has caused much of the underwater plant life to disappear and has also produced algal blooms. Only a few Broads cut off from boat traffic remain as examples of their original richness *(above right)*, with white water-lilies, mare's tails *Hippuris vulgaris*, and reeds in the background.

fenland breeding birds, like the bittern *Botaurus stellaris*, the marsh and Montagu's harriers *Circus aeruginosus* and *C. pygargus*, and the bearded tit *Panurus biarmicus*, now restricted to a handful of sites and surviving only through active protection, would once have been quite abundant. Wintering waterfowl would once have gathered in great numbers where there are now ploughed fields. So too, would large numbers of dragonflies, beetles and other aquatic invertebrates. But, unlike our records of bird species, we do not really know how many invertebrates we have lost. The amphibians have certainly suffered badly, and continue to do so, with a clear link between recent declines in frogs and newts and the loss of small ponds and overgrown ditches in so many areas.

On the whole, the vast majority of the large oligotrophic lakes and the innumerable small dystrophic pools of the least inhabited parts of the British Isles are safe from almost any threat. Some of the Lake District lakes, it is true, have been turned into controlled reservoirs, which has had an adverse effect on such life as they contain because of the greater fluctuations in water level. However, it is the lowland waters that are most vulnerable. They are closest to the bulk of the human population seeking recreation, and to the conurbations producing sewage effluent.

The ever-demanding search for greater farm efficiency has led to an enormous increase in the quantity of artificial fertilizer being poured on to our farmland, a proportion of which inevitably finds its way into the rivers and lakes nearby. So it is the eutrophic waters – our chalk streams, fens and lowland lakes – which suffer most, and it is these waters which hold the greatest variety of plant and animal life, and so these suffer too.

The only counterbalance to these threats and pressures has come from man's need for drinking water and for sand and gravel. Large reservoirs and gravel pits are now common features over certainly the southern half of Britain, though rarer in Scotland and in Ireland. They have increased substantially the areas of standing water available for plants and animals, and these have not been slow to colonize them. The fact that most new waters are in the lowlands has ensured that they will be eutrophic and support the maximum amount of fauna and flora. It has also meant, of course, that they are much in demand for recreation. Zoning of interests has been tried, at any rate on the larger waters or where there are several gravel pits close by, and has been a moderate success.

It is not as if there is not enough water for all. Freshwaters cover roughly one per cent of Britain, and perhaps a greater proportion of Ireland. There is no reason why the magnificent richness that they contain cannot be preserved in all its splendour.

Plants

The plants of freshwater wetlands grow in a variety of ways. The first group, usually tall and robust, live in the damp mud at the water's edge and grow in a natural succession from shallow water back to dry land. The plants at the water's edge may grow out into the water where they join another group for which this is a natural habitat. The roots of these plants are anchored in the mud, sometimes a metre or more under water, but their leaves and flowering heads stand up above the surface, or float upon it. In still water, pondweeds, water-milfoil and water-lilies grow in this way, while in rivers and streams, water-crowfoots predominate.

A third group of plants grows entirely submerged. Again they are rooted in the bottom mud but although growing upwards they do not reach the surface. They include stoneworts and other species of pondweeds. The depth to which the plants can grow under water is dictated by how far the light can penetrate; this in turn is related to the density of plankton in the water. The richer, more fertile lakes have a plentiful growth of plankton which blocks the light and so prevents plants from growing much more than a metre down. In waters with few nutrients, plankton cannot flourish so, consequently, plants can grow six metres or more below the surface.

A final group of plants overcomes the problem of where to root by dispensing with such attachments altogether. The duckweeds and other tiny-leaved plants float upon the surface, drifting with the wind. They can completely cover a small pond, regardless of depth, taking in nutrients through fine filaments hanging down in the water. For them, as for the other groups of water plants, their variety and abundance in a particular lake or river is directly related to the amount of nutrient contained in the water and the mud.

1

2

3

1 There are many species of stoneworts, *Nitella* and *Chara,* growing principally in eutrophic and marl waters. This stonewort *C. vulgaris* was growing in a New Forest pond. They are not flowering plants but large and robust algae. They grow entirely submerged and are eaten by diving ducks, swans and coot.

2 An over-wintering bud or turion of frogbit *Hydrocharis morsus-ranae* sprouting under water in the spring. As the leaves grow they float up to the water surface and white flowers appear in summer.

3 The stems and leaves of water-milfoil *Myriophyllum* remain submerged but the flowering spikes reach up above the surface.

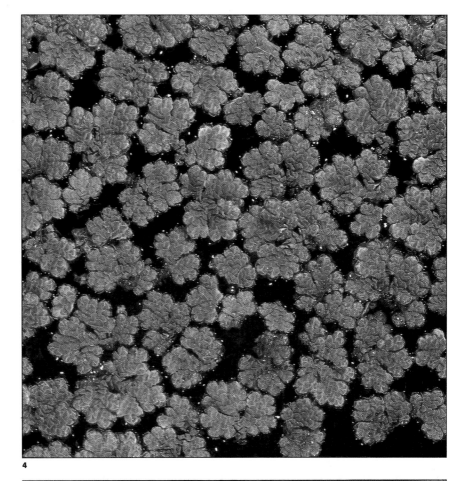

4 The water fern *Azolla filiculoides* was introduced from North America. It can be found in ditches and gently flowing canals in southern England where it only just tolerates hard winters. It is bluish-green in summer and turns pinkish-red in autumn.

4

5 Although they do develop small flowers, floating duckweeds normally spread very rapidly by vegetative reproduction. *Lemna* and *Wolffia arrhiza* can here be seen budding-off new plants. At barely one millimetre across, *Wolffia* is Britain's smallest flowering plant.

5

Plants *(continued)*

1 The pondweeds *Potamogeton* are very numerous with species occurring in all types of water. Bog pondweed *Potamogeton polygonifolius*, however, is restricted to acid water.

2 This starwort *Callitriche obtusangula*, unlike some of its relatives, is typical of eutrophic waters. Here it is growing with water-crowfoot *Ranunculus* and bur-reed *Sparganium erectum*.

1

2

3 Shoreweed *Littorella uniflora* is an emergent plant of oligotrophic lakes. It grows in water to depths of four metres but can survive on dry land if the water level drops, as here on the shores of Coole Lake in Ireland.

3

4

5

4 Bogbean *Menyanthes trifoliata* is a submerged aquatic plant but its leaves and flowers are borne above water. The pinkish-white flowers, which appear in May and June, are densely covered with white hairs.

5 If left ungrazed, the banks of eutrophic lakes and streams develop a luxuriant and often colourful vegetation which includes purple loosestrife *Lythrum salicaria*.

6 The flowering spikes of butterbur *Petasites hybridus* usually precede the large, heart-shaped leaves which when mature are green above, and greyish and woolly underneath.

6

Invertebrates

There are five main zones for invertebrates in and around freshwater. Some groups are restricted to a single zone, others occur in two or more, while a few move from one zone to another at different stages of their life cycles. At the bottom of most lakes and rivers is a layer of mud which is frequently lacking in oxygen. Midge larvae, small worms and a few snails are often all that can live in these conditions. Where there is only shallow water over the mud, leeches, caddisfly larvae and molluscs are common. Fast-flowing streams and the larger, oligotrophic lakes have stony bottoms where stonefly nymphs, freshwater shrimps and certain molluscs are adapted to live.

Water plants form a very important underwater habitat for many invertebrates since they provide both food and protection. The larvae of many flying insects live among the submerged stems and leaves, for example dragonflies, caddisflies, mayflies and midges. Many species of snail can be found here also. When the larvae of the flying insects are ready to metamorphose into adults, they climb up the stems into the air. Many other invertebrates use the aerial parts of water plants for feeding, resting, laying their eggs and for shelter.

In the water itself is the zooplankton, the microscopic animal life on which most invertebrates and fish feed. Swimming through the water are the free-living invertebrates such as beetles, bugs, mites, leeches and flatworms.

The final zone for freshwater invertebrates is the actual surface layer of the water. There are a large number of insects perfectly adapted for life here such as pond-skaters, water-measurers and whirligig beetles. Snails, too, can move around suspended upside down from the surface film.

1

1 Freshwater shrimps *Gammarus pulex* live in fast-flowing streams. They live under stones and, if disturbed, move quickly through the water, swimming on their sides. Breeding can take place at almost any time during the year. The male seizes the back of the female and they may stay joined together for up to a week.

2

2 The largest of the pond snails, the greater pond snail *Lymnaea stagnalis* can grow a shell up to five centimetres long. Pond snails, like land snails, travel on a secretion of slime, and even when moving under the surface film with their shells hanging down, they are moving along on a very thin layer of slime attached to the water surface. Their eggs are laid in ropes attached to stones or plants or, as here, to the shell of another snail.

3 A flatworm *Dendrocoelum lacteum* crawling over a skeletonized leaf. Flatworms have amazing powers of survival and reproduction. They can live for months or even years without food, often in a desiccated state. Although they reproduce by laying eggs, they more usually divide in two. If a tiny piece of a flatworm is detached it will grow into a complete animal, while any damaged part will repair itself.

4 The fairy shrimp *Chirocephalus diaphanus* may be found in large numbers in tiny pools which dry up in the summer. The female shrimp carries the tough, drought-resistant eggs in a brood pouch. When the pool dries up and she dies, they sink into the mud, to hatch when water returns, perhaps after several months.

5 The larvae of the alderfly *Sialis lutaria* live under water for a year or more, feeding mainly on midge and caddisfly larvae. When ready to change into adults, they crawl out of the water and dig a small hole several metres away. There they pupate, emerging as adults two or three weeks later.

6 The water flea *Daphnia obtusa* has two kinds of eggs. The majority are small and unfertilized, from which hatch only females. They are carried in a brood pouch and develop into miniature adults in about two days. The young escape from their mother through a split in the brood pouch wall. At the end of the summer, fertilized eggs are laid, which develop into both male and female water fleas.

7 Although resembling plants, *Hydra* are animals related to the sea-anemones. Like them they have stinging cells along their tentacles to aid the capture of prey. Small protrusions on the side of *Hydra* develop into complete animals and eventually drop off. They move around by turning slow somersaults, standing first on their base and then on their tentacles.

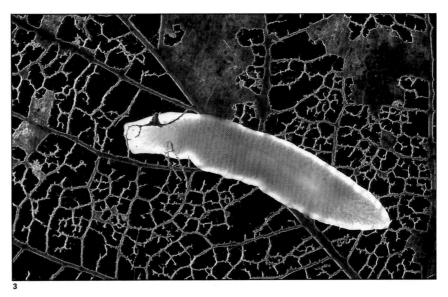

3

4

5

6

7

Invertebrates (continued)

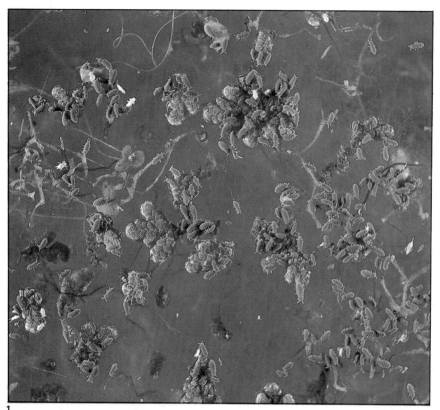

1

1 Springtails *Podura aquatica* are about one and a half millimetres long and live on the water surface. Their common name comes from their unusual mode of progression. The tail is bent under the body and held in place by a hook-like structure. When this is released by the insect, the tail strikes the surface of the water sufficiently hard to make the springtail leap into the air.

2

2 Like its terrestrial namesake, the water stick-insect *Ranatra linearis* is extremely difficult to see when sitting motionless among debris. It feeds on water insects, tadpoles and blood-worms, as seen here.

3 Almost any small pool or ditch has on its surface pond-skaters *Gerris gibbifer*. They rest on the surface film, protected from getting wet by a dense pile of hairs on their undersides. They normally skim over the surface, but can jump or even fly. They feed on dead insects falling into the water.

3

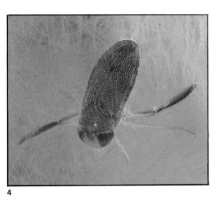

4

5

4 Lesser water-boatmen *Corixa punctata* take in air on the surface before diving, and being buoyant have to hold themselves under water by clinging to plants.

5 The adults of the mayfly *Ephemera danica* cannot feed, and live for just a matter of hours, a day or two at the most. The male dies immediately after mating, and the female soon after egg-laying.

6 The club-tailed dragonfly *Gomphus vulgatissimus* has a very long underwater larval life lasting between one and four years. It spends most of the time buried in soft mud with just its eyes and jaws protruding, ready to seize worms, tadpoles or even small fish.

6

Fish

Freshwater fish can be divided very broadly into two groups. There are those which live in the larger oligotrophic lakes and fast-flowing rivers and streams, and others which inhabit the slower-moving rivers and most eutrophic lakes. Man, however, has inferfered with this grouping, particularly by stocking many waters with trout and salmon. They rarely become established though and stocks have to be maintained by feeding or by continued restocking.

Among the larger fish of well-oxygenated streams and rivers are the salmon, trout and grayling. They also occur in the clear waters of lakes from which the streams and rivers flow. Bull-heads and minnows are smaller kinds which also live in such conditions. An essential requirement for them all is a bed of clean gravel or sand in which to spawn. If there are gravelly areas in lowland chalk streams, where the prolific growth of water plants is kept in check, they will also be able to inhabit such waters. Invertebrates are the principle food source of these fish, the larger ones also taking small fry, tadpoles and even fish eggs.

As the rivers broaden and their current slows, mud accumulates on their bottoms and water plants becomes more plentiful. These conditions are closely akin to those found in fertile, lowland lakes, and the fish living in the two types generally include the same or very similar species. Among them are carp, bream, rudd and roach. Although some species in this habitat lay their eggs in clean areas of gravel, most of them spawn in the dense beds of underwater weed. The small fry remain concealed among the vegetation while they grow. All these species eat considerable amounts of animal food, mainly invertebrates caught while swimming or sifted from the mud. Many fish species also feed on algae, and the leaves and seeds of water plants.

1

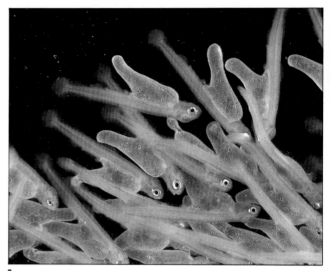

2

1 Bullheads *Cottus gobio* are bottom-living fish of fast-running streams and the edges of clear lakes. They live mostly under large stones, and swim very little, since they lack a swim-bladder, the usual buoyancy organ of more mobile fish.

2 When young salmon *Salmo salar* hatch from the eggs, they are known as alevins. The large, yellow, yolk sac nourishes them for the first few weeks of their life, before they start taking live food and are known as fry or fingerlings.

3

3 A brown trout *Salmo trutta* swims among starworts growing in a gravel-bottomed tributary of the River Test. In the wild, these trout spawn in early winter in a gravel depression known as a redd. Like salmon, they lay large yolky eggs which hatch into alevins.

4

4 Minnows *Phoxinus phoxinus* gather in large shoals for spawning in early June. At spawning time the male's belly and fins turn orange or red, while the upper parts darken.

5 Dace *Leuciscus leuciscus* typically live in the middle reaches of rivers, below the very fast-flowing water of the upper stretches, and above the muddy lower parts. Occasionally, however, they can be found in lakes.

6 Perch *Perca fluviatilis* lay their eggs in long ropes which become entangled around underwater plants. Young, developing fish embryos can be seen inside the eggs.

5

6

Birds

Freshwater wetlands provide birds with nest-sites, food, and sanctuary. The majority of nests are well hidden in plants in the water or around its margins. For the divers and gulls which nest in the open, predators are kept at bay by a barrier of water or bog. These species often nest by relatively infertile waters containing little food for them, and they have to feed elsewhere. Most breeding birds of wetlands, though, find their food where they nest. The richer waters support both thick growths of vegetation in which nests can be built and the necessary quantities of animal and plant food.

A considerable diversity of bird life exploits the varied food present in a fertile, freshwater wetland. The wholly aquatic species such as the grebes and diving ducks find all their food under the water, including fish, small invertebrates, and the soft stems and leaves of underwater plants. The dabbling ducks feed on insects and seeds floating in the surface film, while a third group, including swans and coot, may feed on plants in the water or come out to graze on vegetation growing along the banks. By contrast a large, deep lake with little plant growth may only be able to support a few specialist feeders such as fish eaters.

Many winged insects spend the early stages of their life under water. As well as providing food for diving birds at this time, the midges and mosquitoes, in particular, are fed on by many species of small birds when they emerge into the air. Warblers, wagtails and swallows may not have direct contact with the water but they rely on it to a great extent to provide their main food. A handful of species take their food directly from the water, yet cannot swim; the kingfisher is perhaps the best known of these. By digging its nest hole in a vertical river bank, the kingfisher also uses the water as a barrier against predators.

1

2

3

1 Coot *Fulica atra* build their nests in clumps of vegetation at the water's edge. They feed on water plants and frequently graze on plants in the surrounding floodlands.

2 A moorhen *Gallinula chloropus* picks its way carefully across water-lily leaves. It builds a large, untidy nest of plant material, close to the water, and has the unusual habit of jerking its tail when nervous.

3 Whooper swans *Cygnus cygnus* are winter visitors from Iceland. Like coot, they feed on underwater plants by extending their necks under the water. When up-ended, they can reach down as far as a metre.

4 A reed warbler *Acrocephalus scirpaceus* feeds insects to its young in a nest built in a stand of *Phragmites*. The small reed warbler nests often receive an egg from the parasitic cuckoo *Cuculus canorus*.

4

5

5 The grey wagtail *Motacilla cinerea* pauses on a stone in a stream with a beakful of food for its young. A year-round resident, it nests beside water and feeds on insects.

Birds *(continued)*

1

2

1 The tufted duck *Aythya fuligula* is often seen on lowland lakes and reservoirs. It dives for food, and feeds on invertebrates, small snails in particular, which it picks off underwater plants and sifts from the bottom mud.

2 The red-throated diver *Gavia stellata* catches fish by chasing them under water. It breeds in north and west Scotland, nesting beside small lochs, and flies to larger ones, or to the sea, for its food.

3 Kingfishers *Alcedo atthis,* although not water birds, rely entirely on water for their food. This hen bird is resting on a feeding post prior to diving for a fish.

4 A little grebe, or dabchick, *Tachybaptus ruficollis* sitting on its nest on the Basingstoke Canal. The nest is made from a floating mass of water plants and is securely attached to the half-submerged branches of a willow.

5 The great crested grebe breeds only on shallow lowland lakes in Britain and Ireland, where it feeds on fish. Like the little grebe, it builds a floating nest which it anchors to water plants.

3

4

5

Lowland grasslands and heaths

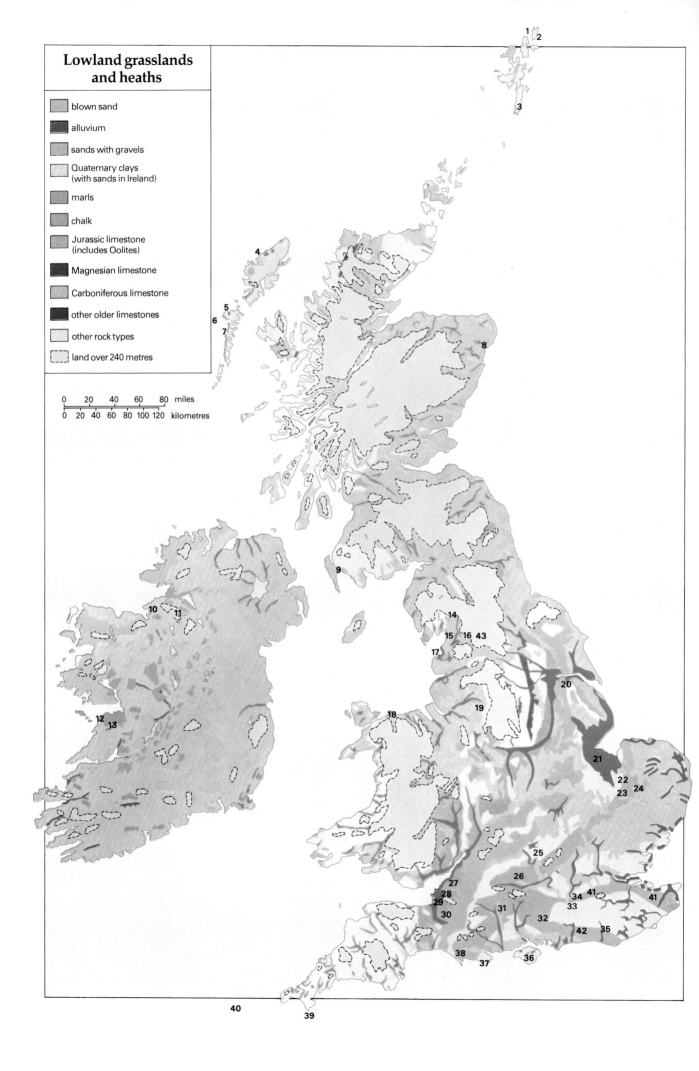

Lowland grasslands
and heaths

- blown sand
- alluvium
- sands with gravels
- Quaternary clays (with sands in Ireland)
- marls
- chalk
- Jurassic limestone (includes Oolites)
- Magnesian limestone
- Carboniferous limestone
- other older limestones
- other rock types
- land over 240 metres

```
0   20   40   60   80  miles
0  20 40 60 80 100 120 kilometres
```

This map shows the surface distribution of limestones and marls, and of the clays, sands and alluvia which have been deposited over the limestones, and other rocks, during the last two million years. Calcicolous and neutral grasslands occur on these rocks. The locations marked are those referred to in this chapter. (1–7 are sites of machair grassland.)

The origin and history of lowland grasslands and heaths

Reconstructing primeval landscapes and their vegetation is a fascinating occupation, although, until quite recently, it has been largely the product of guesswork. By studying the pollen record, however, we are now able to suggest the way plant communities developed in the British Isles following the retreat of the glaciers after the last ice age. The ice melt was obviously a slow process and, for a long time, arctic conditions prevailed over large areas of land to the south of the ice. The landscape 10,000 years ago was probably something like the tundra of the present-day arctic regions of Europe or North America, open and treeless with low-growing plants between the rocks and glacial debris. As the climate improved, with higher summer temperatures, forest colonized the new ground, first with birch and pine followed later by oak, elm and lime. The forests were soon occupied by numerous large herbivorous animals such as wild oxen, rhinoceros, elephant and deer, together with their natural predators.

For a long time this was their world, and man did not influence it significantly until the Neolithic period, about 5000 years ago. The evidence is again from the pollen record, and it shows that the British Isles were forest-covered until the beginning of the Neolithic. But there were some areas, for example in Teesdale and on the Breckland sands, where the tree cover was probably rather open because plants have survived which are not tolerant of shade.

Before 3000 BC, man had not modified the environment more than any other vertebrate hunter or food gatherer. The forest dictated the nature of his food, tools, clothing and dwellings, controlling, therefore, almost every aspect of his life. His small, local clearings would have quickly grown over. But, as man learned to cultivate the ground and domesticate grazing stock, he depended less on hunting and was able to create permanent settlements. In order to till the soil, he had to destroy the forest, but his stone tools were inadequate, and he had to resort to fire when the trees were too large. In addition, his grazing animals needed open areas, and the grass grew better there than under a tree canopy.

In Britain, as the edge of the forest was pushed back, less tree pollen was deposited in the peat. In contrast, the pollen of herbaceous plants increased, particularly those of weeds of cultivation. A good example of a pollen record in which this has happened comes from Hockham Mere in Norfolk. This site, at the northern margin of Breckland, was a lake in immediate post-glacial times and, over a very long period, it gradually filled up with muds and silts which, by excluding oxygen, preserved the pollen. Finally, a peat layer developed over the ground surface.

For centuries, Breckland had been open grassland, and early ecologists were, therefore, not certain whether trees had ever grown there. But, the pollen record at Hockham Mere confirmed that there had been forests until the early Neolithic, and the virtual disappearance of the rabbit *Oryctolagus cuniculus* in 1954 showed that trees would grow readily if grazing animals were removed. Abundant archaeological evidence indicates that Neolithic settlements were widespread throughout Breckland; in fact, it is probable that, during the Neolithic, more people lived in this region than in any other part of Britain. A famous site which illustrates this is the extensive area of flint mines at Grimes Graves, about 16 kilometres away from Hockham Mere. The light soils of Breckland would have been easy to till and, once the fertility of the soil was exhausted, the early farmers would have moved on to make another clearing in the forest.

Although open areas of grassland and heathland were created in this way, the forest would immediately have re-invaded as soon as man and his

grazing animals had left. Bushes and trees such as birch *Betula* and hazel *Corylus avellana* soon colonize such areas unless they are regularly burned or else grazing continues. There is one factor, however, which is sometimes overlooked, and that is the influence of wild herbivores. Large numbers of game animals, particularly deer and cattle, must have lived in the more open forests before the arrival of man. When the first European explorers penetrated the African savanna during the early nineteenth century, they saw enormous herds of grazing animals of many different species. These grazers had an important influence on the maintenance of grassland and it is possible that, in Neolithic Britain, wild herbivores had a similar function. We know that the red deer *Cervus elaphus* was abundant in Neolithic Breckland because many hundreds of their antlers have been recovered from the Grimes Graves flint mines, where they were used as picks. Elsewhere in Britain, in the river valleys where periodic flooding would have inhibited the growth of trees, wild herbivores would have made good use of the rich grazings and have helped to prevent colonization by trees.

In other areas where the forest may have been open, for example on the chalk downs, grazing animals may likewise have created and maintained open grassy areas. Unfortunately, pollen does not survive in chalk soils so this can only be speculative. But Neolithic deforestation probably occurred in the chalk regions as well as in Breckland. The chalk soils could also have been easily cultivated by primitive implements, and there is substantial archaeological evidence of man's early occupation. Furthermore, radio-

Areas whose soils were easy to cultivate were probably the first to be tilled by Neolithic man, and the chalk downland is one of these areas. Ever since Romano-British times man has cultivated sheep and so grasslands have been maintained. Where traditional methods of sheep management have been abandoned though, as has happened along the South Down way, a succession has begun, back to the earlier woodlands which according to pollen records existed 5000 years ago. The trees in this succession are whitebeam, beech and yew.

carbon dating from sites in Kent, where an abundant weed flora and a high non-tree pollen were recorded, suggests that the downs of southeast England were largely deforested as early as 3700 years ago, when the Neolithic period was coming to an end.

About 2800 years ago, the climate became cooler and wetter, with an extensive development of surface bogs and rapid growth of peat. This was particularly so in northern and western Britain and in Ireland. During this period, from the late Bronze to the early Iron Age, agriculture was extended and new invaders from central Europe colonized the country from the south and the east. Then, as the Iron Age progressed into Romano-British times, so sheep grazing appears to have increased. Up until then, pigs and cattle had dominated the animal remains found in settlements. That sheep were grazing on the land is a clear indication that there must have been considerable areas of grassland.

Forest clearance continued as the human population grew and cutting tools became more efficient, and was accelerated during the Iron Age by the need for charcoal for smelting. The people from central Europe had introduced the ox-drawn scratch plough. This new device was so primitive that it produced the small and square 'Celtic fields', which are so widespread on the chalk in southern England, and in places give a stepped profile to the hillsides. Later ploughs were more efficient and both cattle and horses were used to pull them. Eventually, the Anglo-Saxons used big ox teams to draw a true plough and were thereby able to cultivate larger areas and also to exploit the heavy clay soils of the English lowlands where forests had survived. The pollen record shows that arable crops grown by the Anglo-Saxons near Thetford in East Anglia included wheat, rye, flax and hemp, and that the fields were infested with many weeds, such as plantains, associated with this type of cultivation. Also in East Anglia, in the Fenland basin around the shores of the Wash, a rather unusual type of grassland appears to have been created by man, and then disappeared without historic record. The Romans drained and occupied almost all the siltlands in this area which were then maintained as cattle-ranching country not unlike parts of the present-day Camargue in southern France. Arable land would have been present only in the driest parts. But, as drainage techniques became more efficient, arable land was extended, and today it is difficult to find a grass field because the fertile soil gives much higher yields under cultivation.

Forest clearance continued in Britain through the Anglo-Saxon period, and, by the time of the Domesday survey in the eleventh century, the landscape pattern which was to continue for hundreds of years had already been established. Today, lowland Britain and Ireland form a mosaic of arable fields and grasslands, forested areas and conurbations.

The different types of grasslands and heaths

Lowland grasslands and heaths are widespread throughout the British Isles but in general they have evolved in the southern half of England. With increasing altitude and latitude there is a transition to upland and northern grassland complexes and a gradual replacement of the species which are common or even dominant in the south. In the north and west of Britain, and especially in Ireland, the much higher rainfall has resulted in the formation of peat in low-lying situations, but at similar altitudes in southern and eastern England some type of heath or grassland has developed. Although their plant species are very different, grassland and heathland are closely related ecologically because they have both been modified by many centuries of grazing and, sometimes, by burning.

The corncockle *Agrostemma githago* is one of several attractive cornfield weeds which were introduced to Britain by the Romans. Unfortunately, due to the recent practice of spraying, the rose-pink flowers with their long, green, star-like sepals, are now rarely seen in the wild. This plant was growing at the Iron Age farm reconstruction of the Butser Ancient Farm Project Trust in Hampshire.

Acidic grasslands and heaths

There are several types of heathland which have developed on acidic lowland soils derived from sands, gravels or clays. These environments have survived probably because their low fertility makes them not worth cultivating. But they may also have escaped the plough because they were common lands and noone had the sole right of use. Heather *Calluna vulgaris* is the commonest heathland dwarf shrub although in some areas bell heather *Erica cinerea* may be abundant. Certain grasses may, in places, appear as dominant species. Both heathers were highly prized as kindling, bedding for stock and for grazing. Heather-dominated, or ericaceous, heath is a vegetation of an oceanic climate, growing particularly in the northwestern part of Europe. It is often associated with other scrub species, such as common gorse *Ulex europaeus*. This species is found almost everywhere, but in the south and west of Britain a smaller species, western gorse *U. gallii*, often dominates. In the south and east, especially in Dorset, the New Forest, Sussex and Surrey, dwarf gorse *U. minor* may also be common. Mosses and lichens are often found growing with heather and, where it is patchy, they may cover considerable areas of the ground. This type of heath is also found on leached sand dunes by the coast.

Some species of plants in acid grasslands have a very local distribution, for example, bristle-leaved bent grass *Agrostis setacea* in the south of England, Dorset heath *Erica ciliaris* mainly in Dorset, and Cornish heath *E. vagans* on the Lizard peninsula in Cornwall. All are more widespread further south in western Europe but can survive in the southwest of Britain and Ireland because of the mild climate. Where drainage is poor or the watertable is close to the surface, as in valleys and depressions, a wet heath, classified as 'valley mire', develops, with a much richer flora. With increasing altitude and latitude, the lowland heather heath grades into an upland type but without any clear boundary between the two. Additional plants such as the bilberry *Vaccinium myrtillus*, cowberry *V. vitis-idaea* and crowberry *Empetrum nigrum* begin to appear, and gorse declines.

In Surrey, Sussex and Hampshire there are large areas of acidic heathland on Cretaceous and Tertiary sands and gravels. The Surrey heaths are very fragmented but several distinct sites remain, the best of which have become National Nature Reserves. Thursley Heath was originally one of the largest in southern England, and is an excellent example of a lowland type growing on mineral soils where there are low levels of plant nutrients. Nevertheless, these areas would have reverted back to forest if grazing had not destroyed the invading tree seedlings and so maintained the heather

Dorset heath *(below left)* and Cornish heath *(below right)* are two plant species of acid grass lands with a very local distribution. The Cornish heath, for example, grows only on the coastal serpentine of the Lizard peninsula.

Thursley Heath was severely burned in 1976. The initial response to the fire was a growth of mosses and lichens, but by 1980 bell heather and birches were beginning to colonize the area where previously gorse had predominated.

cover. This was achieved partly by domestic stock but rabbits and deer were also important, and burning would have had a similar effect. Today, grazing is no longer an important factor but frequent fires, mainly due to careless tourists, help to control tree growth.

The open heathland of Sussex, Hampshire and Dorset is said to have originated in the Bronze Age. Although climatic variations and human population movements would have allowed the forest to re-invade from time to time, there is evidence that some open heath was maintained from at least the Iron Age until the eighteenth century when nearly 40,000 hectares of heathland are thought to have existed in Hampshire and Dorset. From the eighteenth century, the extent of heathland declined mainly due to reclamation for agriculture, planting of conifers for timber, urban development and mineral extraction. Today, there are barely 6000 hectares; many fragments are less than a tenth of a hectare in extent and only 14 sites have an area greater than 100 hectares. On the Isle of Purbeck in southeast Dorset there are other important tracts of heathland, although these too are now considerably reduced in extent; they are characterized by the very local Dorset heath. Further west, in Devon and Cornwall where the oceanic climate is milder and more humid, there is a great deal of western gorse and a strong representation of other oceanic species.

North of the Midlands and East Anglia, heathland areas are very limited. In Lincolnshire, there are several grassland and heath sites which have developed on the layer of thick sands overlying the oolitic limestone. The most interesting of these is the surviving part of Risby Warren, near Scunthorpe. This area shows considerable ecological diversity, ranging from unstable dunes to closed vegetation and from calcicolous grassland to acidic heath. Lowland heath is rare in Scotland and very local in Ireland; its place is taken by other types of vegetation because of the wetter conditions. However, the coastal dune system at the Sands of Forvie National Nature Reserve in Grampian has a large area of heath, and Torrs Warren in Dumfries and Galloway is a similar west coast example.

Calcicolous and neutral grasslands
Most pure grassland areas are situated on basic or alkaline soils distributed over several different but related rock formations. Chemically, these are all limestones (or calcareous) ranging from soft chalk through moderately hard oolitic rocks to the harder rocks of the Carboniferous. Variants of these grasslands are also found on limestones with a large amount of magnesium,

such as the magnesian limestone of northern England and dolomitic Durness limestones of Scotland. On these chalks and limestones have developed brown earth soils containing free calcium carbonate. These calcicolous grasslands are frequent in southern England but tend to be very local in Wales, Scotland and Ireland. In contrast, the neutral grasslands are widespread and varied in the British Isles and include southern and northern types as well as grasslands associated with mature salt marshes and drained wetlands. They occur on a much wider range of parent materials and superficial deposits, such as alluvium, clays and marls, and their soils are mostly deficient in free calcium carbonate.

Chalk and limestone soils tend to be porous and are therefore dry, but where they contain clay or there is a compacted drift material overlying the limestone, drainage may be poor, producing a transition from dry grassland to marsh or fen. In dry weather, ground water in the chalk may become available to plants by capillarity whereby this water rises up to the surface through the small spaces between the particles of chalk. It was clear that this was happening during the long hot summer of 1976; many people noticed that the vegetation in some chalk districts remained green where the perennial plants had deep roots, whereas elsewhere the plant life was withered and brown. Calcicolous grasslands are perhaps the best known for their rich collections of lime-loving grasses and broadleaved plants. This variety is often associated with low values of major soil nutrients other than calcium. When important elements such as nitrogen, potassium and phosphorus are in short supply, plant growth is slow and the competitive power of some species is reduced; more plants can co-exist in a particular unit area of ground because no single species is dominant. The addition of fertilizers can upset the competitive balance and impoverish the flora since the fast-growing species depress the growth of the others.

In addition to soil and vegetation differences, calcicolous and neutral grasslands have traditionally been under different management regimes. The open chalk and limestone downs were grazed originally mainly by sheep, and later by rabbits. Neutral grasslands, on the other hand, tend to be smaller in area, enclosed by hedges or walls and grazed by cattle and horses as well as by sheep. It was also common practice to take a hay crop on

The profusion of buttercups growing in this field is an indication of the type of management the field has undergone. Usually, by mid-summer, the grass is tall enough to disguise the buttercups, but intensive early spring grazing, combined with a hot, dry summer, has suppressed the grass growth and the buttercups are flourishing due to lack of competition.

Poppies and other cornfield weeds often survive along the margins where selective weed killers fail to reach. Here is a roadside view of a Berkshire wheat field in August.

neutral grassland before grazing took place. Some of these old, neutral pastures have either never been cultivated or else have escaped deep ploughing for a very long period. The vegetation is therefore composed almost entirely of native species and, although created by human influence, may be regarded as semi-natural. Permanent grassland of this type has become increasingly scarce, particularly since the last war when food was rationed and much grassland was ploughed up for the production of cereal and root crops. Since then, our system of agricultural subsidies has made it more profitable to reclaim soils which can be easily worked rather than use them for grazing.

It is common practice today to rotate temporary grassland with other crops; fast-growing grass species are often sown to produce two or three hay crops or else to enable the farmer to feed more cattle per hectare. These temporary grasslands, known as leys, are very poor floristically. Traditionally, arable land has been the home of a variety of weeds of cultivation, of which poppies *Papaver* are the most striking. Herbicides have eradicated many of them in areas of high cultivation.

Why are there so many species of plants associated with chalk soils compared with the flora on other substrates? Botanists have not produced a simple answer. It has been suggested that chalkland vegetation evolved

in Europe in semi-arid environments at low altitude. The climatic fluctuations characteristic of such areas would have maintained a greater degree of vegetation disturbance than is usual, and would, therefore, have created a wide variety of ecological niches available to species with different requirements. Such a situation would have been conducive to rapid rates of plant speciation and diversification. In the course of time, when man began to exploit the plant life of calcareous soils, there was a natural reservoir of many species adapted to this environment that were able to take advantage of the soils disturbed by primitive cultivation.

However, this flora, so typical of the downs for hundreds of years, is now fast disappearing. Old permanent pasture 'unimproved' by fertilizers or herbicides may soon vanish altogether except on the steepest slopes and on areas protected as nature reserves. Elsewhere there are similar floras on calcareous soils although they are generally less rich in species.

Along the rocky west coast of Britain, the vegetation is influenced by wind and salt spray, which contains nutrients such as calcium and magnesium, and creates conditions approaching those of basic soils, but in some places, notably the Channel Islands and the Isles of Scilly, heather, bell heather, and bracken *Pteridium aquilinum* are dominant. In the extreme north of Scotland this sub-maritime heath grades into a coastal type of montane heath with mountain avens *Dryas octopetala* and bearberry *Arctostaphylos uva-ursi*, a formation which occurs where there is a calcium-rich soil derived from a loam shell sand.

On the west coast of the Outer Hebrides, the famous machair grasslands on shell sands have many of the typical chalk-grassland plants which are only local elsewhere in Scotland. Machair is a Gaelic word which describes grass-dominated coastal plains on low-lying sands which in places extend more than two kilometres inland from the shore. They are of considerable agricultural importance and form excellent grazing for sheep and cattle. The first deposits of sands, consisting of shell fragments, are thought to have been laid down 60,000 years ago, although in the post-glacial period some siliceous material from glacial drift was mixed with it. The machair forms one of the most distinctive features of the Outer Hebrides and has been much studied by ecologists, geographers and agriculturalists. There are areas of machair also on some of the Inner Hebrides, on the northwest coast of Scotland, and even farther south.

Old Winchester Hill, Hampshire *(above left)*, is a very steep, south-facing slope which has not been cultivated. The chalk grassland is fescue dominated and the rich, chalkland flora includes the round-headed rampion *Phyteuma tenerum (above right)* seen here growing with lady's bedstraw. When hawthorn scrub invades the grassland, other shrubs and, eventually, trees such as whitebeam and yew become established and a woodland develops.

Opposite

Top left Sea campion and gorse growing on a Cornish cliff. The vivid red strands climbing over the gorse are common dodder *Cuscuta epithymum,* a parasitic plant which penetrates and feeds upon its host plant, usually gorse, heather or clover.

Top right A wind-pruned heath and dead bracken growing among granite rocks on Tresco, Isles of Scilly, show the effects of the strong winds usually associated with an island climate. Behind the bay, the white, silicious sands support a coastal grassland of marram.

Right The famous machair grasslands have a similar flora to chalk grasslands due to the shell sands on which they grow. At Ormiclate on South Uist, the July display includes ragwort, buttercups and dune pansies.

The flora of lowland grasslands and heaths

In most European countries, there is an accepted taxonomy of plant associations whereby it is possible to classify the vegetation of a particular region. These studies, combined with plant geography, help to explain the origin and distribution of many of our plants. An example of this from grassland is the rock rose *Helianthemum apenninum*, which is restricted to the outcrop of Devonian limestone in southwest England and to certain areas in the Mendips, and represents one of the oceanic-southern elements in our flora. Another species, the grass *Koeleria vallesiana*, is restricted entirely to the Mendips. The Continental element is well represented, with a high concentration of species in southeast England. Many of these are associated with the chalk and include the early spider orchid *Ophrys sphegodes*, the lady orchid *Orchis purpurea*, and the monkey orchid *Orchis simia*. All are restricted to the chalk in Kent, while the late spider orchid *Ophrys fuciflora* is found in Kent, Sussex, on the Isle of Wight and on the oolitic limestone in Dorset.

The Breckland flora

The 1000 square kilometres of sandy soils in the Breckland area of East Anglia have long been of particular interest to the biologist because of their soil types. These vary from deep acid sands, whose nutrients have been leached away leaving a residual and impoverished podsol, to shallow, highly calcareous and more fertile soils. The latter are particularly rich in species including a fine turf of fescue *Festuca* and bent *Agrostis* grasses,

On Cavenham Heath, grasses and sedges grow among a carr of willow, alder and birch. As the heathland becomes drier the vegetation merges to sand sedge *(below right)*, while on top of the heath, where the soils are leached and acid, heather takes over *(below left)*.

meadow oatgrass *Helictotrichon pratense*, crested hair-grass *Koeleria*, squinancy wort *Asperula cynanchica*, hairy rock-cress *Arabis hirsuta*, purging flax *Linum perenne*, knotted pearlwort *Sagina nodosa* and wild thyme *Thymus serpyllum*. On the acid sands, the flora is much poorer, often characterized by heath bedstraw *Galium saxatile*, shepherd's cress *Teesdalia nudicaulis*, hair-grass *Deschampsia flexuosa*, and a number of lichens, of which *Cladonia arbuscula* is often dominant.

The calcicolous grasslands in Breckland have been described as a variant of the chalk grasslands of the downs and can be seen on parts of Lakenheath Warren, Weeting Heath, Foxhole Heath, and the sheep-grazed grasslands north of Icklingham. The more acid soils on deep sands produce a heather heathland on Berner's Heath, Horn and Weather, Cavenham and Thetford Heaths, and parts of Lakenheath Warren. A number of coastal species also occur on the Breckland sands, the best known being sand sedge *Carex arenaria*, widely distributed particularly on the sites of earlier rabbit warrens, the grass *Corynephorus canescens* which is rather local on the East Anglian coast and occurs in only one place in Breckland, the sand cat's-tail *Phleum arenarium* and a subspecies of the wild pansy *Viola tricolor curtisii* normally found on the coastal dunes.

The Continental element in the flora includes some rare and interesting plants. The perennial knawel *Scleranthus perennis* survives in open areas while the beautiful spiked speedwell *Veronica spicata* with its tall heads of deep blue flowers still occurs in a few areas where there is a fine turf on calcareous soils. Another plant is the field southernwood *Artemisia campestris*, which is nearly always associated with places where the sandy soil is disturbed. A number of these plants have become quite scarce in recent years, mainly because of the loss of close-cropped grass swards and open ground maintained before 1954 by rabbits.

Chalk and limestone floras

In 1966, it was estimated that, of the total 1.3 million hectares of land on chalk, only about 44,000 hectares were still occupied by unenclosed and untilled chalk grassland. The largest continuous areas of chalk grassland which survive today are in Wiltshire, mostly in the military training area of Salisbury Plain, although there are important sites on the North and South Downs. At Porton Down there are about 1600 hectares of grassland which makes it the second largest remaining chalk grassland in Britain. Most of this remarkable area is only lightly grazed by rabbits and hares, and in the summer there is a profusion of colourful flowers and a spectacular abundance of butterflies. In places there is much open scrub – particularly juniper *Juniperus communis* – and also a wide expanse of stony, lichen-rich chalk sward reminiscent of the East Anglian Breckland. A study of the land use history of Porton Down shows that in 1840 a large part of the downland was cultivated but later in the nineteenth century, particularly after 1870 when the price of wheat fell dramatically, much of the arable land was abandoned and reverted to grassland. Old maps and documents make it possible to date some of the grasslands and this evidence suggests that not much of it can be older than about 110 years. It is perhaps not surprising therefore that, in spite of the very colourful vegetation, there are comparatively few rarities in this large area of grassland.

The commonest type of grassland at Porton is a sheep's-fescue *Festuca ovina* and red fescue *F. rubra* mixture which is thought to occupy the areas which have not been cultivated, at least for many years, whereas grasslands which have developed on land previously cultivated are dominated by the oat-grass *Arrhenatherum elatius* and red fescue. On slopes that face from

southeast to southwest where the soil is shallow, there is an interesting grassland type which consists of sheep's-fescue and rough hawkbit *Leontodon hispidus*, together with the dwarf thistle *Cirsium acaule*, bird's-foot trefoil *Lotus corniculatus* and wild thyme. This grassland can look extremely attractive in the summer, when the orange-yellow flowers of the bird's-foot trefoil colour the downland slopes as far as the eye can see.

Carboniferous limestone floras

In southwest England there are many famous Carboniferous sites, from the numerous gorges of the Mendip Hills, particularly those at Cheddar, Ebba and Burrington, to the popular caves at Cheddar and Wookey Hole. In Bristol, the Avon Gorge has precipitous cliffs falling 91 metres, on which grow several *Sorbus* species, some of which are endemic. The limestone grassland which has developed on the soils of the rock ledges includes many interesting plants such as the rock rose *Helianthemum canum*, the burnet saxifrage *Pimpinella saxifraga*, bloody cranesbill *Geranium sanguineum*, the spiked speedwell, and the autumn squill *Scilla autumnalis*. At Cheddar, the ledges of the gorge may be pale rose pink in the summer with the rare Cheddar pink *Dianthus gratianopolitanus*.

Carboniferous limestone floras extend into Wales in Glamorgan, Powys, Clwyd and Gwynedd, into Derbyshire and the Pennines, Morecambe Bay and Shap Fell area of northern England. The landscape, particularly in South Wales and the Craven Pennines, has characteristic features of typical karst country – open, flat limestone pavements with many holes and fissures, known as grykes. In North Wales, the most famous sites are the Great and Little Orme's Heads in Gwynedd. The Great Orme is a particularly important exposure, although many of the interesting plants are on the cliffs, and the grassland is heavily grazed by sheep as well as being trampled by the many visitors. In northern England the Dales of Derbyshire and Yorkshire are some of the best known areas. The Dove valley is perhaps the most visited, but other areas are Lathkill Dale, Cressbrook Dale, Monks Dale, Lodden Dale, Gratton Dale, Miller's Dale, Deep Dale and Coombs

Parsonage Down in Wiltshire *(above left)* has escaped the plough because it has traditionally been cattle grazed. At the edge of the pasture musk thistles *Carduus nutans* are an indication of disturbed ground; here due to rabbit activity.

The fairy ring champignon *Marasmius oreades* illustrates well the way that the underground mycelium of fungi tend to radiate out in ever increasing circles *(above right)*. Large fairy rings are produced by other fungi, such as the St George's mushroom *Tricholoma gambosum*, and they can date back for several centuries. Large rings show up clearly on aerial photographs of grassland areas, and are possible indicators of permanent grassland sites.

Cheddar *(above)* is a deep, carboniferous limestone gorge lined with vertical cliffs up to 120 metres high. The open grassland vegetation on the ledges grades down into a scrub of rowan and ivy.

Malham Cove in the Yorkshire Dales *(right)* is a natural amphitheatre of Carboniferous limestone cliffs. Several species of *Sorbus* colonize the ledges and ash borders the stream.

Dale. At the south end of the Lake District the main exposures are around the head of Morecambe Bay, in Lancashire and the old county of Westmorland. There is a particularly famous group of low hills around Arnside, Hutton Roof and Witherslack, where there are large areas of limestone pavement, scar and scree.

Carboniferous limestone is widespread in Ireland, occupying the whole of the central plain, but much of this is covered by surface deposits, particularly glacial drift, and the high rainfall has resulted in extensive peat formations and the growth of bogs. The limestone outcrops in several places around the central plain: for example, in Fermanagh where the remarkable Marble Arch gorge is a nature reserve, and again in Sligo and Leitrim where the magnificent limestone plateau of Ben Bulben is intersected by two steep-sided valleys. The most interesting limestone plants are found on the scree and rocky slopes; the flat areas are covered by peat and calcicolous grassland is very local.

The most famous Carboniferous limestone area in Ireland is the Burren in Co. Clare and Galway. It is an area of rounded hills, about 300 metres high, which covers some 375 square kilometres. Much of this landscape is bare rock lying in horizontal beds with 'stepped' slopes when seen in profile. Many hill tops give the impression of being completely bare but in fact a luxuriant plant life lives in the cracks and crevices. The rainfall is soon lost from the limestone surface but the moist winds from the Atlantic sustain the vegetation.

No account of the Burren fails to quote the comment of one of Cromwell's officers that 'there was no water to drown a man, no timber to hang him and no soil to bury him'. This description is misleading because there are green fertile fields in the Burren valleys and a thick growth of hazel on many hillsides. The open, herbaceous vegetation can hardly be called limestone grassland, except on parts of the coast where a fine turf has developed, with the autumn ladies' tresses *Spiranthes spiralis*. Nevertheless, the assemblage of plants in the Burren is one of the most remarkable in Ireland because it contains southern or Lusitanian species mixed with northern and alpine plants, the last growing close to sea level. Some typically montane species grow in abundance, for example the mountain avens and bearberry, while the southern element is represented by the Burren orchid *Neotinea intacta* and the maidenhair fern *Adiantum capillus-veneris*. But there are numerous rarities such as the dark red helleborine *Epipactis atrorubens*, shrubby cinquefoil *Potentilla fruticosa*, the rock rose, the fen violet *Viola stagnina* and the red broomrape *Orobanche rubra*, which is parasitic on wild thyme. The rich flora of the Burren consists entirely of indigenous plants; there are no aliens or species of doubtful origin but so far botanists have only been able to speculate on the origin of this peculiar mixture of species.

Although most of the species mentioned are typical of calcicolous grasslands, a few are not, the commonest being heather which even grows in the limestone crevices. Elsewhere there may be a thin layer of peat, as on Black Head, where heather, crowberry, bearberry and the spring gentian *Gentiana verna* are abundant.

Neutral grassland floras

Neutral grasslands are sometimes referred to as meadow grasslands because their chief agricultural use is as hay meadows or for a combination of grazing and hay production. The main types are characterized by their plants and by the water regime and form of management.

Five types have been recognized. These are, first, the man-made Washlands in East Anglia, which are inundated during the winter when they take

The Burren in Ireland is one of the most important Carboniferous limestone regions in western Europe. The climate is cool and moist, which counteracts the rapid loss of water through the grykes of the limestone pavement. These grykes support a rich profusion of limestone plants such as bloody cranesbill, burnet rose and bird's-foot trefoil. Few shrubs can grow on such an exposed site, but a few, stunted hawthorns have survived severe wind-pruning.

flood water from nearby agricultural land, but for the remainder of the year are grazed by cattle. These areas are primarily of interest because of their rich bird life. A second type are the flood meadows. These are river valley meadows flooded in wet winters and normally used for grazing and hay production. Water meadows, a third type, were formerly widespread, particularly in the south of England. They consisted of an elaborate system of ditches or carriers for irrigating the meadow, and were usually successful in bringing on an early growth of grass in the spring – perhaps three weeks earlier than elsewhere. However, the maintenance of the ditches and sluices is very labour-intensive and today the system is virtually extinct. Fourthly, there are areas where the water level is almost at ground surface for most if not all of the year and the meadow land is maintained by grazing and cutting. Without this form of management these freshwater marsh meadows would revert to a tall marsh vegetation with reed. Finally, there are permanent meadows usually found on clay–loam soils and not directly associated with a river, so that any flooding which occurs is the result of imperfect drainage. These damp grasslands may occur on calcareous soils and show some relationship with the more typical lowland calcicolous grasslands.

The floristically rich flood meadows have become rare in lowland Britain because herbicides and fertilizers have improved the sward and productivity for agricultural purposes. One of the most interesting, however, is North Meadow, Cricklade, in Wiltshire. It is bounded by the River Churn on the north and the Thames on the south, and flooding usually occurs for short periods in the winter and early spring.

North Meadow is a 'lammas land' and has for many centuries been subject to a particular form of management which stipulates that grazing may take place between August 12th and February 12th, the grazing rights being granted in perpetuity to the people of Cricklade. After mid-February the grass is allowed to grow to a hay crop and sections, called hay doles, are put up for sale from time to time, and may be cut by any person who is prepared to offer the appropriate price.

There are numerous common meadow plants in the sward, each adding to its rich and attractive colour, but the most striking is the abundant fritillary *Fritillaria meleagris*, which turns the whole meadow a delicate mauve-purple in early May. Today, North Meadow is probably the best site in Britain for this species because the meadow has not been exposed to modern methods of grassland 'improvement'. In the same county and adjacent to two small tributaries to the River Thames is another very interesting meadow. This meadow with its distinctive flora is private land, but has been used for centuries to produce a hay crop in May and June, followed by grazing by cattle and sheep until the end of the year or the early part of the following year. This form of management allows a plant community to develop in which no one species is dominant, although grasses form the main proportion of the vegetation. At Oaksey, the farmer has never used inorganic fertilizers or herbicides although farmyard manure has been applied, as is the traditional practice. Some winter flooding occurs but not to the same extent as at Cricklade. The different forms of management received by each field may account for the fact that in one the green-winged orchid *Orchis morio*, the twayblade *Listera ovata* and the fritillary occur in large quantities, while in another there will be an abundance of meadow saffron *Colchicum autumnale* and in yet another the cowslip *Primula veris* and pepper saxifrage *Silaum silaus* may be most common.

The flood meadow grassland is particularly well developed in the broad flood plains of the upper Thames, south Midlands and parts of East Anglia. Port Meadow and the Yarnton and Pixie Meads in Oxfordshire are some

The deep pink ragged robin is a plant typical of freshwater marshes, damp meadows and fens in May and June.

Fritillaries are local, bulbous plants of neutral grassland sites, notably wet meadows in southern England. Each bell-shaped flower hangs down from a slender stem. Both purple chequered and plain white flowers appear in this Berkshire field in May.

of the best examples; the last two, having been managed as hay meadows for many centuries, are rich in species without any one plant being dominant. In some of the wet meadows in southern England and Ireland, the beautiful Loddon lily *Leucojum vernum* is a rare and declining member of this vegetation association.

Artificial grasslands and disturbed ground

Never before has there been so much interest in improving our urban environment and preventing the spread of industrial dereliction. We cannot afford to waste a single square metre, and grasses have provided us with the means of improving or restoring to public use large areas of land which have been derelict since the industrial revolution.

The use of grasses for amenity purposes is now an important research activity so that appropriate mixtures of species or cultivars can be recommended for different purposes, whether for a playing field or a bowling green. Much of this work has been done by the Sports Turf Research Institute, which advises on the wearing qualities of different grass mixtures for football pitches and other sports turf areas. In addition, other organizations have studied the establishment of a grass cover on new roadside

verges. The purpose here is to stabilize the soil and develop a vegetation which is both pleasing to the eye and which requires the minimum of maintenance. On calcareous soils, particularly where new motorways have cut through the chalk downs, it is possible to grow colourful mixtures of low-growing calcicolous plants such as bird's-foot trefoil.

Grasses are also important in the reclamation of spoil heaps resulting from mining. Where the spoil has high levels of toxic substances such as lead, zinc or aluminium, resistant strains of grasses must be found either in nature or by selective breeding. But, even when grass can be made to grow on this spoil, the leaves cannot be eaten by stock since they contain too much poison.

Where the spoil is non-toxic, as on colliery waste, pulverized fuel ash from power stations or waste from china clay excavations, other methods of reclamation are available. In these cases, the main difficulties are the absence of a proper soil structure and a lack of major nutrients, particularly nitrogen. In Cornwall, the waste products from the china clay mines are of two kinds, a coarse sand made up of quartz particles, and fine fragments of mica. The sheer quantity of the coarse sand poses great problems; the white cones are visible for many miles and alter the landscape completely. The shape of the cones can be modified so that the outlines fit in with the natural contours of the surrounding hills, but the application of topsoil in order to grow grass would be far too expensive. Grass can be grown directly on the coarse sand by sowing the seed together with a suitable fertilizer. However, the sand is itself very permeable and, in the high rainfall areas of Cornwall, the nitrogen is soon leached away, and the grass dies. Research has shown that if the grass is mixed with white clover *Trifolium repens*, the root nodules of the latter accumulate nitrogen which is liberated to the soil surface and is sufficient to keep the grass alive. It is also important to graze the new grassland with sheep so that the turf is kept short; this gives the clover

When gorse flowers in April, it brings a bright splash of colour to the verges of the M3 *(above left)* and other motorways. This species is one of 60 plants which were planted along motorway verges in the early 1970s.

Late afternoon sun spotlights the grassed-over mica dam in front of the china clay workings at Hawks Tor on Bodmin Moor *(above right)*. This dam, which was landscaped and planted with a mixture of universal, lowland and upland grass and legume seeds in 1973, now provides richer grazing than the adjacent moorland. The distant peak is an old tip which has been naturally colonized by a variety of plants including willows.

plenty of space to spread. In addition, the dung from the sheep supplies further nitrogen. Great progress has been made in recent years in land re-vegetation by combining landscape technology with plant ecology, but more research is needed to speed up the process of restoring the ever-growing areas of dereliction.

Considerable areas of disturbed ground have resulted from changes occurring in the countryside. This has attracted an often colourful flora typically of thistles, docks and dandelions. All are able to take advantage of these areas because they are able to colonize them quickly. Fires provide similar conditions and no plant is quicker than rosebay willow-herb *Epilobium angustifolium* to take hold.

The invertebrates of grasslands and heaths

This brief survey of the great variety of vegetation types on our lowlands suggests that the fauna might also be very diverse. This is almost certainly the case but many groups of invertebrates are difficult taxonomically and there are insufficient specialists to study them thoroughly. So, comparisons of the faunas of different grasslands and heaths are usually made on the basis of easily recognized species such as the butterflies, moths, beetles and spiders, and smaller groups such as the woodlice and the snails and slugs.

In general, a richer flora will support a richer fauna because there are more food sources for plant-eating animals. Many animals feed on several species of plants or else on both plants and other animals. Others are entirely carnivorous or parasitic on other animals. And there is yet another group, known as detritus-feeders, which consume dead organic material.

Burying or sexton beetles derive their name from the extraordinary habit of burying carcasses of small vertebrates in the ground; an activity associated with their highly specialized reproductive process. They burrow under the carcass until a narrow cavity is formed into which the carcass falls, and the soil fills in on top of it. The female remains to lay her eggs and feeds the young larvae on the rotting flesh. On this dead rook are the orange and black *Necrophorus investigator* and the black *N. humator.*

It is, therefore, quite clear that a grassland formation might have a very large number of different invertebrate animals living in it.

The structure of the vegetation is important for all species, whether they are carnivores, parasites, or plant-feeders. This is best illustrated in an undisturbed grassland, and we must, therefore, distinguish between managed grassland, which is exploited for agricultural purposes and may have a sward no taller than five to ten centimetres, and the ungrazed grassland where the vegetation may reach a metre or more. The upper layer of the latter contains the flowering heads of grasses and other plants, and therefore attracts those insects which feed on the nectar or directly on the flowers, fruits and seeds. Below this layer are the leaves and stems, which again are the habitat of other specialist plant-feeders, and closer to the ground is the all-important litter layer. Here there is a high concentration of different groups of animals concerned with feeding either on the accumulation of dead material or on the animals themselves. This structure has a considerable influence on the carnivorous species which either hunt through the grassland leaf canopy or lie in wait on the flowers and the field-layer plants, or search for their prey through the tiny crevices and air spaces within the ground leaf litter. If we consider the number of animal species and the number of microhabitats within such a profile, we can see that there is a pyramid of numbers. The broad base of the pyramid incorporates the soil surface, humus and litter where the largest number of microhabitats and species are found, and the apex is situated in the zone of the flowers, fruits and seeds, where there are fewer niches and consequently a smaller number of species.

Grass tussocks also add variety to the grassland structure. They are important as habitats for many insects and a place of refuge during the winter months. This is because the tussocks are unpalatable to sheep and are usually undisturbed, while the other species of grasses are nibbled down until the sward is no more than two or three centimetres high. It is, therefore, clear that grazing imposes its own structural pattern on grassland.

A temporary structure such as a grass ley, which is maintained for only three or four years and consists of very few plant species, generally has a poor invertebrate fauna. This is partly because of catastrophic habitat changes, such as ploughing and reseeding, which take place before a stabilized fauna has been able to develop, and partly because there are few plant species and no accumulation of litter. The same is found in heavily grazed pastures, where the vegetation is kept very short and the treading effect of the grazing animals breaks up and disperses the litter. Litter accumulation is very slow, in any case, because the vegetation is consumed by the grazers.

In hay meadows, particularly in lowland river valleys where herbicides and fertilizers are not used and grassland has persisted for several centuries, the flora is often rich. One would expect to find a fauna of equal interest. In fact little is known about the fauna of these meadows. The removal of the crop followed by grazing – the usual pattern of management – is probably sufficient to reduce the numbers of species able to live there, although grazing animals do introduce additional species with the accumulation of dung. Without the help of dung-feeding insects it would take a very long time for dung to break down and for nutrients to be returned to the soil.

Burning is not extensively used on grasslands in the British Isles, although it is of course traditional on many *Calluna* heathlands where new young shoots are important for grouse and hill sheep. From time to time, tor grass *Brachypodium pinnatum*, which covers large areas of the downs, has been burned in order to expose the fresh green shoots in the spring.

For small insects, a grassy sward represents a jungle of leaves and stems through which they have to crawl or fly to feed or find a mate. Here, a sawfly starts its journey up to the grass tip from where it will take off for a short flight. Its larvae feed on the grass leaves.

Sheep will eat the shoots when young and the grass is kept under control. Deliberate burning on lowland heaths is occasionally used to control tree growth but most fires are caused by carelessness and ignorance. In dry weather, such fires burn not only the live vegetation but also the accumulated litter, and destroy the greater part of the invertebrate fauna. Recovery during the next few years is slow while the heather and other vegetation grow up again. Here again, tussocks which are resistant to burning provide refuges for some of the animals.

Even less is known about the effects of human treading on the invertebrate life of grasslands and heaths. Popular public beauty spots sustain heavy human impact during holidays and at fine weekends, and it appears that invertebrate life is disrupted at lower treading levels than the plants. For example, on dry soils, the vegetation may be resistant to fairly heavy trampling, but continual physical disturbance will make it a habitat unsuitable for many animals; grassland litter subjected to only five treads per month for a year can cause a fall in numbers of most groups of invertebrate animals by at least 50 per cent, whereas the vegetation itself is scarcely affected. On the other hand, not all animals are reduced in number; one or two species actually increase as the nature of the litter changes.

Treading breaks up the litter and therefore accelerates its decomposition by bacteria and fungi. The contribution made by animals to this process has been demonstrated by the intensive use of insecticides on pasture land. This destroys most of the fauna and, when there is no grazing, the litter accumulates at such a rate that it eventually depresses the vegetation growth and becomes a hazard during hay-making by obstructing the cutter bars of the machines. It seems that the larger invertebrates are important in breaking down the litter into small pieces or else passing it through their gut so that a further process of decomposition can take place when fungi and bacteria grow on their faecal pellets. When, in experiments, litter was enclosed in a nylon mesh bag so that the larger invertebrates were excluded, the rate of breakdown was noticeably reduced.

The application of fertilizers to grassland also has a considerable effect on the fauna. These nutrients, particularly nitrates and phosphates, greatly increase grassland productivity but the response is selective; certain plants grow more vigorously than others which are then eliminated. This, in turn, reduces the numbers of plant-feeding animals, and the changes in the structure of the vegetation influence the predatory animals.

If we take one well-defined group of animals, such as the spiders, which are all predatory, and examine how they exploit a grassland environment, some interesting facts emerge. In ungrazed or very lightly grazed grassland, where a litter layer has formed, most of the species, out of a total of about 140 normally occurring in this habitat, will be found in that zone. The majority are tiny species, one to two millimetres long, which spin fragile webs in the crevices between the fragments of dead plant material. Here, they feed on collembolans, mites and the young of many small flies and plant-bugs. And, even below the litter, there are other species which exploit the surface of the soil. Where it is well drained, the burrows of the purse-web spider *Atypus affinis* may be very common. It occurs mainly on the chalk downs but is also found further north, on the Carboniferous limestone grassland in Lancashire. *Atypus* excavates a vertical burrow, lined with silk and extended on to the surface of the ground as a horizontal silk tube rather like the finger of a glove. The spider, which is quite large and powerful, waits within its burrow until a beetle walks over the tube on the surface. It then rushes up, seizes the prey, make a slit in the silk tube and drags the beetle down into the burrow.

Where grassland is more open and short, several species of wolf spider may be active. In longer grassland the wolf spider most frequently found is *Pardosa nigriceps*, well known for its ability to climb high in the vegetation. Its body has dark and pale, longitudinal stripes which are cryptic against a background of grass stems. A near relative, *Pardosa pullata*, lives deeper in the vegetation so that if the grassland is grazed or cut *Pardosa nigriceps* disappears but *P. pullata* can survive. The stem and leaf zone is preferred by a number of interesting spiders which are beautifully camouflaged in the light and shade of grass stems and leaves. One of these is a hammock spider *Linyphia triangularis* and another is an elongated crab spider the same colour as a grass stem. The crab spider holds its long legs parallel to the grass stems so that it cannot be seen in profile. And, patterns of light and dark markings conceal *Singa pygmaea*, as it spins a small orb web in the spaces between the leaves.

Some species which hunt in the lower zones of the grass climb to the upper parts to construct their egg sacs. *Agroeca brunnea* attaches its eggs to the top of a grass stem and then plasters a layer of hard mud over them as protection against predators and parasites. Tall grass stems are also of considerable use to the tiny, so-called money spiders which live in the grassland litter and normally do not leave their dark, moist environment. At certain times of the year, they emerge from the litter and climb to the top of grass stems where they extrude a strand of silk. This floats like a parachute in the moving air and the spider is carried away. Aeronautic dispersal is common among the smaller species of spiders, and is obviously the means by which they reach distant parts – even oceanic islands.

The upper part of the grassland profile has its own spider fauna of species which lurk in the florets of the larger flowers waiting for visiting

The dew-covered web of the hammock spider consists of many vertical strands of silk which are suspended from the sides of its hammock. The spider sits upside down in the centre of the web, waiting for small flying insects to crash into the strands and drop on to the hammock.

flies. One of these species, *Misumena vatia*, is able to change its colour from white to yellow to yellow-pink according to the flower chosen. Unnoticed by a visiting fly or bee, it sits motionless until its prey is within striking range. Like many crab spiders, the first two pairs of legs are stout and strong, and the large spines on their inner sides hold their prey firmly.

Heather heathland has a rather different fauna from that of grassland, with fewer species unless there are wet patches. This is because dry heather heath has a poor flora and acid soils also support few invertebrate species. However, the same zonation of animal life exists. Even the burrowing spider *Atypus* has its counterpart on the heather heath, although the species concerned, *Eresus niger*, is very rare in this country. It also constructs a tube in the soil, which is usually sand, but there is no 'silk purse' on the ground surface. Instead, strands of silk radiate from the mouth of the burrow and into the surrounding vegetation. When a beetle walks by, it disturbs the silk strands and the spider rushes up from its burrow to seize it.

Many insect groups are well represented in grassland but only a few of the hundreds of species can be mentioned here. The rufous grasshopper *Gomphocerippus rufus* is only known from the chalk in Britain and its best localities are on the North Downs. A similar example is the stripe-winged grasshopper *Stenobothrus lineatus*, which also occurs on chalk grassland where high ground temperatures may develop. Butterflies are some of the most attractive insects of grasslands and contribute as much to the pleasure of walking on the downs as do the wild flowers. Well-known species include the small heath *Coenonympha pamphilus*, meadow brown *Maniola jurtina*, grayling *Hipparchia semele*, small tortoiseshell *Aglais urticae* and the large skipper *Ochlodes venatus*. Two groups are found on calcicolous grasslands: those which occur on the chalk and oolitic limestone, and others which prefer Carboniferous limestone in the north of England. The distinctive chalk species are the chalk-hill blue *Lysandra coridon* – a beautiful insect, more or less confined to areas where its larval food plant, the horseshoe vetch *Hippocrepis comosa* grows – the more local Adonis blue *L. bellargus*, the small blue *Cupido minimus*, which feeds on leguminous plants, and the silver-spotted skipper *Hesperia comma*. The marbled white butterfly *Melanargia galathea* is also characteristic of chalk and limestone, although it is now not so common. In the north of England, the Scotch argus *Erebia aethiops* is confined to Carboniferous limestone.

The Breckland grass heaths are known for a number of species of moths which are perhaps more typical of coastal sand dunes. The widespread cinnabar moth *Callimorpha jacobaeae* is abundant because its food plant, the common ragwort *Senecio jacobaea*, is so common. On acid heathland, the grayling is one of the most characteristic butterflies, together with the green hairstreak *Callophrys rubi* and silver-studded blue *Plebejus argus*. Neutral grassland is associated with some widespread and common butterflies, among them the small white *Pieris rapae*, the green-veined white *P. napi*, the orange tip *Anthocaris cardamine*, the meadow brown and the ringlet *Aphantopus hyperanthus*.

The mammals, reptiles and birds

By far the most important and familiar mammal on British grasslands is the rabbit. Although so widespread and common, it seems to have been absent in this country before the twelfth century, when it was probably introduced by the Normans. For a long time after its introduction, it was local in distribution; it was kept strictly within warrens as a valuable source of food and fur and never succeeded in escaping to the open countryside. Warrens were established anywhere where the soil was light and well drained – the

Weeting Heath is a calcicolous grassland found in Breckland. Rabbits have become widespread on the northern part of the heath and the grassland is a close-grazed, moss and lichen-rich turf.

best conditions for breeding – and, not surprisingly, the Breckland region and the chalk downs were favoured places. In the seventeenth and eighteenth centuries, warrening began to decline as the land was converted to more profitable agricultural use. Rabbits managed to escape and started to spread throughout the countryside, eventually multiplying and so becoming a serious agricultural pest. However, the rabbit's value as a game animal ensured that its numbers were maintained even when there was a conflict with agriculture.

In 1953, myxomatosis reached Britain and within a year or two vast numbers of rabbits were wiped out. The vegetation responded with a remarkable and glorious flowering of many plants which had not been seen for years. In Breckland, for example, maiden pink *Dianthus deltoides*, spiked speedwell, Spanish catchfly *Silene otites*, and sand catchfly *S. conica*, and field southernwood *Artemisia campestris* delighted the eye. The chalk downs showed a similar response, with the flowering of rare orchids. Unfortunately, this process lasted for only a short time because, in the absence of grazing, the more vigorous grasses and plants grew taller, bushes began to invade and the low-growing plants were suppressed.

Some birds were also influenced by the disappearance of the rabbit, particularly hole-nesting species such as the wheatear *Oenanthe oenanthe*, stock dove *Columba oenas* and, in coastal areas, the shelduck *Tadorna tadorna*. The numbers of the first of these dropped dramatically on the Breckland heaths and in spite of attempts in some localities to provide them with artificial holes, there was no sign of recovery.

The rabbit is of course an important prey species for stoats *Mustela erminea*, weasels *M. nivalis* and foxes *Vulpes vulpes* and, in the west country, for the buzzard *Buteo buteo* which was probably the most seriously affected. But stoats also declined, being apparently less adaptable than foxes or weasels. When the vegetation grew tall and thick, small rodents, such as the field vole *Microtus agrestis*, increased in numbers. The common brown hare *Lepus capensis* is a familiar, grassland mammal and an important game species. In the absence of rabbits, it increased for a time as it was immune to myxomatosis. The mole *Talpa europaea* prefers lowland grassland on richer soils, and is scarce in the base-poor soils of acidic heaths where there are few earthworms. The hedgehog *Erinaceus europaeus*, common and

An adder sunbathing on a lichen sward. Common on acid heathlands of Breckland, it occurs in a wide range of habitats, and is rarely far from water. It feeds mainly on small mammals and, occasionally, birds.

pygmy shrews *Sorex aranaeus* and *S. minutus* are all widespread, while the harvest mouse *Micromys minutus*, the smallest British rodent, is often quite plentiful in the taller grasslands which are not grazed.

All six species of British reptile are found on lowland heaths and grassland. Of these the scarce, smooth snake *Coronella austriaca* and sand lizard *Lacerta agilis* are very local and only occur on certain, dry, open heathlands in parts of southern England, although the lizard is also found on the coastal sand dunes at Ainsdale in Lancashire. The common lizard *L. vivipara*, slow-worm *Anguis fragilis* and grass snake *Natrix natrix* are all widely distributed in Britain in hedgerows and woods as well as on grasslands and heaths. But the common lizard is the only reptile known in Ireland. The sixth species, the adder *Vipera berus*, is rather local. It likes to be close to water as well as to have open ground for sunbathing and is common in some coastal areas where there is sandy heathland with scattered pools. It is also numerous on some of the more acid Breckland heaths, notably on the heather and sand sedge at Cavenham Heath National Nature Reserve, where there are pools and other wet places.

The bird fauna of the lowland heaths and grassland has always been rather poor in species. For example, in the 1930s when large areas of sheep-grazed grassland still remained, surveys taken of birds on the chalk downs recorded a rather restricted fauna of meadow pipits *Anthus pratensis*, skylarks *Alauda arvensis*, grey partridges *Perdix perdix* and lapwings *Vanellus vanellus* as breeding species. The last three are about the only breeding birds on arable land in lowland Britain. The stone curlew *Burhinus oedicnemus* formerly nested on most of the chalk downs and Breckland heaths and extended as far as Lincolnshire. But it declined considerably as its habitat was converted to arable farming or forestry plantations.

In recent years, the common curlew *Numenius arquata* has increased in numbers in Breckland because it prefers the taller vegetation, particularly heather, which grew up when rabbits became fewer. Vegetation changes have also affected two other characteristic Breckland birds, the woodlark *Lullula arborea* and the ringed plover *Charadrius hiaticula*. The latter needs a good deal of open sandy ground for nesting, but the decline of the woodlark is harder to understand. The heaths and downs of lowland England were also formerly the home of the great bustard *Otis tarda*. This mag-

Rooks, herring and lesser black-backed gulls are often to be found feeding on newly disturbed ground, for example where freshly mown grass has just been removed for silage.

nificent bird has not been seen in this country as a breeding species since the 1830s. Although an attempt is now being made to re-introduce it to Salisbury Plain, many people feel that the lowland landscape of England has changed far too much for the re-establishment to be a success.

Heaths which have a good cover of gorse, bracken and heather often attract the nightjar *Caprimulgus europaeus*, another species which, in recent years, has disappeared from many traditional nesting areas. The New Forest, Dorset, and parts of Sussex comprise almost the total breeding range of the Dartford warbler *Sylvia undata* in Britain. It is a species more at home in the Mediterranean maquis than the English countryside, preferring heather heaths with scattered gorse bushes or seedling birch which can be used as song perches. It is another example of a species which has lost much of its habitat during the last 40 years. Because it is a resident in Britain, it suffers severely in hard winters. Fortunately, gorse, which is so important for its survival, is thick enough to provide protection from cold winds, and has a rich invertebrate fauna even in winter. The stonechat *Saxicola torquata* and the red-backed shrike *Lanius collurio*, two other heathland birds of southern England, also often nest in gorse bushes. Overgrown grassy areas, where there is plenty of cover, attract the grasshopper warbler *Locustella naevia* and, as the bushes grow, the whitethroat *Sylvia communis* and the lesser whitethroat *S. curruca* move in. The corn bunting *Milaria calandra* is characteristic of open grassy places, but seems to prefer the edges of cultivated land or hay meadows rather than the open heath. Birds of prey are not common as breeding species on heathlands, but Montagu's harrier *Circus pygargus* still nests on rare occasions on some of the Norfolk heaths, and the short-eared owl *Asio flammeus* is seen regularly.

The great meadows in the lowland river valleys are often interesting ornithological areas, particularly where a hay crop is first taken so that nesting birds have cover during the incubation period. Damp meadows of this type are favoured by the reed bunting *Emberiza schoeniclus*, redshank *Tringa totanus*, lapwing, mallard *Anas platyrhynchos*, common partridge, yellow wagtail *Motacilla flava* and snipe *Gallinago gallinago*. In the Washlands, the wet grassland and pools of shallow water with mud margins attract other species which excite the birdwatcher. Some of the rarer ducks, such as garganey *A. querquedula* and gadwall *A. strepera*, breed, as do the black-tailed godwit *Limosa limosa* and, occasionally, the ruff *Philomachus pugnax*. In the 1930s, most of the hay meadows in lowland Britain were the haunt of the corncrake *Crex crex* but this bird has now almost vanished from areas where mechanized cutting is practised. Its strongholds remain in parts of Ireland and in the Hebrides where the hay crop is cut later in the season.

In winter, the meadows are favourite roosting and feeding sites for large flocks of gulls, rooks *Corvus frugilegus*, lapwings and golden plover *Pluvialis apricaria* as well as for visiting northern thrushes, the redwing *Turdus iliacus* and fieldfare *T. pilaris*. So, an environment inhospitable for birds in the breeding season may provide an invaluable winter food supply both from the soil fauna and from scattered seeds.

Plants

Many factors have contributed to the distribution of plants in lowland Britain as we see them today. The type of soil, the climate, competition with other species and, not least, man's own activities, have all played a large part in the shaping of vegetation patterns. Weeds are opportunist plants which quickly take advantage of waste ground laid bare, but many of the more interesting native plants are becoming scarcer owing to the loss of their preferred habitat. Plants which are on the edge of their range are especially sensitive to both climatic and environmental changes. Such changes may take place gradually by natural means; but they also occur – usually more rapidly – as a direct result of man. Draining of wet lowlands, ploughing of grasslands, as well as changes in farm management and the collection of plants, have all contributed to locally distributed plants becoming rare. Both green-winged orchids and pasque flowers are plants of permanent grassland areas which will not survive if the land is ploughed. Also, since permanent grassland is not a natural vegetation climax, these plants will survive only if the grassland is maintained either by grazing, or by mowing. Otherwise, shrubs begin to invade and eventually a woodland climax develops.

Wild clematis, common rock rose and salad burnet are all lime-loving or calcicole plants; while calcifuge plants such as heaths will not tolerate growing in limy soils. Such plants, which are choosy about the type of soil in which they will grow, may have a limited distribution, but if they are specially adapted they may compete very favourably with ubiquitous, but less well-adapted plants.

1

1 Adder's tongue *Ophioglossum vulgatum* is a striking fern which grows in grassland and open scrub, most commonly in the southeast of Britain. Each year, a single tongue-shaped leaf appears above ground. Arising from the base of the leaf an erect fertile spike appears slightly later, bearing two rows of sporangia in which the spores develop.

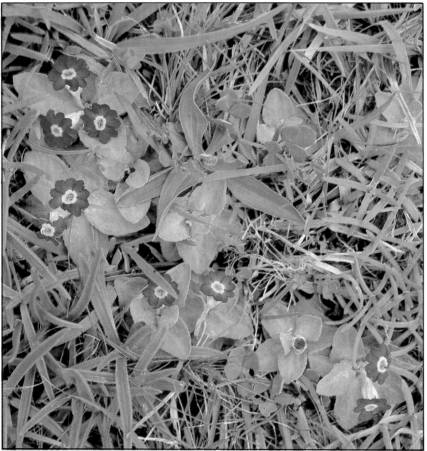

2

2 Scottish primrose *Primula scotica* is the smallest native member of the primrose family. Confined to the extreme north of Scotland and also present on Orkney, it grows in short coastal turf and on dunes. It has two flowering periods; the first is during May–June and the second July–August.

3

4

4 Round-leaved fluellen *Kickxia spuria* is one of two species of fluellens which grow as annual weeds on arable land, especially in cornfields on calcareous soils. It is a local plant in parts of southern England and does not extend up beyond the Midlands and South Wales. It is most easily seen in corn stubble.

3 Smaller than early purple orchids, the green-winged orchid *Orchis morio* grows in short grasslands, preferably on calcareous soil, and can be locally abundant on permanent pastures in southern England. This attractive orchid which flowers in May and June has no spots on the leaves and the purple sepals are distinctly veined with green.

5 Lichens are some of the most attractive small, heathland plants, especially the *Cladonia* species which bear contrasting spore-producing apothecia on their tips. The range of flowering plants which grow on poor heathland soils is limited and so the slow-growing lichens can establish themselves without much competition.

5

Plants *(continued)*

1

1 Knapweed broomrape *Orobanche elatior* is a plant which completely lacks chlorophyll. Unable to photosynthesize its own food, it lives as a parasite on greater knapweed which grows on calcicolous grasslands. Once the underground broomrape tubers have attached to the roots of their host, the parasite can develop its dense flowering spike. Each plant produces many seeds, which increase the chance of some landing beside a host plant.

2 *Briza media* is the most common of the two native quaking grasses. Growing in both wet acid or dry calcicolous meadows and grassy places, it is widespread all over Britain, although absent in north Scotland. When in flower, the purple-green spikelets quiver in the slightest breeze, giving rise to the common name.

2

3

4

3 The attactive, blue spring gentian *Gentiana verna*, here growing in coastal turf on an Irish limestone outcrop, is now rarely seen in Britain, as the plant is confined to grassland areas in north England and in western Ireland. The flowers which appear in May or June are pollinated by bumble bees, and in ungrazed areas capsules containing up to 250 seeds will form. Even if no seed is produced, gentians can still spread by underground rhizomes.

4 Neat feather moss *Pseudoscleropodium purum* is widespread, equally tolerant of chalk or acid soils in open grassland or woodland sites. This pale green, branching moss loosely weaves itself among the grass on calcicolous grassland slopes.

5 The hoary rockrose *Helianthemum canum,* here growing on the Burren in Ireland, is an attractive local shrub of rocky limestone pastures. The golden-yellow flowers of this rockrose are smaller than the more widespread common rockrose *H. nummularium.*

6 Maiden pink *Dianthus deltoides* is an attractive, locally scattered plant of dry, grassy and sandy places from Surrey up to Scotland. The solitary, scentless flowers have toothed pink petals with white spots. These plants are growing with lady's bedstraw on a sand dune system on the east coast of Scotland.

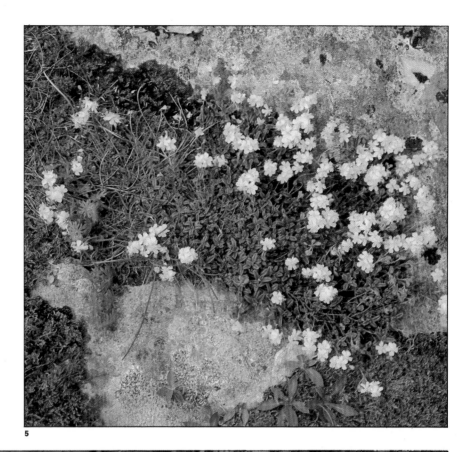

5

6

Invertebrates

Almost every structural component of a grassland or heath-land is exploited by the plant-feeders. The roots are eaten by the larvae of butterflies, moths and beetles, and the stems by these insects and by sawfly and fly larvae. The leaves are eaten, mined, sucked and galled by larval and adult insects of different groups, while the flowers, fruits and seeds are exploited by insect specialists. An abundance of flower species provides nectar and pollen for adult flower-visitors, such as bees, moths, butterflies and hoverflies. All this activity by invertebrate animals contributes to a flow of energy and nutrients away from the green plants.

The structure of the vegetation is also important for the carnivores and parasites. Some hunt through the leaf canopy, while others lie in wait on flowers or search through the crevices and air spaces in the ground leaf litter. Parasitic wasps fly low over vegetation and bare ground in search of suitable living animals in which to lay their eggs.

At each stage in this food chain, a proportion of the energy is lost in the form of dead material which is added to the decomposer system. This organic material supports fungi, detritus-feeders and scavengers, all of which break down the material and release the nutrients back to the soil so that they can be recycled through the green plants.

1

1 The chalkhill blue *Lysandra coridon* is one of several species of blues which are largely confined to southern England. This species which can be seen in July and August is locally common on chalk hills and in limestone areas. The male, shown here, is a silvery blue, and the female dingy brown.

2 The meadow brown *Maniola jurtina* is widespread throughout Britain and is on the wing in fields and woodland rides from June to September. The larvae feed on grasses, hibernate, and do not pupate until after the winter.

3 The individual pollen grains from the knapweed flower can be seen all over this bumble bee's body *Bombus lucorum*. Like the smaller honey bee, bumble bees play an important role as insect pollinators.

2

3

4

5

4 A Mother Shipton moth *Euclidimera mi* rests on a mountain avens flower in the Burren, Ireland, in early June. The moth, which is widely distributed over England, Wales, south Scotland and Ireland, gets its name from the markings on the forewings which are thought to resemble the profile of an old woman.

5 These small moths *Micropteryx calthella* are feeding on the pollen in a marsh marigold flower; they will also feed on buttercups. The moths have unequal sized mandibles with interlocking teeth which grind up the pollen before it is passed into a pouch.

6 On grassy places inland and by the sea the striking six spot burnet moths *Zygaena filipendulae* can be seen on the wing on sunny days in July and August. These moths are pairing on the outside of a cocoon on the Lizard in August. The greenish caterpillars, which have black markings and yellow spots, feed on vetches and clovers. They hibernate in the winter and complete their growth in the spring, crawling up stems to make their cocoons where it is difficult for birds to attack them.

6

Invertebrates *(continued)*

1

2

1 The structure of spiders' webs shows up well when etched with dew on autumnal, misty mornings. *Araneus quadratus,* a relative of the garden spider, sits on its orb web with its prey.

2 The crab spider *Misumena vatia* sits inside or behind a flower, lying in wait for unsuspecting insects which visit the flower to feed. It then emerges into the open to grab its prey. This yellow spider is feeding on a hymenopteran on a wood spurge flower. Adult spiders can change colour from yellow to white and back again in a few days.

3 The great green bush cricket *Tettigonia viridissima* is the largest bush cricket found in Britain. In midsummer its loud, continuous song can be heard in the fields and hedgerows near the south coast of England and Wales. Food includes seeds and other insects such as this male bog bush cricket.

4 The sand-digger wasp *Ammophila sabulosa* digs a flask-shaped hole in sandy places on heathland areas. It then goes in search of a non-hairy caterpillar which it paralyses and drags back down into the hole and upon which it lays an egg. The hole is then sealed with a stone and the site concealed by flicking sand grains over it. When the young wasp emerges it feeds on the caterpillar.

5 Road casualties such as this hedgehog are quickly utilized as a food source by many insects. These greenbottle flies *Lucilia caesar* are laying their eggs on the soft, bare skin.

6 *Arion ater* is a large slug which may be totally black, grey or brick red. Slugs, like snails, tend to be most active at night, but they will also emerge in the daytime if it is wet. Most are omnivorous, eating algae, fungi and lichens and also rotting vegetation.

3

4

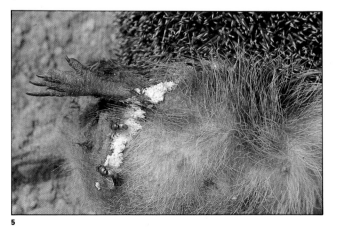
5

6

Birds

The bird population of managed grassland and arable land fluctuates seasonally. Very few species find it suitable for all the activities of the breeding cycle: feeding, display, nesting and rearing broods. Over vast areas of farmland, skylarks and lapwings may be the only two breeding species. The early mowing of hay and the even earlier harvesting of silage crops have made the habitat unsuitable for birds which need thick cover for nesting and hiding their young. In southern Britain this applies especially to game birds, but on large estates pheasant stocks are often replenished artificially.

But the fields may be invaded at all times of the year by huge flocks of birds which roost in trees, like the crow family, by freshwater or even on the coast, like gulls, geese, swans, ducks and waders. Some feed on invertebrates and grain and therefore they strike a balance in the farmer's scales. But geese and swans are unpopular since they attack crops and graze the early bite. Occasional birds of prey career over the fields sending clouds of birds sky high.

Among them will very often be meadow pipits, the most abundant small birds of open country. They winter in the lowlands where there is a good invertebrate food supply and breed on rough pastures at all altitudes. Although meadow pipits also nest on lowland heaths, this habitat has a very distinctive bird life. But the pressures under which it has been placed mean that it is now the relict home of several rare breeding species. In winter its food potential is very low and it is virtually deserted except for the passing predator intent on small mammals such as mice or voles.

1

2

1 When a nightjar *Caprimulgus europaeus* sits on its nest on bare ground in heathland areas during the day, its mottled body markings blend in with the surrounding vegetation. Although present all over Britain and Ireland, it is showing a decline in numbers and is now very scarce in Scotland. After dusk the characteristic mechanical churring song can be heard.

2 This curlew *Numenius arquata* is sheltering from winter winds in a stubble field on Wexford North Slob in Ireland. Although curlews frequently nest inland on moors and meadows, they are also a familiar sight on mud flats and estuaries where they can be seen feeding with other waders.

3 Rough coastal scrub, moors and heaths are the typical terrain of the stonechat *Saxicola torquata.* They are widespread in Ireland where this male was seen, and tend to have a southern and westerly distribution in Britain.

3

4

4 Apart from some exposed upland areas, there are few parts of Britain and Ireland where starlings *Sturnus vulgaris* do not occur. The birds seen here are feeding on the insects disturbed by cows trampling over the ground as they feed.

5 The jackdaw *Corvus monedula* feeds in fields alongside starlings and rooks. Typically gregarious, it will also scavenge on tips. This jackdaw is feeding on the external parasites of a red deer hind.

5

Uplands

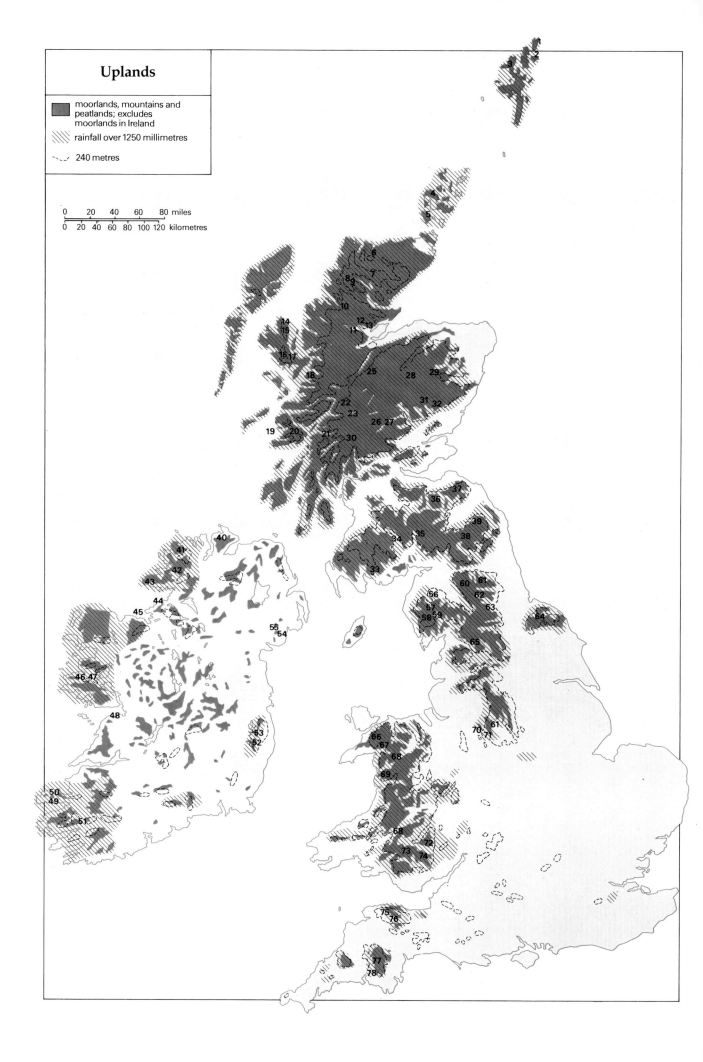

Uplands

- ▨ moorlands, mountains and peatlands; excludes moorlands in Ireland
- ▨ rainfall over 1250 millimetres
- ⌇ 240 metres

| 0 | 20 | 40 | 60 | 80 miles |
| 0 | 20 40 | 60 80 | 100 | 120 kilometres |

This map shows the distribution of mountains, moorlands and peatlands. The locations marked on the map are those referred to in this chapter.

A history of uplands

The uplands – hills, moors and mountains – provide much of the most splendid scenery to be found in Britain and Ireland, rivalled in magnificence only by some of the rugged, craggy coastlines. They are also by far the most extensive of the major terrestrial habitat types, containing vast reservoirs of wildlife. Areas not given over to forestry or intensive agriculture comprise about one eighth of England and Wales, over a quarter of Ireland and nearly two thirds of Scotland. Yet the vegetation, except for that of the mountain peaks and the wetter bogs, is man made. We now know that the moorlands of Britain and Ireland formerly bore a cover of scrub and woodland which was largely destroyed in prehistoric and historic times.

Most of this knowledge comes from examining fossilized plant remains. Deep peats, and the muds and silts at the bottom of lakes, are devoid of oxygen. This prevents the complete rotting away of plant material by micro-organisms, and is the reason why peat can accumulate. Because both peat and lake-bottom muds gradually build upwards with time, any plant remains present at a given depth are evidence of the vegetation existing when that layer was deposited. Such deposits often contain some identifiable macroscopic remains like fruits, seeds and leaves. These, however, are generally outnumbered a thousand-fold or more by microscopic pollen grains and spores. The outer skins of these are very resistant to decay; even when the inner parts have decomposed, the size and shape of grains are still apparent. Different groups of plants can be identified, sometimes even to species level, by the different sizes and shapes of the grains and by distinctive sculptured patterning on the skins. The study of preserved pollen grains found in the deposits has given tremendous insights into the vegetation that has existed in the British Isles during the 10,000 years since the upland glaciers disappeared.

For the past two million years, the hemispheres have been subjected to a series of alternating warmer and colder periods. During the last few cold periods glaciers formed in the mountains, then expanded and merged into massive ice sheets which covered most of northern Europe. During the intervening warmer 'interglacial' periods, the ice sheets retreated and temperate-living plants and animals recolonized the area. These glaciers and ice sheets have sculptured most of the British and Irish uplands. While glacier ice itself is fairly soft, glaciers pick up and carry with them gravel, stones and boulders which scrape the underlying rock surfaces in a giant sandpapering effect. So soft rocks were worn away and the harder rocks smoothed off. The movement of glaciers formed the U-shaped valleys found in all the mountain regions of Britain and Ireland, and also gouged out the valley heads to form the mountain corries. As the ice sheets retreated while the climate warmed, most of the lowlands were left under a covering of the scraped-off materials; these superficial deposits now mask much of the bedrock. In the uplands, lakes formed in scooped out hollows and in valleys and corries dammed by deposits of glacial debris. Those of the English Lake District are particularly obvious when seen on a map, radiating like spokes on a wheel from the cluster of mountains.

Differences in the bedrock have resulted in great differences in the shapes of different mountains. No better contrast exists than between the Black Cuillin Mountains and adjacent Red Hills on the Isle of Skye. The rugged, jagged Cuillins are formed largely of hard gabbro and softer, more easily weathered dykes of basalt. The granite and granophyre of the Red Hills have weathered into screes, giving smoother, more rounded hills. Mountain peaks owe their ruggedness, when compared to the glacially smoothed valleys, to two causes. First, on the steeper slopes the moving ice sheets

The U-shaped, glaciated valley of Glen Shee in Perthshire *(above)* flanked by hills on each side, is clearly outlined by sun breaking through storm clouds in August. Shee Water meanders through the valley to join the River Ericht at Bridge of Cally.

A few, lone, pine trees remain on a small island at the edge of Loch Dee, Kirkcudbrightshire *(left)*. The surrounding man-made moorland and scene has been devoid of large trees for a long time, but a recent planting of young spruce trees in the foreground will change the landscape in years to come.

Mountain avens *(above)* is a native alpine plant, remains of which have been identified in Britain that date back more than 20,000 years. The flora growing at the edge of the ice sheet in southern England, at that time, resembled the Arctic flora of today.

tended to pluck large chunks away from the rock faces rather than to smooth them off. Second, as the ice sheets shrank it was the mountain peaks that first emerged. They were then subjected to very severe frost action, which on the higher and more northerly mountains has continued to the present day. This produced crumbling rock faces and cliffs, rocky outcrops, and great screes of the frost shattered debris.

In the last glaciation southern England and most of the Midlands were free of ice, as was southern Ireland except for a local ice sheet in the south Kerry mountains. These unglaciated areas bore a vegetation very like arctic tundra today; tree-less, mossy, lichen-rich swards, with abundant sedges *Carex*, willows *Salix*, mountain avens *Dryas octopetala* and dwarf birch *Betula nana*. Then, as the climate gradually warmed and the ice receded, woodland spread across the land, mainly of birch *Betula* at first, but with hazel *Corylus avellana* and Scots pine *Pinus sylvestris* soon becoming abundant. Their very rapid spread suggests that scattered trees may already have been growing at especially favourable sites. Other broadleaved species later largely displaced them in the lowlands, but birch and pine remained dominant in the uplands. Soon after, the climate became wetter and a striking development of bogs, characterized by the lush growth of the *Sphagnum* mosses, began on poorly drained ground, especially in the west of Britain and in Ireland.

Other plants and animals also migrated back. To begin with, land bridges joined Ireland, Britain and the Continent together, and permitted the rapid re-invasion of species. These bridges existed because as water became locked up in the glacial ice sheets the sea level fell by over 100 metres. But as the ice caps melted the seas rose again, and by about 6000 BC Britain was once more an island. Ireland seems to have been cut off from Britain rather earlier. The new Irish Sea probably prevented many species from recolonizing, so accounting in part for the relative poverty of the Irish fauna and flora compared with Britain's. The development of the North Sea and the Channel had a similar effect on the flora and fauna of Britain compared with that of the Continent.

About 3000 BC, Neolithic man began to make his presence felt; this coincided with a return to drier conditions and a slowing down of bog growth. Previous Mesolithic man led a nomadic hunting and food-gathering existence, and seems to have had little effect on the land. But Neolithic man introduced farming and began to clear forests for this. Clearance continued fairly steadily, despite some short-lived phases of forest regrowth, so that

Fox Tor Mire on Dartmoor *(right)* is a treacherous mire which is dominated by green *Sphagnum* bog mosses. In this water-logged area an extensive blanket bog has developed and the associated flora is limited to plants which will tolerate permanently wet conditions.

East of Glen Coe lies the desolate moorland landscape of Rannoch Moor. This glaciated area is a mixture of lochs, morainic and granitic knolls, peat-filled hollows and blanket mires. Here, the peat has eroded away to expose stumps of ancient Scots pine, known as bog pine, which have been preserved for several thousands of years. In the raised drier parts of the mires, and also on the tops of the old stumps, clumps of woolly hair-moss *Rhacomitrium lanuginosum* grow.

today only small fragments of the original woodland cover still exist. Deforestation was aided by a reversion to a wetter climate in Britain from about 800 BC, though perhaps nearer 2000 BC in Ireland. This began a new phase of active bog growth which has continued to the present day. The spread of *Sphagnum* prevented many forests from regenerating. The tree stumps so often exposed at the bottom of bogs by peat cuttings attest to the former extent of forest, though these stumps are generally anything from 2000 to 6000 or more years old.

Deforestation did not proceed at equal rates all over the uplands. There was a great increase in farming in Bronze Age Britain, and the North York Moors, Dartmoor and much of the Lake District, for example, seem to have been substantially denuded by about 500 BC. In contrast, many of the remoter parts of the Scottish Highlands were not deforested until the late eighteenth century. Bronze Age deforestation in Ireland was not so marked. The economy seems to have been based more on semi-nomadic cattle ranching than settled arable farming. But land clearance there greatly increased during the agricultural developments of the Celtic monastic period before the ninth century. The renewed felling of woodlands during the seventeenth century saw the country effectively devoid of its native woods by 1700. Yet perhaps as much as 15 per cent of the land was still well wooded only a hundred years or so before. Elizabethan state papers could claim that extensive woods sheltered both rebels and wolves.

Thus, although the peat bogs and some of the blanket peats are due simply to the wet climate, most of the moorlands were created from forest. Whether or not forests were felled, tree regeneration was prevented by grazing from domestic livestock as the farming population increased, and also by fire. Many of the areas today under blanket peat probably only succumbed to peat growth after deforestation by man or his animals. Trees are very efficient at drying out soils and preventing *Sphagnum* growth.

On the grassy hills surrounding Llyn Idwal in the Snowdonia National Park, trees are rare. Here one hawthorn has managed to grow above the sheep browsing level, but the distorted shape of the other plant is proof of constant pruning by sheep which graze the whole area. To the right, dark green clumps of rushes grow untouched by sheep, on the wetter ground.

The natural woodlands of the British and Irish uplands were dominated in particular by pine, birch, hazel, oak *Quercus* and alder *Alnus glutinosa*, with some ash *Fraxinus excelsior* in limestone areas. Their replacement by grass and heather *Calluna vulgaris* moorland had profound biological consequences. The woodland wildlife largely disappeared, to be replaced by other species which previously occurred mainly in woodland glades or above the tree line (the altitude above which trees cannot grow). The most important effect, however, has been on the soils, on which all land-dwelling wildlife is ultimately dependent. Most of the uplands have intrinsically poor soils, developed from hard, acid rocks like granite, gneiss, gritstone and quartzite. With the high rainfall, lime is leached out of these soils faster than it can be replaced by weathering of the rock particles. The soils become progressively more acid and less fertile. This process is accelerated by the acid litter produced by heather and has resulted in the widespread formation of particular kinds of soils called podsols, where a bleached layer is found near the surface from which almost all organic matter, lime, iron and other minerals have been leached out. Often a 'pan' has formed below this leached zone where the iron has concentrated. Such pans can be hard and impermeable to roots and water, causing surface waterlogging and starting peat formation.

Above the tree line it is not clearly known to what extent the vegetation has been modified through man's activities. The montane heaths and grasslands have probably been relatively little affected, though all have been grazed by the ubiquitous sheep. The lower regions between the high tops and the tree line are likely to have been influenced more. Sheep grazing pressures have been higher, and much of the vegetation is inflammable and must have been burnt over by run-away fires in the past. These slopes were probably once much more shrubby in appearance, with much willow and juniper *Juniperus communis* scrub.

Upland habitats

Upland is a vague and ill-defined term, but we use it here to denote those areas of the British Isles which are generally over 240 metres and bear moorland-type vegetation. Also included are lower areas which for climatic reasons carry moorland-type rather than lowland heath-type vegetation, such as the blanket bogs of Scotland and Ireland. This chapter excludes detailed descriptions of the plants and animals of Carboniferous limestone areas because of their affinities with lowland calcicolous grasslands.

Uplands include a wide variety of vegetation types and habitats. The upland heaths and moors form a continuum with the lowland heaths which were formed from woodland in the same way as the moors and have undergone the same changes in their wildlife and soils. Most species extend from the lowlands to the submontane zone, for example, heather, purple moor-grass *Molinia caerulea*, heath rush *Juncus squarrosus* and meadow pipit *Anthus pratensis*. A few even occur over 1200 metres, like mat-grass *Nardus stricta*, bilberry *Vaccinium myrtillus* (called blaeberry in Scotland and whortleberry in southwest England), and the common lizard *Lacerta vivipara*. The transition is marked only by the gradual appearance and disappearance of a few species. Crowberry *Empetrum nigrum*, stag's-horn clubmoss *Lycopodium clavatum*, golden plover *Pluvialis apricaria* and, very characteristically on heather-dominated areas, red grouse *Lagopus lagopus* appear with increasing altitude. However, the lower temperatures found with increasing latitude allow montane species to grow nearer sea level. The vegetation at 300 metres on Ronas Hill in Shetland is like that around 900–1000 metres in the central Highlands, and quite unlike anything found on the highest Irish mountains.

There are no standard names to describe and distinguish between different kinds of upland, whether above or below the tree line. In places a 'moor' implies a peaty soil, and an upland 'heath' a mineral soil, but the Scottish grouse moors are all 'moors' regardless of the nature of the soil. The term 'peatlands' is often used for upland or lowland areas covered with peat. Soil surveyors restrict its use to soils with more than 30 centimetres of peat. 'Heath' is sometimes used for areas where heather and other species of heath in the botanical sense predominate, as on Exmoor. Often, however,

Crowberry *(below left)* is widespread on moorlands and the drier parts of blanket bogs in the northern parts of Britain though less common in Ireland. It is rare in southwest England and absent in the southeast.

The bilberry *(below centre)* is much more widespread than crowberry, growing on acid soils all over the British Isles on moors, heaths and in woods. The attractive pink flowers are pollinated by bees and are followed by luscious bluish-black berries.

Cocoons of the greyish-white rush moth *Coleophora alticolella* on heath rush *(below right)*. The caterpillars feed on the seeds of the rush before they pupate. The cocoons persist all winter on the dead flower spikes.

Grouse moors which are burnt in rotation produce a striking mosaic on the hillsides west of Aberdeen in July. Young heather shoots produce food for the red grouse, which take cover and nest among the taller, older plants. A light snow fall in winter lies as a white sheet on the freshly burnt ground, but falls through the tall heather which appears as contrasting dark strips.

areas dominated by grasses or even mosses are also called heaths. Regional names exist, like 'fell' and 'wold' in parts of northern England. Most moors in the central and northwest Highlands are 'forests', despite the general lack of trees, the term being used to denote a hunting preserve, as in the New Forest of southern England. A further complication is that any Scot walking in the uplands, whether at 300 or 1200 metres, speaks simply of being 'on the hill'.

Heather is an important part of the vegetation of most moorlands, whether on mineral soil or peat. Only where soils are very lime-rich (calcareous), or where grazing has been particularly intense over long periods, as in Snowdonia and the Cheviots, is heather scarce. The finest flourishing of heather is on the grouse moors of eastern Britain. Here, the heather is managed by burning. Small strips, ideally of half a hectare or so, are burnt in a rotation of 10 to 15 years which produces a patchwork effect on the moors. Burnt heather quickly sprouts again from the stool if it is not too old, and yields a fresh supply of young shoots which are the main food of red grouse. A mosaic of small patches provides young heather for food close to tall heather which provides both cover from predators and sites for nesting. Grouse rarely feed more than about 15 metres from the cover of tall heather. They are territorial birds, so each territory must have both short and tall heather. Burning in a mosaic thus gives the greatest number of territories on a moor. A well-managed moor on a good soil may support a pair of grouse for every two hectares, but a moor on blanket peat may have fewer than one pair for every 50 hectares.

The uplands include extensive grasslands which show wide variations in species composition, depending on aspect, soil, climate, age and past history, especially their grazing history. On calcareous soils, upland grasslands were formed directly from deforestation. On neutral and acid soils, woodland clearance resulted in a predominance of heather and other dwarf shrubs, but heavy grazing has converted many heathery areas to grassland, a process aided by too frequent burning. On average, a stocking rate of more than five sheep on two hectares of heather moorland will cause a trend to grasslands variously dominated by bents *Agrostis* and fescues *Festuca*. The higher the grazing intensity, the quicker the change will be. Somewhat lower stocking rates may cause a slow change to a predominance of mat-grass or purple moor-grass, especially on more poorly drained soils. Sheep barely graze these latter species unless they are forced to, so the plants have a competitive advantage over others in the sward and tend to increase. The prevalence of mat-grass in parts of the Southern Uplands and of purple moor-grass in the Welsh uplands has come about in this way. Grasslands dominated by heath rush develop in a similar way, and are locally extensive in the Pennines.

Peatlands are also common, especially in Ireland and the west of Britain. Many bogs formed initially in wet hollows where drainage was poor. Although often base-rich to begin with, such bogs become more acid as peat accumulates and the bog surface is removed from the influence of the ground water. In the end they are irrigated by rainwater only, and are covered with a carpet of heather, *Sphagnum* mosses and other acid tolerant plants. An interesting feature is that they tend to become slightly convex, with their centres often several metres higher than the edges. These are called raised bogs. In the rainier uplands, however, more extensive peat formation occurs on flat and gently sloping ground. Such blanket bogs or blanket peats are particularly frequent in the English Pennines, the north-west Highlands and Islands of Scotland and in western Ireland. Expanses of blanket bog often encompass raised and valley bogs. In Scotland such bog complexes are called 'flows'. Valley bogs occur where the ground is irrigated by spring water, and are common in both the uplands and lowlands. Their vegetation is very variable depending on the acidity of the water and ranges from *Sphagnum* carpets through purple moor-grass and bog myrtle *Myrica gale* to fen.

Bristhie Bog in Silver Flowe National Nature Reserve in southern Scotland is a blanket mire with well developed pool and hummock systems. In December the purple moor-grass has turned a golden colour and so contrasts well against the dark green heather.

A rowan or mountain ash tree grows out from a rocky gulley near Cwm Idwal in Snowdonia. Providing there is enough soil present, trees are able to grow on these precipitous faces where sheep are unable to graze. In August, the rowan berries have turned red and provide food for various birds.

Most of the uplands have more than 1500 millimetres of rain per annum. The bulk of this runs off in the streams, burns or becks that tumble down the hillsides, and form a distinctive sub-habitat traversing the moorland scene. The spray-splashed boulders carry a luxuriant growth of mosses and liverworts. Steep banks often occur which have escaped the ravages of moorland fires and grazing. They shelter relics from the former woodland cover, such as ferns, primrose *Primula vulgaris* and wood anemone *Anemone nemerosa*, plus occasional trees and shrubs, notably the rowan or mountain ash *Sorbus aucuparia* and the eared sallow *Salix aurita*.

Southwest England

The only substantial uplands are Exmoor and Dartmoor, unglaciated plateaux rising only to just over 500 and 600 metres respectively. However, their winter climates are severe. Remarkable glazed frosts occur, when every blade of grass, twig, post or rock can be sheathed in ice. In other respects they are very different. Dartmoor sits largely on granite, and blanket bog covers most of the plateau, dominated by heather, cross-leaved heath *Erica tetralix*, cotton-grasses *Eriophorum* and purple moor-grass. On sloping ground the vegetation is mainly of heather, often with abundant bilberry, but on the lower slopes heather is replaced by grass and bracken *Pteridium aquilinum* under the influence of higher grazing pressures. In contrast, Exmoor lies on softer sandstones and other sedimentary rocks which have weathered to give deep, relatively fertile soils. Because of this, large areas have been reclaimed for agriculture. The plateau is dissected by very steep-sided, largely wooded valleys, locally called 'combes'. The plateau surface bears mostly heather moors, though with much grass and bracken, and with a large expanse of blanket bog in the centre. Despite being 'islands' of upland in a lowland setting, both districts contain a wide range of moorland species, including ring ouzel *Turdus torquatus*, merlins *Falco columbarius* and, in Dartmoor, golden plover.

The East Lyn River flows through the famous Doone Valley in the north of Exmoor National Park. In the foreground bell heather and gorse flower in August. Dissecting the upland area are deep, wooded valleys.

The bright green leaves of least willow grow up with mosses and lichens as part of a snow-patch community on an exposed ridge on Ben Lawers. This tiny willow grows on mountain tops up to an altitude of 1300 metres. It produces catkins in June soon after the leaves have opened.

Wales

Almost 39 per cent of Wales lies above 240 metres, the Welsh hills and mountains forming an upland massif bordered by a lowland coastal fringe. The main uplands of South Wales are the Old Red Sandstone ranges of the Brecon Beacons, rising to 886 metres. These bear grasslands, variously dominated by bents, fescues, mat-grass and purple moor-grass, but with some dwarf shrub heaths of heather, bilberry and crowberry, especially in the Black Mountains to the east, and with areas of blanket bog on the moorland plateaux. There are sufficient outcrops of calcareous rocks to find lime-loving (calcicolous) plants, such as purple saxifrage *Saxifraga oppositifolia*, filmy fern *Hymenophyllum wilsoni* and green spleenwort *Asplenium viride*. There is also enough montane habitat to give the least willow *Salix herbacea* its southernmost British sites. The Carboniferous limestone cliffs above Crickhowell, south of the Black Mountains, are famous for harbouring many rare whitebeams *Sorbus*.

The Cambrian Mountains of central Wales are formed largely of slates and shales, soft rocks which have worn down to give a tamer landscape than either to north or south. The moors are covered mainly with purple moor-grass and mat-grass grasslands, with a little heather or bilberry. Large areas of blanket bog occur on the plateaux, while bent–fescue grasslands and bracken predominate on the lower slopes. This region is the remaining refuge of the red kite *Milvus milvus*. Over 20 pairs nest in the hillside woods, feeding on the adjacent moors and farmlands.

North Wales is dominated by heavily glaciated mountains. They extend from Snowdonia in the north, with Wales' highest peak Snowdon at 1085 metres, to Cader Idris (892 metres) in south Gwynedd. Intensive glaciation has produced narrow-topped mountains with steep, precipitous slopes. The summit vegetation includes fescue, bilberry and *Rhacomitrium* moss. The slopes are grassy, due to centuries of grazing by domestic livestock, though some heathery areas remain. High-level outcrops of calcareous rocks are a refuge for many mountain plants commonly found on more northerly mountains and in arctic regions. They are the only location in the British Isles for the mountain lily *Lloydia serotina*, a plant like a small white tulip. Dotterel *Eudromias morinellus* are occasionally seen, and bred for certain in 1969.

Northern England

South of Hadrian's Wall lie the massive Pennine uplands, with broad, sweeping moorlands rising gently to large summit plateaux. They are formed mainly of Millstone Grit, giving poor acid soils, but major exposures of the underlying Carboniferous limestone in the central and southern Pennines are associated with richer floras. The Pennines include the Yorkshire Dales and the Peak District.

The northern Pennines rise to 893 metres on Cross Fell. The gently sloping eastern faces are mainly heathery, in contrast to the bent–fescue, mat-grass and heath rush grasslands of the steeper, western scarp slopes. The drier parts of the plateaux bear *Rhacomitrium*–fescue heath and fescue grasslands. The more extensive wetter parts bear blanket bog, much of it severely eroded, in which heather and hare's-tail cotton-grass *Eriophorum vaginatum* predominate, and cloudberry *Rubus chamaemorus* commonly occurs. The region embraces Upper Teesdale, famous for the number of rare mountain plants growing there, mostly on the 'sugar' limestone. This uncommon rock was changed into its crumbly crystalline state by contact with a hot intrusive magma. These rarities are a locally surviving remnant of a once widespread immediate post-glacial flora. They include spring

The extensive stretches of bare limestone pavement, as here above Malham Cove, are known as 'karst' plateaux. The surface is dissected by grykes which develop by the action of rainwater. It is in these grykes that a rich limestone flora develops, protected both from wind and grazing.

gentian *Gentiana verna*, bog sandwort *Minuartia stricta* known only from Teesdale in the British Isles, and Teesdale violet *Viola rupestris*.

The central Pennines are notable for the many Carboniferous limestone exposures of the Craven district, which rises to 723 metres on Ingleborough. The limestone cliffs, screes and pavements support a rich flora.

The finest part of the southern Pennines is the High Peak moorlands, rising to 636 metres on Kinder Scout. There are extensive heather moors, often with plentiful bilberry, with bent–fescue and mat-grass grasslands where grazing has been heavier. The moorland plateaux are substantially covered with blanket bogs, many heavily eroded. Hare's-tail cotton-grass is very abundant in these, as it is throughout the Pennines, but here it is often the only vascular plant over great areas. Heather is infrequent and *Sphagnum* is almost entirely absent. This unusual condition seems to be due to heavy grazing and burning from the fifteenth century. Atmospheric pollution from the surrounding industrial towns seems finally to have eliminated *Sphagnum* from all except the very wettest parts of the moors, and certainly to have prevented any recovery. South of the High Peak the Pennines tail off into the Carboniferous limestone country of the Derbyshire Dales. The steep-sided dales still have a good deal of natural hazel and hawthorn *Crataegus monogyna* scrub and ash wood as well as cliffs, crags and grasslands supporting a sizeable flora.

The North York Moors are a great rolling plateau of Jurassic sandstones with an average elevation of from 250 to 350 metres. There are steep scarp slopes to the west, but the moors descend more gently elsewhere. Heather moorland covers the plateau, and provides some of the best grouse moors in Britain. The plateau is dissected by a number of steep-sided and often wooded dales, mostly running north to south. The combination of these with the rolling moorland gives the region much of its scenic appeal.

The Lake District has a considerable diversity of landforms, geology and wildlife, and its mountains and valleys have been heavily glaciated. Topographically there are three main areas. To the south lies a relatively soft moorland landscape on Silurian sandstones, slates and grits. The northern part is on ancient Ordovician slates and mudstones, and has weathered into fairly smoothly contoured mountains like Skiddaw and Grasmoor. Central Lakeland is formed from a variety of hard, volcanic rocks which have weathered into rugged, jagged mountains like Scafell Pike (the highest Lakeland peak at 978 metres) and Great End. The vegetation is extremely varied. The southern parts bear a mixture of heather and other dwarf shrubs, of grassland and of bracken. Indeed bracken is very abundant throughout the Lake District up to about 300 metres. Central Lakeland has little heather and the slopes above the heather are mainly grassy. The north is more heathery, and there is grouse moor on the western fells of the Skiddaw Forest. The mountains have a rich flora, including alpine catchfly *Viscaria alpina* on Hobcarton Crag, one of only two British stations, and oblong woodsia *Woodsia ilvensis*. The Lakeland mountains are a haven for ravens *Corvus corax*, peregrines *Falco peregrinus* and golden eagles *Aquila chrysaetos*; the last has recently returned after being exterminated in the eighteenth century. They are also the only place in England or Wales where the mountain ringlet *Erebia epiphron* occurs, Britain's only alpine butterfly.

North of the Pennines the rolling, grassy and now heavily afforested, Northumberland hills rise northwards into the rounded, equally grassy Cheviots. The grassy areas are due to intense sheep grazing. The Cheviot itself reaches 815 metres, and has a large summit plateau over 760 metres. This bears heather and hare's-tail dominated blanket bog, and cloudberry

A typical autumnal Lakeland scene looking north from Watendlath Fell with Skiddaw behind. The ubiquitous bracken is at its most attractive when the fronds have coloured up at the end of the summer. This plant, which can exceed the height of a man, is a serious grassland weed. It is difficult to eradicate since, even after a fire, new fronds will soon sprout up from the underground rhizomes.

occurs plentifully. Several unusual mountain flowers can be found, including dwarf cornel *Chamaepericlymenum suecicum*, a very rare plant in England though frequent in the Scottish Highlands.

Southern Scotland

The Southern Uplands stretch from Nithsdale to the east coast, range upon range of smooth rounded hills with many summits over 750 metres. They are now mainly grassy, thanks to sheep, though some stretches of heather still occur, particularly in the Moorfoot Hills and the Lammermuirs. Wide-scale afforestation has taken place in recent years, and many hills are now changing their character yet again. Many northern plants occur, and the cliffs above the Moffat Water have the highest concentration of these in the Southern Uplands. Galloway to the southwest of Nithsdale presents a very different aspect. Massive granite intrusions have formed a block of rugged hills. Once mainly heather clad, they have now been more completely afforested than any other upland region in the British Isles, totally altering their former character. However, some moors remain, notably at Cairnsmore of Fleet. The fauna is very Highland. Peregrines, merlins, ravens and golden eagles breed in the moorland zone, and dotterel have bred of late on the high ground. Red-throated and black-throated divers *Gavia stellata* and *G. arctica* breed in the hill lochs, at their southernmost station in Britain. The Scotch argus butterfly *Erebia aethiops* occurs and the dragonfly *Aeshna caerulea* breeds at its only British location south of the Highlands.

Scottish Highlands and Islands

No few paragraphs can do justice to the Highlands. They contain the largest tracts of upland in the British Isles, the highest mountains, the greatest stretches of mountain top vegetation, and the greatest diversity of geology, landforms and wildlife. Parts of the Highlands are the nearest we get to true wilderness in the British Isles.

The upland bird fauna is at its richest, not only with spectacular predators like the golden eagle, of which there may be up to 30 pairs in the Isle of Skye alone, but characteristic breeding waders such as the golden plover, dunlin *Calidris alpina* and snipe *Gallinago gallinago*, with the rare greenshank *Tringa nebularia* often on the bleakest moorland flows. On the high tops three montane species breed: the ptarmigan *Lagopus mutus* widely, dotterel mainly in the central Highlands, and snow bunting *Plectrophenax nivalis* confined to the Cairngorm Hills. The nesting of the snowy owl *Nyctea scandiaca* on the Shetland island of Fetlar from 1967 to 1795 was the most striking example of recent penetration of northern Scotland by tundra species. Since then, shore lark *Eremophila alpestris* (1977), Lapland bunting *Calcarius lapponicus* (1977, 1978) and purple sandpiper *Calidris maritima* (1978) have all been found nesting in closely protected localities. Birds of the northern forests and bogs – redwing *Turdus iliacus*, fieldfare *T. pilaris*, brambling *Fringilla montifringilla*, wood sandpiper *Tringa glareola* and Temminck's stint *Calidris temminckii* – are also nesting regularly.

Characteristic of the fast-flowing stream anywhere in the uplands are three passerine birds: grey wagtail *Motacilla cinerea*, dipper *Cinclus cinclus* and ring ouzel. Where the flow slackens, common sandpipers *Actitis hypoleucos* nest on the banks and red-breasted mergansers *Mergus serrator* in thick cover or under boulders. But sandpipers nest also by stony lochans. Where there are peaty banks or islets, the red-throated diver may nest; the black-throated prefers larger waters, as does the Slavonian grebe *Podiceps auritus*. The very rare red-necked phalarope *Phalaropus lobatus* nests beside

Lochan-nan-cat is a small loch at the base of Ben Lawers in Perthshire. In the distance are snow pockets which can remain on the hills as late as June in some years. The Ben Lawers region is famous for its alpine flora and the cliffs provide inaccessible places where plants can grow out of reach of grazing animals.

shallow, often peaty, pools which are usually fringed with emergent plants such as bogbean *Menyanthes trifoliata*.

Most of the montane vascular plants found in the British Isles occur in the Highlands, many only growing there. Thus southwest England has 5 per cent of the montane vascular flora of Britain and Ireland, Ireland 29 per cent, southern Scotland 34 per cent, Wales 35 per cent, northern England 52 per cent, but the Scottish Highlands and Islands 93 per cent. Dwarf birch, for example, occurs locally in the Highlands, though two colonies are known in northern England. In Britain it grows on blanket bog, rarely reaching much above heather height.

In terms of geology and landforms the Highlands and Islands can be divided into five regions: the Grampians; the north-central Highlands; the northwest Highlands and the Outer Hebrides; the Inner Hebrides and other western islands; Shetland, Orkney and the northeast Highlands. The Grampians lie between the Highland Boundary and Great Glen faults. They are the worn-down stumps of a former great mountain chain, with a general level of between 600 and 900 metres. There are numerous peaks over this, including Ben Nevis to the west, Britain's highest mountain at 1344 metres. The grassy Breadalbane mountains of Perthshire are formed largely of calcareous mica schists, and all have rich, montane floras. The most famous site is Ben Lawers, the richest upland site in the British Isles with over 60 per cent of the montane flora. The same calcareous rocks outcrop at the head of Caenlochan Glen, and in the twin corries of Glen

Seen from Beinn Ghlas is the grassy summit of Ben Lawers in Perthshire. Unlike many other Scottish mountains, Ben Lawers is composed of calcareous mica schists. An interesting assortment of flowers grow in the varied habitats which include grasslands, wet flushes, bogs, scree slopes, cliffs, ledges and late snow beds as seen in the foreground.

Reindeer foraging beneath the snow cover in the Cairngorms (below). The original herd was introduced from Sweden in 1952 since when over 500 calves have been born and all the animals in the present herd have been born in Scotland. The size of the herd is kept down by culling and also by the sale of animals to parks.

Doll and Corrie Fee at the head of Glen Clova, in Tayside. Caenlochan has more montane plants than any other single corrie in Britain. These include many of those growing on Ben Lawers but with a few others on more acid rocks like alpine sow-thistle *Cicerbita alpina*. The adjacent Clova corries also have large species lists, with some fine montane willow scrub and the only known station in Britain for alpine coltsfoot *Homogyne alpina*.

The Cairngorms in the east are a great dissected granite plateau. They owe their main biological interest to the large area of plateau above 1100 metres, including six summits over 1200 metres, although the total of montane plants present overall makes the district second only to Ben Lawers in numbers found. The plateau vegetation includes montane blanket bog, *Rhacomitrium* heaths, moss and liverwort communities associated with the longest-lasting snow patches, and also large areas dominated by the three-leaved rush *Juncus trifidus*. An interesting feature is the managed herd of domesticated reindeer *Rangifer tarandus*, introduced in 1952. The lower slopes are heather clad to 900 metres, and bear large areas of natural Scots pine forest. Rannoch Moor in the west is a complete contrast, being some 250 square kilometres of poorly drained plateau at about 360 metres, surrounded by a rim of mountains. This was the site of accumulation of the ice sheet that eventually covered the Highlands in the last glaciation. Severe glacial erosion produced a confused, undulating relief, now showing as a patchwork of lochs and lochans, basin and blanket bogs, and rocky knolls. Bog pools here are the last remaining place in the British Isles where the small rush *Scheuchzeria palustris* grows.

The north-central Highlands are a mountainous belt roughly 60 kilometres wide, north of the Great Glen. The rocks are mostly Moine schists. The southern part comprises complex ridge and valley systems, with many peaks over 1100 metres. This gradually changes to the more open rolling uplands of the north, with occasional isolated mountains like Ben Klibreck (961 metres) and Ben Loyal (763 metres). The two most important mountains botanically are Beinn Dearg (1084 metres) and Ben Wyvis (1046 metres). Beinn Dearg, lying 18 kilometres southwest of Ullapool, is composed of both acid and calcareous rocks. It consequently bears a wide variety of vegetation types, with both calcicolous and lime-avoiding (calcifuge) plants. The summit area has considerable bare ground showing the stone stripes and polygons formed by soil movements over frozen soil. As a botanical site it is rated second only to Ben Lawers and the Cairngorms, with specimens of 56 per cent of Britain's montane flora. Ben Wyvis, lying

Shetland mouse-ear chickweed *(above)* grows among the debris on a serpentine fellfield on Unst in Shetland. Woolly hair-moss *Rhacomitrium lanuginosum (below left)* grows on the lee side of boulders near the summit of Ronas Hill on the mainland of Shetland. Wind-pruned vegetation on a stony, moraine slope on Beinn Eighe *(below right)* includes the green prostrate juniper.

northwest of Dingwall, is a large, flat-topped mountain particularly notable for the large expanses of *Rhacomitrium* heath on the summit plateau.

The northwest Highlands and the Outer Hebrides are formed largely of Torridonian Sandstone overlying Lewisian gneiss, the oldest rocks in Scotland. To the south, the Torridonian Sandstone forms the Torridon hills, and has weathered to give striking stepped escarpments as on Liathach. Further north, the sandstone cover has been largely eroded, leaving a low but rough terrain of lochs, peaty hollows and rocky bosses rather akin to Rannoch Moor. The few remaining outcrops of sandstone form isolated peaks like Canisp, Suilven and Quinag, perhaps the most spectacular and hauntingly beautiful mountains in Scotland. Although none exceed 850 metres, they achieve their visual effect by rising so abruptly and steeply from the surrounding low moorlands. Some of the northwest mountains are capped with white quartzite, like Beinn Eighe and Canisp. This, as it is largely devoid of vegetation, adds to their grandeur. Calcareous rocks outcrop in places giving locally rich floras. The best site is Inchnadamph, just west of Ben More Assynt, where cliffs, screes and pavements of the Durness limestone occur. Mountain avens is abundant here, as are plants like holly fern *Polystichum lonchitis*, dark red helleborine *Epipactis atrorubens* and Norwegian sandwort *Arenaria norvegica*. Typical breeding birds are wheatear *Oenanthe oenanthe* and ring ouzel. The rocky knob and lochan terrain of Sutherland is also typical of the highly eroded and glaciated gneiss exposures of the Outer Hebrides. Much of it lies below 30 metres, though there are mountains on Harris and South Uist.

The Inner Hebrides and the other western islands show a great variety of geology, landforms and vegetation. Perhaps the most interesting are those with the worn-down remains of a former great tableland of basalt lavas: northern Skye, the Small Isles, Mull and of course Staffa with the famous Fingal's Cave. These eroded lavas now form flat-topped hills, terraced hillsides, sweeping moorlands and vertical escarpments. These outcrops commonly support an interesting flora, for example, on Beinn Iadain in Morvern, a reserve of the Scottish Wildlife Trust. The Trotternish ridge in northern Skye has many montane species, including the tiny, and very rare, Iceland purslane *Koenigia islandica* in damp gravelly spots. Alpine rock-cress *Arabis alpina* has its only known station in the British Isles in the Black Cuillins.

The northeast Highlands, Orkney and Shetland form mainly rolling country with well-rounded hills. Caithness is mostly very low lying, and has the largest expanse of blanket bog in Britain. Much of Orkney has

On the west coast of Sutherland *(above left)*, the landscape has been worn down by glacial action to form a series of small hills and hollows known as 'knob and lochan' terrain. As the ice advanced to the west it smoothed the eastern faces of the knobs but tended to pluck away pieces of rock to leeward, leaving a jagged face. The hollows between the raised knobs are now either peat or water filled.

Landslipping and erosion in Tertiary lava flows in Trotternish Peninsula, in the northeast of Skye, has resulted in a series of rock pillars and pinnacles, including the spectacular Quirang *(above right)* and the famous Old Man of Storr, to the south.

been reclaimed for agriculture, but there are moorlands on Hoy and the north Mainland. The latter are notable for their population of hen harriers *Circus cyaneus*, and also have many merlins, kestrels *Falco tinnunculus* and short-eared owls *Asio flammeus*. Shetland is geologically complex, but appears as a series of valleys and low ridges, substantially covered with blanket bog. It is particularly notable for its bird life and its outcrops of serpentine, a basic rock containing often toxic levels of nickel and chromium, and with a magnesium content exceeding that of calcium. The vegetation of serpentine areas is often an unusual mixture of species, and many rare plants can occur in quantity. Typical northern and arctic birds nesting on coastal moorlands are the great skua or bonxie *Stercorarius skua* and the arctic skua *S. parasiticus*. Many birds dive-bomb intruders on their breeding grounds, but the bonxie quite often actually strikes the intruder on the head.

There are many tracts of the Highlands which are biologically very poorly known, including Lochaber and Lorne to the west and the 800-odd square kilometres of the Monadhliath Mountains. The sharp-eyed walker may well spot a plant previously unrecorded for that district, or even just possibly for Scotland and the British Isles. The tiny wormwood *Artemisia norvegica*, Iceland purslane and diapensia *Diapensia lapponica* have all been recognized since the Second World War for the first time in our islands, and all are quite abundant where they do grow.

Ireland

Central Ireland is a low limestone plain, between 60 and 120 metres above sea level, and the largest continuous area of Carboniferous limestone in Europe. It is, however, mainly covered with glacial drift. This includes the great belt of drumlins, extending from Co. Down in the east to Sligo Bay in the west, which is one of the largest in the world. The drift impedes drainage, which accounts for the presence of the many raised bogs which locally, and especially in the west, give parts of the plain their upland

A great skua, or bonxie as it is known in Shetland, flies over its breeding ground on cotton-grass moorland on the island of Unst. It feeds mainly on birds and their fledglings, but like the Arctic skua it also chases other sea birds until they disgorge their food.

character. These bogs appear as uniform reddish-brown expanses, coloured by the predominance of *Sphagnum rubellum*, raised several metres above the general level of the plain. This central lowland is surrounded by a discontinuous border of hills and mountains bearing a variety of moorland vegetation types.

All the common moorland plants of Britain are present. Only a few of the less common are missing, like petty whin *Genista anglica*, a spiny, yellow-flowered, leguminous dwarf shrub, and the dainty, white-flowered chickweed wintergreen *Trientalis europaea*. Moorland birds are generally scarcer than in Scotland and the black grouse *Tetrao tetrix* is unknown in Ireland. The relative rarity of buzzards and the absence of golden eagles is due to their earlier extinction there by man. Adders *Vipera berus* are of course missing, as are wild cats *Felis silvestris*, but the common lizard and frog *Rana temporaria* are abundant. Ireland's montane flora is very reduced however. Ireland's mountains, in a region with a mild oceanic climate, are just not high enough to allow the development of the kind of vegetation found on summits in North Wales or the Lake District, let alone the Scottish High-

A valley bog in the Dingle Peninsula, on the west coast of Ireland as seen from the road up to the Conair Pass. Such bogs develop in valleys and depressions where water draining off the surrounding land accumulates; carpets of bog mosses grow and thereby help to trap more water.

lands. The summit of Carrantual (1041 metres), Ireland's highest mountain, bears a mainly grassy moorland vegetation. Here and elsewhere the limited montane flora is largely confined to cliffs. However, although the montane flora is insignificant in a British Isles context, its very rarity in the Irish context increases the excitement of finding a mountain plant and makes the few montane sites truly precious.

Antrim and east Londonderry in the northeast lie on a high plateau of basalt. This has weathered into rich agricultural soils, but the rocky out-crops support several montane species. The best locality is Benevenagh (384 metres), whose cliff flora includes mountain avens, purple saxifrage, moss campion *Silene acaulis* and least willow. Progressing clockwise around the country, the famous Mountains of Mourne in southern Co. Down are a group of granite hills rising to 852 metres on Slieve Donard. Weathering has produced some fine cliffs and pinnacles. The hill slopes are mainly heathery, while the handful of montane plants include least willow, starry saxifrage *Saxifraga stellaris*, which is found on most of the Irish mountains, and parsley fern *Cryptogramma crispa* in its main Irish station. South of Dublin is the great granite mass of the Wicklow Mountains, the largest continuous area of upland in Ireland, with some 530 square kilometres above 300 metres. The broad, rounded summits are covered with blanket bogs dominated by deer-grass *Trichophorum caespitosum* and common cotton-grass *Eriophorum angustifolium*, the convex slopes with heather moor above about 380 metres, and with gorse *Ulex europaeus* infested grasslands below. The montane flora is almost non-existent, probably because there are no cliffs. Roseroot *Rhodiola (Sedum) rosea* and mossy saxifrage *Saxifraga hypnoides* formerly grew on Lugnaquilla (926 metres) but may now be extinct.

Kerry is a very humid region with high rainfall, mild winters and regu-larly mist-shrouded mountains and it is the headquarters of the Lusitanian elements of the Irish flora whose usual habitats are in southwest Europe. While these southern species flourish mainly in the lowlands, St Patrick's cabbage *Saxifraga spathularis*, kidney saxifrage *S. hirsuta* and the large-flowered butterwort *Pinguicula grandiflora* all ascend over 800 metres, the first growing at 1041 metres on Carrantual. Kerry's climate is also responsible for a remarkably plentiful and diverse array of mosses, liver-worts and ferns. These grow prodigiously well here, with a lushness rarely encountered in Britain. Much of Kerry appears as a series of alternating mountainous ridges and valleys, the higher ground being mostly of Old

St Patrick's cabbage *(above)* is a Lusitanian species which grows well in damp, rocky places and as an epiphyte on trees in west and southwest Ireland.

Starry saxifrage thrives on wet, rocky ledges and beside mountain streams.

Red Sandstone. The best known range is MacGillicuddy's Reeks, which includes Carrantual. The vegetation above 200 metres is very heathery, gradually giving way to grassy swards near the summits, with several montane species occurring over 900 metres. Brandon (953 metres) on the Dingle Peninsula is another fine Kerry peak, with a precipitous scarp slope dropping straight into the Atlantic.

The best exposures of the Carboniferous limestone underlying the glacial drifts of the central plain occur to the west in Co. Galway and Co. Clare. The most famous botanically are those of the low Burren Hills, covering about 360 square kilometres of west Co. Clare. Limestone pavement, which spreads over their slopes, shelters a flora distinguished for its richness and luxuriance of growth, exceeding that at any British site.

The Connemara district of west Galway is a bleak windswept area dominated in the north by the quartzite peaks of the Twelve Bens and the Maam Turk Mountains, and in the south by a low-lying wilderness of bogs, lochs and rocky knolls. This knob and lochan terrain is identical to that of the Outer Hebrides and northwest Highlands and is developed on the same worn-down gneiss. The mountains support about a dozen montane species as well as upland ones like rock bramble *Rubus saxatilis*. Connemara is a centre for the Lusitanian heaths: Mackay's heath *Erica mackaiana* in blanket bog, Irish heath *E. mediterranea* in drier bogs, and St Dabeoc's heath *Daboecia cantabrica* on well-drained and rocky ground. The first two are lowland plants, but St Dabeoc's heath occurs up to about 600 metres on the Twelve Bens. Northwest Mayo is equally if not more exposed, but lacks Connemara's knobs and lochans, having the largest area of blanket bog in Ireland. Irish heath is abundant.

Another major outcrop of Carboniferous limestone occurs above Sligo Bay, forming the Ben Bulben range, a limestone plateau at 450 to 600 metres. Steep grassy slopes climb to 350 metres and abruptly give way to vertical limestone cliffs which rise to the peat-covered plateau. The north-facing cliffs bear the finest array of montane plants in Ireland. Irish sandwort *Arenaria ciliata* grows here at its only location in the British Isles, and alpine saxifrage *Saxifraga nivalis* and chickweed willow-herb *Epilobium alsinifolium* at their only Irish stations.

Co. Donegal in northwest Ireland is a land of hill, moor, heather and bog. In the north there are the quartzite peaks of Errigal (752 metres) and Muckish (670 metres), and the rounded granite uplands of the Derryveagh Mountains, rising to 683 metres on Slieve Snaght. Further south there are extensive dissected moorlands, and the Blue Stack Mountains. In the southwest is Slieve League, with spectacular cliffs dropping straight into the sea. Despite the Highland appearance of Donegal, the hills support very few montane plants.

Animal life in uplands

Earthworms and other soil fauna are usually scarce in upland habitats because of the predominantly acid soils and the poor nutritional value of the coarse, moorland plants. But dung is a very good food, and worms congregate in this. An old but not dried-up cow pat may, if turned over, reveal a dozen or more small worms. On less acid soils the reddish worms *Dendrobaena rubida* and *Lumbricus rubellus* may predominate, the latter being the worm so abundant in garden compost heaps. Moles *Talpa europaea* are only found in the uplands in the very best soils, usually those developed in alluvium or in rocks like limestone or basalt where earthworms, their main food source, are abundant. Moles are absent from Ireland, and also from many of the Scottish islands.

There are plenty of insects and invertebrates to be found on heather moorland, but their obviousness varies greatly through the year. In early summer, the hill walker soon notices legs covered in cuckoo-spit. This is the protective froth produced by the sap-sucking nymphs of members of the family Cercopidae. The adults are popularly called froghoppers because of their broad heads which give them a vaguely frog-like appearance, and because of their leaping ability. Anyone who has picnicked out in summer will probably have noticed their sudden arrival in cups of tea and coffee. The magnitude of the web-spinning spider population is most evident on a dewy morning or a day with hill mist, when surprising numbers of orb and carpet webs are picked out by a spangling of tiny water droplets. In late summer, when the heather is in bloom, foraging bees cannot be missed. Honey-bees *Apis mellifera* may be most numerous – beekeepers like to move their hives up to the moors if they can, as the luscious heather honey commands a premium. There will also be plenty of bumble-bees, the large, roundish, hairy bees so conspicuous in flight. Red-tailed ones are likely to be the bilberry bumble-bee *Bombus lapponicus*, and several white-tailed species may be present, particularly *B. jonellus*, *B. lucorum* and *B. soroeensis*. On the move they all look very similar.

Many insects feed on heather. One which locally can reach plague proportions is the heather beetle *Lochmaea suturalis*, a small, dark brown beetle whose larvae feed on young heather shoots. In some years, larval grazing is so severe that expanses of heather turn a characteristic reddish-brown, and many plants never recover. Other heather-feeders commonly encountered are the bright green, yellow-spotted caterpillars of the emperor moth *Saturnia pavonina* and the large, brown caterpillars of the northern eggar *Lasiocampa quercus callunae*.

A female emperor moth resting on heather *(below left)* displays the eyespots on her wings. When the moths emerge during April and May, the female produces a scent which the male moth detects using his much more elaborate antennae.

The hairy caterpillar of a northern eggar moth feeds on heather on Beinn Eighe in July *(below right)*. These, and other large moorland caterpillars, are eaten by cuckoos which are common all over upland areas. The oak eggar caterpillars pupate in autumn and the moths emerge the following May or June.

Unlike heather moors, several species of butterflies breed on and at the margins of upland grasslands, though most are not confined there. Two that are characteristic are the large heath *Coenonympha tullia* and the Scotch argus. Both feed mainly on purple moor-grass. The former is widely distributed in the British Isles, being absent only from southern England and South Wales. The rather variably coloured adults appear during June and July. The Scotch argus is confined to northern England and Scotland. The dark chocolate brown adults can be seen in late summer. Our only alpine butterfly is the mountain ringlet, a relict from the cooler climate of the last glaciation. It occurred in the last century in Co. Mayo and Co. Sligo, but is now apparently extinct in Ireland. In Britain, it is found above about 550 metres in the Lake District and 450 metres in parts of the west Grampians. The caterpillars feed on mat-grass.

The mountain hare *Lepus timidus* is a feature of mountainsides and moors in Scotland, where it is native only to the Highlands. But it has been introduced to several islands, the Scottish Lowlands, the Pennines in England and North Wales. The only hare native to Ireland, it faces competition from introduced brown hares *L. capensis*, which have also been taken to some Scottish islands; on Arran, where there are no mountain hares, they are found well up in the hills. The Scottish form of the mountain hare has a white coat in winter, making the animals very conspicuous on ground without snow, but the Irish race moults only to piebald or not at all. On at least one Scottish moor, mountain hares are sufficiently numerous to keep the heather constantly trimmed down to compact bushes.

Voles *Microtus agrestis* can be numerous in rough, relatively ungrazed upland pastures in Britain, though absent from Ireland. Their numbers undergo marked cyclic changes, sometimes reaching 'plague' levels but then, as abruptly, decreasing. Another small rodent, the wood mouse *Apodemus sylvaticus*, is present throughout Britain and Ireland, and in most of the islands also. It is often the commonest small mammal of heather moors, especially where a deep mossy layer gives cover. A catholic feeder, its diet includes all kinds of seedlings, fruits, seeds and invertebrates. Adders are often encountered basking in the sun on dry, grassy or heathery hillsides. Carnivores, they feed on anything they are big enough to ingest, and their varied diet ranges from insects, slugs, worms and lizards to mice, voles, shrews and even small birds.

Red deer *Cervus elaphus*, our largest native land mammal and herbivore, were once common in woodlands throughout the British Isles, but past hunting and deforestation have restricted them to the uplands and to protected lowland parks. An estimated 270,000 exist in Scotland, mainly in the Highlands, but there are small, unconfined herds in the Lake District, southwest England, Co. Donegal, Co. Kerry and the Wicklow Mountains in Ireland. They are numerous enough over much of the Highlands to prevent natural regeneration of trees in any quantity, necessitating the erection of costly deer-fencing around commercial woodlands. Red deer are a very similar colour to roe deer *Capreolus capreolus*, which are commonly seen on moorlands, with a reddish-brown summer coat becoming greyer in winter. Red deer are almost twice the size of roe deer, with a more prominent white rump, especially in winter, while the stags grow large, many-spiked antlers. They tend to live in groups, unlike the territorial roe deer, with the stags keeping apart from the hinds and young for most of the year. The sexes mingle during the mating season or rut from September to October, when stags compete to attract a harem of hinds and their 'roaring' echoes through the hills. In the Highlands they are most readily seen in winter, when the weather forces them on to low ground.

Red deer stags in velvet browsing late in the day in Sutherland. When the antlers are fully grown, the velvet begins to irritate and the stags use hard surfaces such as tree trunks to clean it off. Above the heathland vegetation in this picture, bracken grows among the birches.

Britain is very poor in mammalian carnivores. The wolf *Canis lupus* was exterminated in historic times and the lynx *Lynx lynx* in prehistoric times. However, foxes *Vulpes vulpes* are common everywhere in mainland Britain and in Ireland. Wild cats were once common throughout Britain, though absent in Ireland, but were confined to the remote Highlands by the end of the last century as a result of persecution and forest clearance. Since the First World War they have been gradually increasing in numbers and range, and now seem to be recolonizing parts of the Southern Uplands. Adults resemble large domestic tabbies, with dark grey or black stripes on a greyish background, and a black-tipped, round-ended and rather bushy tail. They are territorial, and their underground dens are usually in woodland but may occur on the open hill. In the northeast Highlands, wild cats commonly hunt rabbits in the valley bottoms, but those with forest margin or moorland territories prey mainly on mountain hares. Rodents and small birds are also taken, and may be the more important food in the West Highlands. Wild cats are shy and secretive, and are mainly nocturnal, more so even than foxes. Systematic search for them is generally very unrewarding. They are as likely to be seen by chance, illuminated in a car's headlights. Their droppings can be found though, and on snow-covered ground their tracks are readily spotted.

Because wild cats and foxes are usually nocturnal, it is the avian predators which are most readily seen. The buzzard *Buteo buteo* was quite a scarce bird at the beginning of the century because of previous persecution, but it is now commonplace to see one hovering or soaring high on motionless wings, or to hear its high-pitched mewing. Buzzards recolonized Antrim as a breeding species in the 1950s and can now be sighted further south in Ireland regularly. Myxomatosis caused a temporary reversal of the buzzard's increase as rabbits were then their main food. But buzzards take other small mammals, birds if they can catch them, and invertebrates also, and the setback was short lived.

Peregrines have not been as lucky as buzzards. Persecuted heavily during the Second World War in case they intercepted military carrier pigeons, they had just about recovered when their numbers dramatically halved between 1955 and 1965. The cause was traced to their eating birds like woodpigeons *Columba palumbus* which had previously consumed grain treated with the chlorinated hydrocarbon insecticides aldrin and dieldrin. There was some direct poisoning, but the main effect was more insidious, a decrease in eggshell density and thickness. The more fragile eggshells tended to break under the weight of the incubating parent bird, and breeding success plummeted.

Like buzzards, golden eagles have increased this century. The Lake District and Orkney have been recently recolonized, and a pair bred again on the Antrim coast during the 1950s. An eagle soaring high or quartering the ground when hunting is a magnificent sight. Breeding success began to decline in the west Highlands in the early 1960s. This was traced to their eating sheep carrion and thus ingesting dieldrin sheep dip, which made their eggshells fragile also. Fortunately, this was quickly spotted and prompted a voluntary ban on the use of dieldrin sheep dip. A return to near-normal breeding success followed. Apart from sheep and deer carrion, eagles favour largish prey like rabbits, hares, game birds and many sea birds.

There are three other typical upland raptors. The merlin occurs widely in all the uplands of Britain and Ireland but with a low density. Usually nesting in open moorland, it feeds mainly on small birds, though it also takes small rodents and insects. Short-eared owls are somewhat local in the British uplands and do not breed regularly in Ireland where they are winter visitors. They feed mainly on voles and their numbers fluctuate along with the population cycles of the voles; their absence from Ireland may be due to the absence there of voles. Most successful of the three is the hen harrier which, from strongholds in Orkney and the Outer Hebrides, has spread in the past 30 years to the Inner Hebrides, the Scottish mainland, northern England, North Wales and the Isle of Man. Apparently never extinct in

A red grouse sitting on its nest among bilberry and mat-grass. This game bird has a rapid flight with whirring wing beats alternating with a glide. Frequenting upland moors adult red grouse feed mainly on young heather shoots, and the berries and new shoots of bilberry.

Two male black grouse, known as blackcock, displaying on a lek site in southern Scotland. Their loud, bubbling calls make an eerie sound as dawn breaks on an early spring morning. As the males spread out their lyre-shaped tails, they show their white tail coverts. This lek is centred on a stand of deciduous bog myrtle which has been stripped of its male flowers by the blackcock.

Ireland, it has also increased there since 1950. Its prey is mainly skylarks *Alauda arvensis*, meadow pipits, and red grouse.

Of the non-raptorial birds, the curlew *Numenius arquata* is probably the most familiar because of its hauntingly liquid song. It nests in lowland pastures and marshes as well as moorlands. Another familiar bird is the golden plover which breeds only on moorlands. This century has witnessed its decline in some upland areas so that, apart from a few pairs on Dartmoor, it no longer breeds in southern England, South Wales or southern Ireland. But it is still common elsewhere, and its clear whistling call is a frequent sound over the moors. The smaller dunlins have a very similar distribution, though they favour wet ground and blanket bogs for nesting. They also nest on coastal salt marsh and commonly on Hebridean machair. Ptarmigan cannot be missed by anyone venturing over 800 metres in the central Grampians, for example, at the Cairngorm or Glenshee skiing complexes. Very like red grouse, they can be distinguished by their white winter plumage and their white wings and breast in summer. They feed on a variety of plants, at high levels mainly on crowberry and bilberry, and lower down on heather too. They are not known to breed in the British Isles outside of the Highlands and Islands. Black grouse *Tetrao tetrix* are frequent in Scotland wherever moorland and woodlands adjoin, but are scarce elsewhere in upland Britain and absent from Ireland. Their springtime 'lekking', when the black males or blackcock display to the arriving grey hens, is well worth an early rise to view.

No account of moorland birds, however abbreviated, would be satisfactory without mention of that most magnificent corvid, the raven *Corvus corax*. Like the buzzard, the raven has recovered significantly from previous persecution, and is now to be seen in all the uplands of Britain and Ireland. Mainly a carrion eater, its deep, harsh croaking, once heard, cannot be mistaken for that of a crow. The crow is also a frequent moorland bird. In contrast to the all-black carrion crow *Corvus corone corone* of England, Wales and southern Scotland, the hooded crow *C. c. cornix*, typical of the Highlands and Ireland, has a grey back and underparts. The two forms interbreed where their populations overlap. Carrion-eaters, they are also highly predatory, taking eggs and young birds in particular.

The future

The uplands are continually changing. At one end of the scale there is change in geomorphological time, the constant wearing down of elevated ground. The more dramatic examples, like the downhill movement of screes, rockfalls from cliffs, soil movement by flash floods, and peat erosion, can be seen actually in operation. The vegetation changes due to changing climate after the last glaciation were followed by rapid and gross changes due to man. But the tempo of human influence on the uplands has progressively increased. The initial deforestation took place over thousands of years. The effects of the next great event, the introduction of sheep ranching by Cistercian monks and its continuation by succeeding generations, have occurred over centuries and are still slowly working their way through the uplands. Arguably the third great event is the afforestation of the last half-century, particularly since the Second World War. This alters the appearance and wildlife content of significant tracts of hill totally and within only 20 years.

Afforestation of the uplands could be regarded as just a reversal of the historic and prehistoric woodland clearances that created the bulk of the moorlands. However, it is by no means recreating the structure, wildlife content and soils of the original forest cover. It is creating new ecosystems. That trees like Sitka spruce *Picea sitchensis* and lodgepole pine *Pinus contorta* are going to be planted is inevitable, when their timber yield can be twice that of our native Scots pine. Although these new forests have their critics, they have an exciting wildlife potential. A forest with all stages present, sapling, thicket, pole and mature, albeit in a mosaic of large blocks, contains a greater diversity of wildlife than the moorland it replaced. Of course, some species, like heather, red grouse, and mountain hares are reduced, but others, like tufted hair-grass *Deschampsia cespitosa* and black grouse increase, and woodland plants and animals colonize as the forest matures. Imagine the excitement if goshawks *Accipiter gentilis* could be acquired as a regularly breeding and widespread species. Increasing fringe plantings of native hardwoods is another obvious way of further diversifying wildlife. Clearly, however, representative examples of our moorlands and their wildlife must be conserved. They are as much a part of our cultural heritage as any museum artefact.

There are other fields of concern. The uplands are the 'lungs' of many towns and cities, and recreational pressures on the hills are increasing. With good paths, the hills may satisfy the needs of many more walkers with negligible loss of wildlife interest or visual amenity. Good forest walks can absorb more people than the same area of open hill. Yet skiing developments cannot expand indefinitely around their present loci without eventually causing irreparable loss of fragile montane habitat. Areas like the unique Cairngorms plateau must be safeguarded. Water supply is another upland

Llyn y fan fach in the Brecon Beacons is a fine example of a corrie lake. This glacial, moraine-dammed lake is now used as a reservoir. To the left lie escarpments of Old Red Sandstone.

use which could still expand. This is really a question of where reservoirs are sited. Constructing the Cow Green reservoir in Teesdale was akin to opening a giant quarry in Ben Lawers. Yet a moorland reservoir opens new vistas in recreation, with swimming, boating, surfing and fishing, and new habitats for wildlife. Mineral extraction is another potential gross hazard for particular areas, like open cast mining in Snowdonia for low grade copper ore, or in Orkney for uranium ore. Yet a large quarry face can, when working ceases, provide nesting sites for peregrines and ravens in an otherwise cliff-less landscape. A threat of new toxic chemical pollution from agriculture is ever present. The consequences of storing vitrified radioactive waste in deep holes in parts of the uplands are impossible to assess. The risk or chance of accidental release of radioactivity into the environment may be negligible, but the consequences of such an accident are more far reaching than anything man has yet done.

Montane plants

The montane zone is characterized by its severe, arctic-type environment, with low temperatures, very short growing seasons, and prevalence of strong winds. Plants of windswept places minimize the desiccating and cooling effects of exposure by adopting low growth forms which are also more likely to retain an insulating layer of snow; wind speeds at ground level being only a fraction of those even at knee height. Herbs with tap roots tend to form cushions (moss campion, diapensia) or rosettes (alpine saxifrage, alpine rock-cress); others may be prostrate (purple saxifrage) or creeping (three-leaved rush). Woody plants form prostrate mats (least willow, mountain avens). These adaptations restrict montane plants to arctic-alpine environments. They cannot grow tall enough to compete elsewhere, while many are also killed by high summer temperatures. The only exceptions are a few species such as thrift, which also grow in high stress coastal sites. Soil instability from frost heaving and downhill movements is another hazard, accounting for the prevalence of reproduction by vegetative means.

The montane zone, however, offers them a wide range of possible habitats, ranging from stable rock faces to constantly moving gravel screes. The latter, surprisingly, supports quite a few plant species, such as the parsley fern and wavy hair grass for example. The dry cliffs bear only a few plants but the moist, north-facing cliffs and the numerous, inaccessible ledges safely out of the reach of grazing animals are homes for a high proportion of the montane flora. Wet, mossy flushes are ideal sites for the starry saxifrage and the drier, stony flushes provide a home for the yellow mountain saxifrage.

1

1 Drooping saxifrage *Saxifraga cernua* is a rare alpine which occurs in only two locations in Britain; both in Scotland. Flowering infrequently and rarely setting seed in Britain, the plants reproduce vegetatively from the red bulbils which develop in the leaf axils.

2

2 Yellow mountain saxifrage *Saxifraga aizoides* is a common plant beside streams and on wet banks in the Highlands. It also occurs on hills in north England and northwest Ireland. Growing as a mat, it sends up dense groups of erect stems which flower in midsummer.

3 A parsley fern *Cryptogramma crispa* growing in the Lake District in April. An arctic-alpine plant which grows on siliceous soils free from calcium and also on rock screes, it is concentrated in North Wales, the Lake District and northwards into Scotland where it is easily seen on rock faces, screes, stone walls and on quarry spoil tips.

4 Moss campion *Silene acaulis* is a perennial alpine herb which grows in dense cushions on the higher mountains in South and North Wales and on many Scottish mountains, but is rare in Ireland.

5 The yellow map lichen *Rhizocarpon geographicum*, with its black markings, is conspicuous on hard acid mountain walls and rocks. It grows in smooth patches which can easily be spotted from a distance. These lichens were growing on a wall in Cwm Idwal.

6 Alpine lady's mantle *Alchemilla alpina* is locally abundant on Scottish mountains and also occurs in the Lake District. It grows up to an altitude of 1200 metres in the Cairngorms.

3

4

5

6

Plants and invertebrates of bogs

Where drainage is poor and water frequently collects, peat tends to accumulate and bogs form. Most species present are confined to such places, for while a few of the common upland heath and grassland species are found living in these bogs, many cannot tolerate the waterlogged and usually acid soils.

Perhaps the most familiar plants of bogs are the hummock-forming *Sphagnum* moss species, cotton grasses and the yellow-flowered bog asphodel. Also present are a few more widespread moorland plants: heather, purple moor-grass and deer-grass. Bogs and wet moors also support many bryophyte species and, where the bog is not burnt regularly, lichens are abundant. Peaty ground in northwest Scotland and in Ireland often bears purple-red sheets of the liverwort *Pleurozia purpurea*, blackish patches of the moss *Campylopus atrovirens*, and jelly-like lumps of the brick-red alga *Glaeocapsa magna*.

A fascinating group of plants often found growing on bogs are those that trap insects. Bog soils are extremely low in plant-available nitrogen and plant insectivory is a very successful method of supplementing the meagre supply. Three groups are native: the sundews, the butterworts and bladderworts, while pitcher plants are naturalized on bogs in Roscommon and Westmeath in central Ireland.

Animal life in bogs is not obvious, though vast numbers of invertebrate species live in the surface peat, such as midge larvae. However, several distinctive invertebrate inhabitants can be found, for example the bog bush cricket, marsh spider, water-beetles, dragonflies and water-fleas, the last being an important food source for the bladderwort.

1

1 *Sphagnum cuspidatum* is a bog moss which grows in pools and hollows of blanket bogs and in wet places on moorlands.

2

2 *Pleurozia purpurea* is an upland liverwort which is common in western Scotland and Ireland where it grows in conspicuous red tufts and is a striking feature of wet moorlands. On each leaf a small lobe forms a tiny pitcher which holds water.

3

4

3 Bog myrtle *Myrica gale* is a deciduous, aromatic shrub which grows in bogs and wet heaths. Before the spring leaves burst, the golden, erect male flowers open to release the pollen which is blown on to the tiny, red, female flowers growing on separate plants. Highlanders used to sleep on bog myrtle as it is a deterrent to fleas.

4 Bog asphodel *Narthecium ossifragum* is common over most of Britain in bogs, wet heaths and on moors. When the flowers open in July, they can form spectacular yellow swards. In Shetland, the plant has been used as a substitute for saffron in both medicine and for dyeing.

5

5 The pink, bell-shaped flowers of bog pimpernel *Anagallis tenella* open on sunny days adding a splash of colour to a green bog moss carpet. Here they are growing with yellow tormentil *Potentilla erecta* on Dartmoor.

Plants and invertebrates of bogs *(continued)*

1

1 Known locally as the Kerry bog violet, the greater butterwort *Pinguicula grandiflora* is the largest and most spectacular of the three insectivorous butterworts found in the British Isles. Small flies are trapped by glandular hairs on the basal leaves as a source of protein.

2 Lesser bladderwort *Utricularia minor* is an aquatic, carnivorous plant which lives in boggy pools and ditches. The underwater bladders are used to trap water fleas and other crustaceans. Pale yellow flowers appear above water from June until September.

3 A marsh spider *Dolomedes fimbriatus* carries her egg-sac over a bog-moss carpet. Swamps, boggy pools and reeds beside still waters are the favourite haunts of this handsome spider, which is largely confined to southern England and southern and eastern Ireland. When disturbed, she can escape by climbing down plant stems under water.

2

3

4

4 A blue damselfly has been trapped in the sticky leaf hairs of the round-leaved sundew *Drosera rotundifolia*. Digestive juices produced by the sundew break down the insect proteins into nitrogenous substances which can then be absorbed by the insectivorous plant, which grows on soils which are low in nitrogen.

5 A female bog bush cricket *Metrioptera brachyptera* drinks moisture from a fruiting bog asphodel spike. Like all bush crickets, it has a long pair of fine antennae. It feeds on plants and animals living on the bogs and wet moors which it frequents.

5

Woodlands and hedgerows

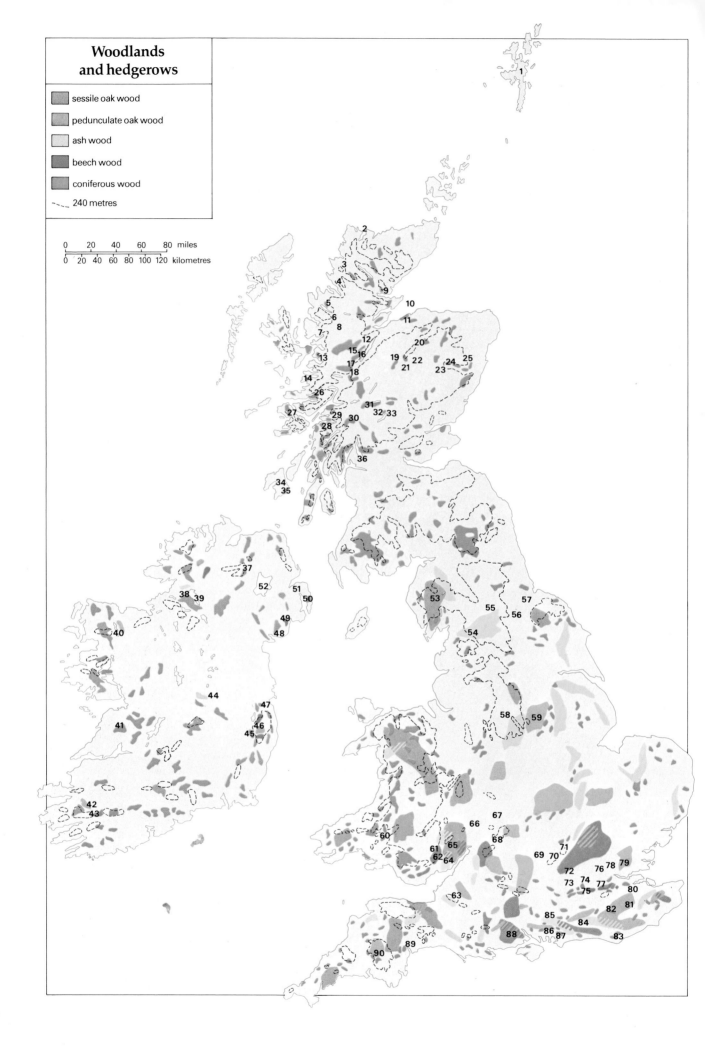

Woodlands and hedgerows

- sessile oak wood
- pedunculate oak wood
- ash wood
- beech wood
- coniferous wood
- - - - 240 metres

| 0 | 20 | 40 | 60 | 80 miles |
| 0 | 20 40 | 60 80 | 100 120 | kilometres |

This map shows the distribution of the major broad-leaved and coniferous woodlands. The locations marked are those referred to in this chapter.

Pedunculate oak woods

Woodland itself is nature's greatest achievement and its variety and fascination can best be appreciated in the early hours of the day. Before the first low rays of summer sun warm the woodland air, the birds have begun to stir, and a wave of sound spreads through the wood heralding the dawn chorus. In a lowland oak wood, this chorus is varied and powerful. Then, as the first insects take to the wing and reflect the rays of light, and the badgers return to their setts, as the rising sun illuminates the glades full of bluebells and wood anemones, the dawn chorus fades away.

When walking through such an oak wood, or any other piece of broad-leaved forest, it soon becomes clear that the wood itself is composed of several vertical layers of vegetation. The topmost layer is formed from the canopies and upper branches of the trees, which are strong enough to support the nests of buzzards *Buteo buteo* and herons *Ardea cinerea*. The second high layer is provided by the shrubs such as holly *Ilex aquifolium*, rowan *Sorbus aucuparia*, wild cherry *Prunus avium* and wild service *Sorbus torminalis* that grow underneath the tree canopy. The shrub layer may also consist of hazel *Corylus avellana* or sweet chestnut *Castanea sativa* which are sometimes coppiced; their trunks are cut back to the ground on a rotational basis of between perhaps 12 and 15 years. The shrubs in many lowland pedunculate oak woods often form a luxuriant layer that has a most important part to play in the wood's ecology. Here breed such birds as the blackbird *Turdus merula*, jay *Garrulus glandarius*, and warblers like the blackcap *Sylvia atricapilla* and garden warbler *S. borin* while in the south and east the nightingale *Luscinia megarhynchos* nests on or near the ground. Besides hazel with its attractive, dancing catkins, there are other regular members of the shrub layer such as hawthorn *Crataegus monogyna*, blackthorn *Prunus spinosa*, guelder rose *Viburnum opulus* and sallow *Salix caprea*. The presence and the size of the shrub layer in a wood are dependent upon the amount of light that penetrates the canopy above. A well-established oak wood with a tightly woven canopy may possess an extremely thin shrub layer whereas, if the trees are scattered, more light can flood in to fill the glades and clearings.

The shrub layer in spring and early summer hums with the wings of countless insects. Here the speckled wood butterfly *Pararge aegeria* follows the moving sun spots and, in the oak woods of the New Forest, the rare white admiral *Limenitis camilla* suns itself. Hover-flies, bumble-bees and fritillaries frequent the tall thistle flowers, while grass snakes *Natrix natrix* and slow-worms *Anguis fragilis* sun themselves beneath their plumes.

Below the shrub layer there is often a rich field layer reaching perhaps some two metres in height. In the spring and summer, this layer contributes much of the beauty to be seen in a lowland oak wood. At first, when the canopy is leaf-less, the ground may be covered with lesser celandine *Ranunculus ficaria*, dog's mercury *Mercurialis perennis* and wood anemone *Anemone nemorosa*. Then, as the canopy begins to burgeon, there follow other plants with varying tolerance of shade, such as ground ivy *Glechoma hederacea*, bluebell *Endymion non-scriptus*, wood sage *Teucrium scorodonia*, yellow pimpernel *Lysimachia nemorum* and red campion *Silene dioica*. Later still, rosebay willow-herb *Epilobium angustifolium* begins to fill the open ground and sanicle *Sanicula europaea* raises its tight umbels of pinkish flowers. The field layer itself may be almost absent in some woods while in others its variety and composition depend on the nature of the soil and the amount of light and water that is available.

Some woodlands are very large and store a vast quantity of energy which they have gathered from the sun. This energy may then be dispersed

Semi-wild fallow deer are common in many oak woods *(above)* but the descendants of the original introduced herds are now confined to only a few areas, such as Epping and the New Forests. A buck is usually five years old before it assumes the broad and characteristic palmate antlers.

Pedunculate oak woods are renowned for their rich field layer, which is at its most colourful in spring and summer. Here, in May, bluebells and clusters of greenish-yellow wood spurge *Euphorbia amygdaloides* brighten a woodland scene *(left)*.

Birds that nest in holes need well-grown and even over-mature timber for nesting sites. Two, three-week old little owls look out on a woodland scene from a nest at the base of an oak tree (above left).

Cherry galls on the underside of an oak leaf (above right) are a sign that a female gall wasp Cynipis quercus has been at work. Galls appear in autumn and a small grub can be found inside each one. The galls are formed in response to a stimulation of the host tree by the insect when it lays its eggs.

The speckled wood butterfly (below right) can be found in Ireland and much of Britain. It is a lover of warm, sunny glades and can here be seen basking in a sun spot on a bramble leaf.

among the other living things that occur in woodland. There are very intricate food chains with predators at one end of the chain such as hawks, owls, carrion crows *Corvus corone*, magpies *Pica pica* and jays feeding on small birds like thrushes, tits and warblers as well as their eggs and young. The birds, in turn, influence the populations of spiders, parasitic insects, carnivorous insects, gall-wasps, leaf-miners, sap-feeders such as bugs and aphids, and leaf-strippers like the caterpillars, snails and slugs. There are also delicate links between the fungi and the insects and other animals that feed on them.

Many species of aphids, for example, feed on the sap of oak leaves and provide a staple food for many kinds of birds and carnivorous insects like ladybird larvae. The caterpillars of the winter moth *Operophtera brumata* and the green oak-roller moth *Tortrix viridana* often infest the foliage of the trees, and a single great tit *Parus major* may eat up to 300 of these caterpillars in a single day. In fact, the breeding season of the great tit in oak woods is synchronized with the annual 'bloom' of oak caterpillars.

The leaf litter under the trees contains many different soil animals. These include earthworms which may turn up each year as much as five tonnes of earth in every half hectare of woodland, other invertebrate decomposers like millipedes, woodlice, slugs and snails and the larvae of flies, and many kinds of beetle such as stag beetles *Lucanus* and click beetles that help in the process of breaking up rotting wood. Dying and dead wood is, in fact, a great natural resource in a forest and may support up to one fifth of the whole fauna. But even healthy trees may bear an enormous variety of living creatures, and altogether some 284 animal species have been recorded on oak trees, a total including nearly 200 different kinds of butterflies and moths.

A number of British mammals are also often associated with oak woods. Badgers *Meles meles* are well distributed, with their underground setts usually on well-drained mounds, whose presence in the middle of an oak wood is often betrayed by elder *Sambucus nigra* which grows around them. Foxes *Vulpes vulpes* are common and may dig out their own earths or even share part of a badger sett. Both mammals will feed on young rabbits *Oryctolagus cuniculus*, rodents and some vegetable food. Wood mice *Apodemus sylvaticus* and bank voles *Clethrionomys glareolus* are frequent and their density was correlated with the breeding success of tawny owls *Strix aluco* in Wytham Woods near Oxford; the proportion of owls breeding was higher in the years when their prey was abundant than in those years when they were thin on the ground. Stoats *Mustela erminea* and weasels *M. nivalis* sometimes hunt for rodents and rabbits in the woods, while shrews and hedgehogs *Erinaceus europaeus* tend to live nearer the edges of the woodland rather than deep inside it. Moles *Talpa europaea* are more common in woodland than is often believed since they are less likely to be noticed there except when making shallow tunnels in water-logged ground. Some oak woods support deer, and fallow *Cervus dama*, red *C. elaphus*, and the introduced Sika *C. nippon* can all be seen in the New Forest. Indeed the belching grunt of the fallow buck, the bovine roar of the red deer stag and the extraordinary wavering whistle of the Sika stag can all be heard during the rutting season. The tiny muntjac deer *Muntiacus reevesi* is now well established in many Midland oak woods but can live unsuspected even in quite well-visited woods. In the evenings, pipistrelle *Pipistrellus pipistrellus* and noctule *Nyctalus noctula* bats can often be seen hawking for flying insects in the rides or above the woods.

Each part of the woodland is filled with certain species that are specialists in a particular way of life. Great spotted woodpeckers *Dendrocopos major* hammer into trees with their chisel-shaped bills while treecreepers *Certhia familiaris* explore the bark and its crevices with their thin, curved bills. Tits exploit different layers of the shrubs and canopy while some warblers may hunt for insects in one layer of the wood and nest in another. Woodcock *Scolopax rusticola* feed and live and nest on the ground while herons,

The woodcock is chiefly a bird of open, damp woodlands of oak, birch and pine, especially those with a rich field layer and a ground zone with wet and decaying leaves. The bird's back is richly marked and it closely resembles the woodland floor. Woodcock spend the day resting and fly at dusk.

Sessile oaks *(above right)* were often coppiced so that their new growth could be used for fuel as well as providing tannins for hides.

One of the features of sessile oak woods are the plants that grow on the trees themselves. In Wistman's Wood, an isolated oak wood on Dartmoor, epiphytic plants include the common polypody fern *Polypodium vulgare (right)*, mosses and liverworts.

which fish in the rivers and lakes, may come to small woods to breed. In winter, many of the insect-eating birds leave the oak woods, with the warblers, redstarts *Phoenicurus phoenicurus* and flycatchers going south, and the robins *Erithacus rubecula* and song thrushes *Turdus philomelus* moving towards human habitations. When autumn comes, some of the tits combine with each other and perhaps also with treecreepers, nuthatches *Sitta europaea* and goldcrests *Regulus regulus* to form loose flocks that wander through the branches looking for spiders and insects. Some woodland birds change to a vegetable diet in the autumn and some of the thrushes will enter the oak woods to feed on the fruits of hawthorn, elder, rowan and holly. Dunnocks *Prunella modularis*, which feed on animal matter in the summer, switch almost entirely to seed during the winter months.

So far we have been looking at the life and ecology of one broadleaved tree, the pedunculate oak *Quercus robur* whose chief characteristics are the stalked flowers and acorns and the leaves without stalks. There is, however, a second native oak known as the durmast or sessile oak *Quercus petraea*, which possesses stalked leaves and unstalked or 'sessile' flowers and acorns. But there are hybrids or intermediate forms between the two oaks which are difficult to distinguish in the field. The pedunculate oak is the dominant oak of lowland Britain, while the sessile is more typical of the highland zone. The dividing line between lowland and highland Britain runs roughly from the mouth of the River Tees in Cleveland to the mouth of the River Exe in Devon. South and east of this line are the more recent rocks and fertile lowland plains with clays, loams, marls and brown earths which favour the pedunculate oak. These oaks can also be found in parts of the north and west of Britain but rarely in Ireland where the high ground forms a saucer-like rim to a great central and often boggy plain. In England, in regions such as Sherwood Forest, both kinds of oak flourish alongside each other.

Sessile oak woods

The sessile oak is very typical of highland Britain and it may well have been growing there before the pedunculate, which we know has been widely planted. Unfortunately, it is not possible to separate the two species during pollen analysis. However, the sessile is certainly the dominant oak of the older siliceous rocks and acid soils in the north and west of Britain and in Ireland, where it grows on hillsides and valley slopes. The trees may be found in close canopy but they are also often stunted and small. There are fine sessile woods in the Lake District, on the Malverns, in the Towy Valley and many parts of Wales, on the Pennines, in western Scotland and in Ireland on the Old Red Sandstone near Killarney and around Lough Conn. On Loch Lomond and on the metamorphic rocks of Galway there are several islands covered with ungrazed semi-natural oak wood lying in a contrasting moorland setting. Sometimes downy and silver birch *Betula pubescens* and *B. pendula*, rowan, alder *Alnus glutinosa* and holly grow among the oaks but the shrub layer is often poorer than in a pedunculate wood and, where grazing by deer or sheep occurs, it may be absent altogether.

The ground zone is usually heathy or grassy and the absence of a shrub layer has a profound effect on the bird life, for example. But where the oak is mixed with birch the fauna is more varied than in tracts of pure oak. Bramble *Rubus fruticosus* is frequent in the field layer, cow wheat *Melampyrum* and yellow pimpernel shine among the mosses, and bluebells occur only where there is no grazing. Red and roe deer *Capreolus capreolus* are regular visitors and there are also red squirrels *Sciurus vulgaris*, rabbits, brown hares *Lepus capensis* and sometimes mountain or blue hares *L. timidus*, shrews *Sorex*, hedgehogs, voles, wood mice, stoats and weasels, and perhaps badgers and pine martens *Martes martes*. Pipistrelle and long-eared bats *Plecotus auritus* are often common as well, while Daubenton's bats *Myotis daubentoni* may hunt for insects through oak woods which are near water. Like pedunculate oak woods, sessile oak woods also support a wide range of butterflies and moths, especially winter moths but, since the invertebrate-eating blackbirds are less common than in pedunculate oak woods, this suggests a poorer insect fauna as well. Chaffinches *Fringilla coelebs* and willow warblers *Phylloscopus trochilus* are the commonest bird species, but these northern sessile oak woods are rather silent places after the bird choruses of the lowland oak forests.

The spread of woodlands in post-glacial times

Although much of the early part of this chapter has been concerned with the dominant oak, it was not the first tree to colonize Britain and Ireland at the end of the ice ages. During the Pleistocene Period, which lasted for about a million years, the ice sheet advanced south, at one time as far as the Thames estuary and the Bristol Channel and the southern parts of Ireland. What vegetation still survived was of a tundra type, with stony and rocky ground frozen for most of the year and bearing only stunted shrubs, mosses and lichens. The landscape must have resembled parts of Greenland today.

As a native in the British Isles, the strawberry tree is confined to the sessile oak woods around the Killarney Lakes *(right)*. Here, the evergreen trees contrast well against the brown autumnal oaks on a November morning. The creamy, bell-like flowers open in September and the warty, red fruits ripen in October. In the Killarney woods it can grow to a height of 10 metres or more.

The greenish-grey, cream-spotted Kerry slug *Geomalacus maculosus (below)* is localized to the extreme southwest of Ireland and in damp or wet weather it can be found on moss or lichen-covered trees and rocks. Unlike other members of its family, it rolls up into a ball when disturbed. In dry weather it disappears beneath moss carpets or into cracks in rocks.

The Scots pine was the dominant tree of the old Boreal forests but only a few fragments of these woods survived where it was too difficult to extract their timber. These snow-laden pines of the original Caledonian Forest are growing in Glenmore in the shadow of the Cairngorms.

From about 18,000 BC to about 7500 BC, the climate slowly improved and the ice sheets began their long final retreat. We can deduce what happened to the vegetation afterwards by analysing the different proportions of pollen grain types preserved in the peat bogs. In this way, it is also possible to determine which trees are native and which have been introduced. As conditions improved in Britain, successive waves of trees and other plants advanced into England across the land bridge that linked it to the Continent until about 6000 BC. Exactly when the Outer Isles and Ireland were detached from mainland Britain is still conjectural, but when the links were broken some animal and plant species had not yet crossed over.

It is clear from the pollen record that, as the tundra moved northwards with the retreat of the ice around 5000 BC, birch trees followed up its progress while not far behind came Scots pine *Pinus sylvestris* with some hazel, oak and scattered elms *Ulmus* and alders. It is possible that the silver and the downy birches had managed to survive the glaciation in a few places; otherwise they would have made their way into England across the existing land bridge. Whatever their origins, the birch woods continued to advance and grow in size. In some regions willows *Salix*, aspen *Populus tremula* and juniper *Juniperus communis* would also have taken a hold. Gradually, the Scots pine came to assert its dominance over the birch but both trees could be found occupying land which was originally tundra in late glacial times.

The climate then changed again, becoming warmer and wetter. It was in this period that the broadleaved trees began their spectacular advance. Deciduous summer forest became established in the British Isles with elm, pedunculate and sessile oak, small-leaved lime *Tilia cordata*, alder and hazel. Out of this assemblage, oak became the most important tree. Alder sometimes accompanied the Scots pine and survived in many of the oak woods

Hazel growing on Islay in December. Where trees cannot grow because of the climate, the ground may be covered with climax scrub. Hazel will establish itself on the west coast of Scotland and Ireland where there is heavy rainfall, strong winds and high humidity.

in the western, damper regions. Hazel passed its zenith but it still forms dense scrub on Islay and elsewhere in western Scotland, and on the lime-stone karst country of the Burren in western Ireland. New colonists arrived with the forest species: shrub-forming plants like hawthorn, blackthorn, rowan, wild cherry, aspen, willows and holly. Later, the climate became drier and beech *Fagus sylvatica* and hornbeam *Carpinus betulus* began to spread across the countryside perhaps as far as Wales and the southwest of England. Together with ash *Fraxinus excelsior* and yew *Taxus baccata*, beech was able to establish itself on the chalky or limestone uplands where oak could not grow so well.

Many species of trees succeeded in gaining strong footholds in the British Isles. But beech, hornbeam and small-leaved lime, which were so characteristic of England, never reached Ireland, probably because they failed to cross the land bridge before it sank under what is now the Irish Sea. This premature severance also had its effect on the animal species of Irish woodlands. There are no dormice *Muscardinus avellanarius*, or roe deer. Woodpeckers, marsh tits *Parus palustris* and willow tits *P. montanus*, nuthatches, nightingales, and pied flycatchers *Ficedula hypoleuca* are missing but some of these species were already on the limits of their range in Britain. A number of butterflies like the purple emperor *Apatura iris* and white admiral do not appear in the island's fauna.

Climate plays an important part in the environment of trees; that of western Europe and the British Isles with its damp, warm summers and cooler winter months favours the growth of broadleaved deciduous trees such as oaks. The trees lose their leaves in winter and so avoid dehydration during a period when very little water could be taken up from roots em-bedded in frozen soil. There is often a clear correlation between high rainfall and altitude, but rainfall and temperature are the more important factors in determining the types of tree that will grow in a region. High wind will stunt the growth of trees, drying out the shoots and causing the canopy of the tree to develop asymmetrically. The parent rocks that produce the soil have a part to play but they seem to be of less importance than the climatic conditions themselves. The maritime nature of Ireland's climate with wet, mild winters, cloudy, cool summers and very strong winds from the west, have all influenced the distribution of its forests. It was once well covered by deciduous forests but local conditions of climate and soil favoured the establishment of blanket bog, and trees now only flourish on land that is reasonably well drained.

Ash woods

Not all woods are pure and so it is not unusual to find other species of trees, such as ash and birch, growing amongst the dominant oaks. However, inside a wood, there is a natural development of tree species called a succession. On light soils, birch may establish itself and then be succeeded by oak wood, while beech, which is also an end or climax succession, may follow on an initial development of ash wood. So, at the end of the succession, there is normally a climax community in a state of balance with the environment. But, in some regions, because of climate and other local conditions, the logical tree species at the end of the succession cannot establish itself and the earlier, pre-climax may come to be the final form of tree. For example, ash is, for a period, often a dominant tree on shallow limestone soils but it is eventually overtaken by beech which suppresses the ash and itself becomes the dominant species. Outside the normal range of the beech, ash may compose the final tree community.

Ash is a very common tree in many parts of the British Isles and often grows on hillsides where the soil layer is too thin to support sessile oaks. Some of the finest ash woods are those on steep limestone slopes: in the Peak District and Somerset, the Mendip Hills and South Wales, in Derbyshire, Yorkshire and North Lancashire, in southwest Scotland and on the uplands of Co. Clare and Co. Galway. In Ireland, ash has probably never been very widespread although it is a fairly common roadside tree. At the higher altitudes, it may be replaced by downy birch with perhaps a few rowans. In the damper ash woods there are often ramsons *Allium ursinum*, yellow archangel *Lamiastrum galeobdolon*, giant bellflower *Campanula latifolia* and spotted orchid *Dactylorhiza fuchsii* as well as many mosses and liverworts, while on somewhat drier soils, ground ivy, bloody cranesbill *Geranium sanguineum*, lily-of-the-valley *Convallaria majalis* and, in more northern regions, baneberry *Actaea spicata* may be found as well.

Ash woods are attractive places in which to walk with the sun casting dappled patterns between the boles as the light filters down through the feathery fronds of the leaves. But, ash itself has attracted a rather thin invertebrate fauna and it is, therefore, much poorer than the oak as a habitat. Chaffinches and wrens *Troglodytes troglodytes* are common in many Scottish ash woods, while the woods around Lower Lough Erne and on the Big Esker at Kilbeggan in Ireland are particularly rich in blackbirds, willow warblers, chaffinches and robins.

Beech woods

It is rather uncertain when the beech – which Gilbert White of Selborne called 'the most lovely of all forest trees' – first arrived in Britain. It seems to have spread during the dry period between 4000 BC and 2000 BC and to have moved naturally beyond its present range even as far as Wales and southwest England. In the Brecon Beacons National Park in Wales is an

Mixed woodlands such as Felshamhall Wood in Suffolk *(above left)*, with its oak and birch standards, are usually rich in wildlife. Here, two years after coppicing, a luxuriant field layer, which includes oxlips and purple orchids, has grown up. This wood has been managed as a coppice since the thirteenth century.

Colt Park Wood *(above right)* is an ash wood growing at 335 metres on the Ingleborough Scar in Yorkshire. On this National Nature Reserve ash, rowan and guelder rose grow from limestone slabs, often known as pavements' while giant bellflower, lily-of-the-valley, baneberry and yellow star-of-Bethlehem *Gagea lutea* grow in the grykes.

The mixed woods of the Forge Valley in the North York Moors National Park *(right)* are rich in flowers. Beds of ramsons carpet the limestone slopes above the River Derwent and the air is redolent with their pungent scent.

Broadleaved woods are often at their most attractive in autumn. These beeches are growing in Bratley Wood in the New Forest. The lack of shrubs is due to persistent grazing by ponies and fallow deer, and dense shade.

extreme westerly, semi-natural beech wood at Cwm Clydach, while beech, small-leaved lime and whitebeam *Sorbus aria* grow on the limestone outcrop of Craig y Ciliau. On chalky uplands, beech will become the dominant tree but in some areas, due to position and topography, the dominance may pass to ash or yew. It is now largely confined to the chalk Downs of southeastern England and the inferior oolite of the Cotswolds; poor and more twisted examples can be seen on the Bagshot Sands southwest of London and the Lower Greensand of the Weald of Kent. Some large areas of beech are in south Oxfordshire and Buckinghamshire where the trees support the local furniture industry.

Many of the woods of southwest England, Scotland and Ireland, which often contain very fine stands of timber, have been planted. Many began as ornaments for eighteenth-century houses and, at this time, conifers were often used as nurse trees for the tiny beeches and felled later. This might explain the surviving and exposed beech clumps in the Pennines and elsewhere. In Scotland, beech can be seen growing in many places from Fife north to Grampian, and the seed of these planted trees often forms considerable woodland. After being introduced to Ireland, probably in the seventeenth century, it now graces countless hedgerows and roadsides with fine groves at Powerscourt, Tollymore, Mount Stewart, Cairnwood and in the Vale of Clara to the south of Dublin.

The shrub layer in a beech wood is largely absent or very thin since little light filters down into a close-canopy wood and the soil is generally rather shallow. The spreading rootlets of the trees also use up a great deal of the moisture in the ground. In dense beech woods, the only plants which can survive are those that draw their nourishment from dead organic material such as fallen leaves. These plants, known as saprophytes, lack colour since they do not have the green pigment essential for the process of photosynthesis. In the more open woodlands where there is more light available, a richer flora often includes oak-wood plants such as dog's mercury, bugle *Ajuga reptans*, wood anemone and sanicle. Chalk beech woods may contain bird's nest orchid *Neottia nidus-avis*, several species of helleborines, spurge laurel *Daphne laureola*, hairy violet *Viola hirta* and Solomon's seal *Polygonatum multiflorum*.

The beech tree itself can support around 200 different kinds of invertebrates which makes it in this respect about eight times richer than the ash tree. This comparative richness in small animal life helps to compensate

The rarest of all beech-wood flowers is the ghost orchid *Epipogium aphyllum (below left)*. Before the mid-1950s it was recorded only in nine of the previous one hundred years. Here it is seen flowering in the Chilterns in August.

One of the common flowering plants in beech woods is the bugle *(below right)* which flowers from April to June. The flowers are normally powder-blue but occasionally they may be white or pink.

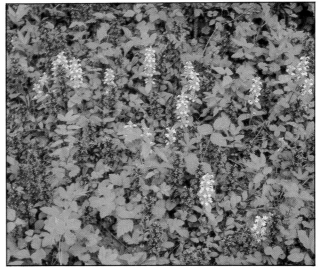

for the adverse factors such as the small amount of incoming light, shallow soil, sparse shrub and field layers, and a dense leaf fall. Where the banks are too steep to retain the fallen leaves, moss often grows and spreads a green carpet. The breeding bird community is somewhat less rich and varied than that of oak woods, because of the sparse shrub layer. Chaffinches are often the commonest species, followed by the blackbird. In English beech woods, there are high numbers of great tits and blue tits *Parus caeruleus*, woodpigeons *Columba palumbus*, willow warblers, wrens and robins while green woodpeckers *Picus viridis* like the open woods as well. Chiffchaffs *Phylloscopus collybita* are often the first summer migrants to sing in the beech woods in spring while in the woods of the New Forest, for example, wood warblers *P. sibilatrix* and redstarts fill the beech groves with their shivering trills, plangent notes and warbled phrases. In old mature beech woods, woodpeckers also take advantage of rotten and poor timber. Badgers often excavate their setts among beech trees in the better-drained chalk uplands rather than on the lower chalk itself. Throughout October in the New Forest, amorous fallow deer bucks roam along the edges of the beech woods proclaiming their territories with loud belching sounds. In Ireland, the dominant species of birds are similar to those found in the Irish sessile oakwoods.

Bird life in autumn beech woods depends on the crop of beechmast. In a good year, hundreds of chaffinches, bramblings *Fringilla montifringilla*, tits, nuthatches, stock doves *Columba oenas*, woodpigeons and woodpeckers will gather in the woods to exploit the harvest but the seeding is irregular and one good crop does not follow another. Some birds, such as nuthatches, coal tits *Parus ater* and marsh tits will hide beech nuts for use in bad weather.

Birches

The graceful birch trees are often associated with Scots pine since both flourish equally well in similar conditions of soil and climate. Together with pine, they form the climax community to the north of the belts of broad-leaved summer woodland. Birch prefers a fair amount of light and is less successful when in direct competition with the Scots pine. Besides a dwarf birch *Betula nana*, which is an Arctic relic growing around high moorland bogs in Scotland, there are two species of well-developed tree. The silver birch is an elegant tree with pendulous twigs and a silvery bark, while the downy birch is smaller with less pointed, downy leaves. The silver birch grows well on sandy, gravelly soils and tends to be commoner and more widespread in the south while the downy prefers damper conditions and so forms a high proportion of the Scottish Highland woods. However, many of the birch woods of the Lake District and northern England are composed of both kinds of tree. In Scotland, the silver birch tends to be found in the eastern and central Highlands and the downy birch in the wetter north and west. The damper, western birch woods often cling to rocky, boulder-strewn slopes which, like the trees themselves, are covered in a velvety growth of green and yellow moss. Ferns and various kinds of grass, among them great wood-rush *Luzula sylvatica*, wood sorrel *Oxalis acetosella*, dog violet *Viola canina* and wood anemone can often be seen growing under the trees. Although once common in the primeval forests of Ireland, birch now chiefly occurs as scrub on some of the hillsides and along the edges of bogs and around lakes such as Lough Neagh.

Birches are not long-lived trees and many woods are not able to re-generate because of intensive grazing by cattle, sheep and deer. Trees age, rot, are attacked by wood-boring insects and fall. Many birch woods present a rather dismal sight; leaning, shattered and fallen, mossy boles

In the Scottish Highlands, Scots pine and
birch are the most commonly occurring trees.
In Glen Affric a rich growth of the graceful
silver birch dominates the landscape.

criss-cross each other and form a tangle of wood covered in fungi and
lichens, often under a pall of low, misty cloud. In these open woods in
Scotland it is possible to find hares, weasels, stoats, voles, mice and even in
places a few wild cats *Felis silvestris*. Badger setts are not uncommon and
these are sometimes occupied in part by foxes. The insect life of the birch
woods is often very varied and includes such interesting moths as the great
brocade *Eurois occulta*, scarce prominent *Odontosia carmelita* and Kentish
glory *Eudromis versicolor*. One kind of shield-bug, *Elasmucha grisea*,
lays her eggs on a birch leaf where she guards them with her body and,
even after hatching, actively protects her young. In many birch woods, the
dominant bird is the willow warbler followed by the chaffinch, tree pipit
Anthus trivialis, wren and robin. There may be coal tits which nest in holes
in the trees or the ground as well as great and blue tits, song thrushes and,
occasionally, redwings *Turdus iliacus*. In the birch woods of Ireland, willow
warblers and robins are common while there are often good numbers of
blackbirds, mistle thrushes *T. viscivorus* and chaffinches.

Other broadleaved trees
In addition to the comparatively widely distributed and well-known trees
that we have been looking at so far – trees that could and do become

When sycamore leaves fall in autumn they form a golden-yellow carpet *(above left)* on the woodland floor. The large, leathery leaves, however, take a long time to decay and so smother the growth of ground layer plants.

Coppiced sweet chestnut *(above right)* is seen here in winter, growing with oak standards. In their early stages coppices are a delight with their bird songs and spring flowers. Just before coppicing is due, however, dense shade may inhibit the growth of the field layer.

Alders growing by a stream in Glen Docherty in Scotland *(left)*. In moist valleys and where the ground is wet the alder often replaces the oak. In Wales, alders are often mixed with ash trees. If there is a shrub layer it usually consists of brambles, hollies, hawthorns and small ashes. The ground zone may be covered with primroses, violets and wood anemones.

dominant over an area or provide important constituents in woodland – there are other broadleaved species. There is the sycamore *Acer pseudoplatanus* introduced from central Europe, which likes deep, loamy soils and is well established in northern England, Scotland and many parts of Ireland. Sycamores can form small woods and are found as shelter belts in exposed coastal situations and grow as clumps around farmsteads. They also tolerate smoky regions and therefore flourish within urban areas. Many of the northern woods are grassy, with celandines, ground ivy and wild raspberry *Rubus idaeus* growing under the trees. The plant-eating invertebrates that flourish on the sycamore are low in number compared with those on oaks but tits will often come to feed on the aphids that gather on the foliage. Sycamore woods to some extent resemble beech woods and Irish sessile oak woods.

Besides the introduced sycamore there are other broadleaved trees of note. Field maple *Acer campestre* often grows in hedges on calcareous soils in the south and east of Britain. Hornbeam is native in southeast Britain where it may occur with oak. It attracts that rare bird, the hawfinch *Coccothraustes coccothraustes*, which eats its seed. Pollarded hornbeams can be seen in Epping Forest, on Enfield Chase and in Hertfordshire and some are regularly used as nest sites by tawny owls. There are also groves of sweet chestnut, which were introduced by the Romans and frequently coppiced, and these are rather like beech woods in their ecology. The horse chestnut *Aesculus hippocastanum* was introduced from Istanbul in 1576 but remains largely a park and avenue tree. There may also be strips of aspen and willow growing on damp ground. Willow woodland or carr is an unusual habitat in Britain since the trees normally fringe rivers and other waterways; there is such a wood on the banks of the Welsh Harp reservoir in northwest London. Box *Buxus sempervirens* is one of our few broadleaved evergreen trees and favours dry limestone soils; it grows well on the North Downs at Box Hill as well as at several sites in the Chiltern and Cotswold Hills.

In damp valleys and water-logged regions, the oak is replaced by the alder with its roundish, serrated leaves, catkins and false cones. When undisturbed, an alder can grow to over 30 metres. It has decreased in the British Isles very largely because of the drainage of wetlands. Alders like a soil rich in mineral salts, and small lines, groves or woods can be found throughout the British Isles north to Sutherland and across Ireland to the west coast. They are most likely to come to one's attention in Wales and Scotland where they grow up the hill slopes. Alder also grows in the fenland and Broadland carrs where trees form a thick jungle rising from a bed of tussock or fen sedge *Carex paniculata*. Elsewhere alder is best known as a riverside tree but it is also a winter haunt of visiting redpolls *Carduelis flammea* and siskins *C. spinus*.

It is clear that some of the woods in the British Isles are formed from several species of trees, and mixed woodlands of this kind are regular features of the countryside. Such mixed woods provide a very varied habitat for invertebrates and for the birds which feed upon them. Although birds and mammals may live in a region, they are generally less affected by the actual species of plant growing there than by the nature of the shrub layer and the availability of cover, nesting and breeding sites. With many invertebrate species, however, there is often a very close dependence upon a few plant species or even just one. The woods formed from some introduced tree species will not, therefore, attract certain kinds of invertebrates which take longer than some birds and mammals to adapt to alien trees. Sycamores are said to support only 15 dependent invertebrate species and Norway spruces *Picea abies* only 37. Forestry often demands large blocks of a single tree species – a monoculture – and this practice reduces the variety in the habitat and with it the range and richness of the wildlife that can be expected to occur there.

Man and the history of woodlands

Man has exploited woodlands for several thousand years. It is probable that, until the early Neolithic period some 5000 years ago, forests of various species were the predominant vegetation over much of Britain's land surface. Oak was a common tree, Scots pine and birch clothed the lighter land and the hillsides, ash flourished on the limestone, and alder and willow filled the marshes and lined the river banks. Recent research suggests that small-leaved lime may too have covered much of lowland Britain. There were also local woods of elm, beech, hornbeam and probably whitebeam, field maple and yew. The early Neolithic settlers began the process of forest destruction that by modern times had reduced the original forest cover by as much as 90 per cent. These early farmers seem to have chosen the lighter and more easily cultivated soils of the chalk and limestone hills for their settlements and it was here that so many forests were first cleared.

From Roman times to the later Anglo-Saxon occupation, a continuous assault was made on the thick forest cover on the clays of the Weald, the Midlands and East Anglia. The Danes continued the clearances so that, by the eleventh century, the forest cover of Britain had been reduced from around 16 million hectares to a quarter of that amount. The Norman Conquest brought in a code of forest law, and Royal Forests were established over perhaps as much as one third of the land area of England. Forest clearances continued, however, probably in the attempt to clear certain regions of wolves and outlaws.

By the twelfth century, southern Scotland was almost denuded of its forest cover, and by 1700, the area of woodland in Ireland had shrunk to minimal cover. To balance this loss of timber, there were Acts as early as 1457 requiring tenants to plant trees but the results were at first rather poor. In Ireland, during the 150 years since 1700, many landlords had planted trees on their estates particularly in the Counties of Dublin, Kildare and Wicklow. There was also an increase in planting in England and Scotland by private landowners. Some of these plantings were of native trees, such as Scots pine, beech and oak, but many were also of exotic, European conifers such as larch *Larix*, spruce *Picea* and silver fir *Abies*. A great deal of woodland was also regarded as a sporting amenity rather than a source of timber so that gamekeeping and the advent of the shot gun sometimes had a catastrophic effect on the woodland wildlife on many estates. In a period of three years after 1837 the keepers on one Scottish estate killed 285 buzzards, 275 kites *Milvus milvus*, 63 goshawks *Accipiter gentilis*, 18 ospreys *Pandion haliaetus*, three honey buzzards *Pernis apivorus* as well as many wild cats, pine martens and polecats *Mustela putorius*.

Hedgerows

A statute of Edward IV in 1483 authorized the planting of hedges around coppices to protect them from the attentions of domestic stock. The creation of hedges continued in southern England so that by 1800 nearly all the fields had been enclosed by quickset hedges often of blackthorn, hawthorn, elder and holly. These hedges usually included forest trees such as oak, ash, beech and elm with occasional crab-apples *Malus sylvestris*, cherries, maples and willows as well, which were allowed to grow naturally. The hedges themselves were usually planted along the old field boundaries and lanesides; most are now composed of hawthorn, but other hedges may contain

This old, stag-headed oak stands in part of the original Forest of Windsor, an unmanaged forest where beech trees predominate. Windsor and the New Forest are two of the most famous of the Royal Forests and were recorded in the Domesday Book.

The countryside of southern Britain seen across the River Severn from Moel y Golfa, one of the Breidden Hills *(above right)*. The land is a patchwork of small woods, fields and hedgerows. Hawthorn is the commonest hedge species in the British Isles having originated with the enclosures.

A vibrant display of red and white campion flowers and bluebells appear in a shady Cornish hedgerow *(right)* after the earlier primroses and violets have faded. Throughout the rest of the summer, a succession of flowers and fruits colour the verges.

shrubby species which are elements in the shrub layer of a broadleaved wood, such as elder and sycamore; these might be sown by the wind or by birds. Thirty years ago, there were perhaps some two and a half million kilometres of field hedgerow in Britain with another one and a quarter million kilometres bordering roadsides, but a great decrease has taken place in recent years with the creation of large prairie-like fields. This has been most noticeable in East Anglia which was also where many medieval hedgerows could be seen.

Hedges remain, however, a regular feature of parts of our countryside, and the plants growing along their lengths and at their bases are often very typical woodland flowers maintaining a foothold in the landscape – among them bluebell, dog's mercury and lords-and-ladies *Arum maculatum*. Many hedge plants are also typical of the scrub that once fringed the edges of woodlands when farming was less widespread and the human population at a much lower level.

Farmland itself, on which so many of the hedgerows survive, is a comparatively unstable environment. It is subject to many dynamic influences such as ploughing, harvesting and the use of chemicals on the land. Hedges may be periodically cut, lacerated by flail-machines and even severely damaged by the largely unnecessary practice of burning the stubbles. The wider and more 'natural' a hedge is, the greater the variety of wildlife can be expected to find shelter there. Well-grown, dense and uncut hedges have strong affinities with the borders of a broadleaved wood. They can often be seen on embankments, on roadsides and along disused railway tracks. Other hedgerows are 'laid' at regular intervals and are reduced to low narrow strips in which branches are bent or cut to form a horizontal barrier against the movements of cattle and sheep. Many hedgerows contain standard and small trees. Untrimmed hedges allow the flowers and later the fruit of their component shrubs to develop: hips, haws, holly berries, honeysuckle *Lonicera*, ivy *Hedera helix*, privet *Ligustrum vulgare*, sloe, black bryony *Tamus communis* and wild cherry. Dense hedgerows also harbour more mammals and birds which can find food, breeding places, shelter and roosts, and some animals may use the cover of a hedge to cross what would otherwise be open and dangerous terrain, so avoiding predators. Many creatures are killed by traffic when crossing from a hedge on one side of the road to that on the other, but the widening and re-alignment of older roads sometimes leads to pieces of enclosed highway being left more or less untended and these are often valuable sanctuaries for wildlife.

Two of the commonest mammals that frequent hedgerows are the wood mouse and the bank vole which live in burrows in the soil below the hedge but clamber about in the structure of the hedge itself looking for fruit and berries. The bank vole also lives in many of the stone walls that serve as field boundaries in the north of England and in Scotland, but it is missing from Ireland. It eats a considerable amount of green vegetable food as well as the flesh of haws and a wide range of insects. In contrast, the wood mouse likes the hard centre of the haws and will often store both them and hips with hazel nuts and grain in old birds' nests, which are used as a kind of feeding tray or platform. In the south and east of England the delightful and attractive harvest mouse *Micromys minutus* may sometimes be found in the hedges that border the ripening fields of corn. Rabbits and common rats *Rattus norvegicus* have their burrows in the earth banks that support many hedges and on occasion the rats will stalk and kill the young rabbits as well as exploring the hedge for the eggs and nestlings of birds. At the base of hedges, tiny shrews search continually for small invertebrates and, throughout the summer, one of the extraordinary sounds along the hedge rows of Britain is the needle-points of sound which emanate from squabbling, screaming shrews.

Hedgehogs, as their name correctly implies, will live and hibernate in hedgerows and also forage at night along their lengths, sniffing their way towards the slugs, beetles, worms, snails and insect larvae on which they feed. Foxes and badgers may travel at night using the hedge for concealment as they move on to a favourite hunting or feeding ground. Even the tiny muntjac deer will use a hedge as a safe green corridor to reach new areas of woodland. Hares also have favourite, well-used runs through hedgerows to enable them to cross from one field to another. But the regular predators along the hedgerows are stoats and weasels. Stoats will work their way along hedgerows and stone walls on the track of a selected rabbit which is pursued until the hunter can kill it with a bite at the back of the neck. In a similar way the smaller weasel, which is absent from Ireland, captures and kills mice and voles which it hunts through their burrows.

Magnificent ropes of scarlet, glossy berries of the black bryony festoon the hedgerows in autumn *(above)*. Though similar to the white bryony *Bryonia dioica*, the two plants are not related. Another hedgerow plant is wild clematis *Clematis vitalba* which is often called traveller's joy or old man's beard. Its attractive, fluffy seed heads are further enhanced by a light dusting of frost in winter *(above right)*. In summer, the hedgerows hum with insect life and the scorpion fly *Panorpa communis (centre right)* with its distinctive, staccato flight is a common sight. Another familiar hedgerow inhabitant is the greenfinch *Carduelis chloris*, which feeds on seeds, berries and fruit buds. A cock greenfinch *(right)* feeds its young in a nest in a hawthorn hedge.

Some of our amphibians and reptiles will make their homes in hedgerows in Britain; many are absent from Ireland. Toads *Bufo bufo* and frogs *Rana temporaria* may be found in the damp grassy places at the foot of the hedge, while slow-worms will burrow at the bottom of hedgerows where they often fall victim to birds of prey, badgers, foxes, rats, hedgehogs and adders *Vipera berus*. Common lizards *Lacerta vivipara* also frequent British hedges, and can be seen basking on a favourite stone or piece of bare ground. The grass snake is an animal of open woodlands and hedgerows in England and Wales particularly where water is not too far away. It is a good climber and will reach the topmost shoot of a shrub to bask in the rays of the setting sun. It may be found hibernating sometimes in groups, in holes in banks and in old rabbit burrows.

Hedgerows also provide a sanctuary for many kinds of bird but here too the richness of the bird life depends on the character, size and treatment of each particular hedge. The more a hedge resembles a piece of woodland, the more birds of woodland origin can be expected in it. A thin, laid hedge may contain only a few. A typical list of hedgerow birds in order of their abundance would be blackbird, chaffinch, dunnock, robin, yellowhammer *Emberiza citrinella*, linnet *Carduelis cannabina* and whitethroat *Sylvia communis*. If the hedge is on farmland, then birds associated with open country, such as pheasants *Phasianus colchicus*, grey partridges *Perdix perdix*, yellowhammers, linnets and corn buntings *Miliaria calandra*, may nest in it or at its foot. Of the seven commonest hedgerow birds, the first four are typical of broadleaved woodland and the other three of scrub and forest edge. In some places, reed buntings *Emberiza schoeniclus* have turned to breeding in drier habitats including hedgerows. Swallows *Hirundo rustica* snap up insects along sheltered hedgerows while sparrowhawks *Accipiter nisus* and barn owls *Tyto alba* regularly hunt along them. But not all hedgerows are good for bird life. The fuchsia hedges typical of southwest Ireland, for example, are attractive and naturalized but lack bird life.

The presence of forest and large trees in a hedge provides an extra habitat for birds. Tits, woodpeckers, owls, kestrels *Falco tinnunculus*, stock doves, tree sparrows *Passer montanus* and redstarts may nest in their holes while carrion crows and rooks *Corvus frugilegus* construct their big platforms of twigs high up in the canopies.

The sun setting behind dead English elms *(below left)*, victims of Dutch elm disease. Dead elms, however, still provide useful nesting sites for many birds such as rooks and kestrels.

After feeding her young, a female kestrel *(below right)*, with a blood-stained bill, looks out from her nest hole in a dead elm tree in a hedgerow. Widespread all over Britain, kestrels are now a familiar sight to motorists who cannot fail to see them hovering over motorway verges.

Hazel scrub on the Carboniferous limestone of the Burren, to the south of Galway Bay in Ireland *(above left)*, is a climax vegetation. Where the effects of wind and grazing are severe the growth is often less than a metre in height, but it shelters many kinds of woodland flowers as well as mosses and lichens.

Hawthorn, gorse and wild rose colonize an old colliery tip at Beechenhurst in the Forest of Dean *(above right)*. The tip was last mined in the middle of this century, and part is now used as a recreational area after landscaping by the Forestry Commission.

Scrub succession

Scrub consists of a mixture of bushes and tree seedlings at various stages of growth. It is, therefore, a step in the succession towards woodland which, in the British Isles, is the climax vegetation. It is generally fairly open and therefore often has a rich flora. The wildlife may be richer in scrub and on the edge of woodland than in the heart of a wood itself due to this wide variety of plant species. In the Chilterns, juniper scrub may herald a succession to beech wood, while on the deeper soils hawthorn may precede ash wood, then beech and perhaps finally oak. Although yew is quite common on downlands, English scrub is dominated by hawthorn. Here, the breeding bird population is a mix of woodland species like song thrushes, robins, bullfinches *Pyrrhula pyrrhula*, and chaffinches, and birds of more open country like whitethroats, linnets and formerly the red-backed shrike *Lanius collurio*. Dense thorn scrub is a valuable bird habitat as well as sheltering foxes and the smaller mammals; it provides safe breeding and roosting sites as well as berries for the winter months. On hillsides, at the upper limit of tree growth, natural scrubby woods of oak and birch appear as broken and twisted fell-woods.

There are many areas of scrub in Ireland. Around Lough Neagh, tracts of birch and willow ring with the songs of willow warbler and chiffchaff and buzz with the rattles of the grasshopper warblers *Locustella naevia*. Birch and alder combine in Co. Donegal to form scrub, while in Co. Cork low willow supports a breeding population of chiffchaffs, reed buntings and stonechats *Saxicola torquata*.

Coniferous woodlands and plantations

Earlier, we saw something of the vast changes that took place in the forest cover of the British Isles. The toll of forest destruction accelerated during the last century with growing industrialization and the building of new towns. In Northern Ireland, there were profound changes in the system of land-holding by which farmers who previously had held land as tenants were now empowered to buy it. Unfortunately, most of the new landowners had not the means to maintain the surviving areas of woodland and very quickly they were cleared. By 1900, most of the woodlands in the British Isles were in private ownership and the former large holdings of the Crown had greatly declined. The First World War imposed an almost intolerable strain on Britain's own supplies of timber with the clear felling of nearly quarter of a million hectares of woodland. In 1919, therefore, the Forestry Act created the Forestry Commission to set up and manage its own State

Ancient yew trees such as these growing in a grove at Kingley Vale, near Chichester, cast a very dense shade which suppresses the shrub and field layers so effectively that even mosses may be scarce.

Forests, to help with the care of private and other woodlands and to undertake research. The Commission began by re-afforesting many of the devastated areas and also by planting up regions of moorland and hillside with introduced coniferous trees.

Gradually the forest cover in Britain has increased until it now occupies about 9 per cent of the land area which is probably higher than at any time in the past 1000 years, even though most areas consist of exotic conifers. In Northern Ireland, there has also been a great deal of planting with an objective of 60,000 hectares of forest. Eire's objective is 440,000 or 6·5 per cent of the land area.

These exotic conifers have become familiar features of many hilly regions and even dominate much of the scenery of Highland Britain and Ireland, spreading carpets of green and serried lines of trees. About three-quarters of our commercial woodlands are formed from around 10 species of exotics some of which are harvested for softwood and pulp. Yet there are only three species of conifer native to the British Isles – the noble Scots pine, the dark and sombre yew and the scrub-forming juniper with its scented, blue-green needles. Yew is often an element in some Welsh oak woods, in the limestone ash woods of the North and in the west country and in many of the beech woods that grace the downs of southern England. But it can become the dominant tree as in parts of southern England, in the valley of the Wye and in southern Ireland. Some of the purest yew woods seem to grow on the slopes around the heads of chalk valleys where they may have been protected when small by hawthorn or juniper scrub and when more mature by a nearby beech wood.

In Britain, the most evocative conifer is the Scots pine with a pyramidal shape when young but a dome-shaped canopy and gloriously coloured reddish-orange bark when mature. It appears as naturalized woods on the heaths of southern England, and as part of the great conifer plantations established by the Forestry Commission and private landowners during the last century. But it is at its finest in the native Caledonian forests of the

Only a few sizeable tracts of the old, indigenous pine forests of Scotland now remain. The Black Wood of Rannoch in Perthshire, where this September scene was recorded *(above right)*, is one of them. The ground cover consists of heather, bilberry and bracken.

One of the floral gems of the Scottish pine woods is chickweed wintergreen *(right)*, with its white, usually seven-petalled, star-like flowers rising on a slender stem from a whorl of shiny green leaves.

Scottish Highlands. Some of these pine woods achieve footholds high up the hill slopes, and goldcrests can be heard singing at 550 metres in some low pines above Glen Feshie. Many of these old pine forests grow in heathery situations, but they are often so heavily grazed by red deer and Scottish black-faced sheep and choked with heather and plant remains that seedlings have little or no chance to establish themselves. Some of these woods are open, others have trees growing in close canopy. There may also be birch and rowan, juniper and alder. The field layer is heathery but the ground zone may hold some rather special plants such as the boreal relic, chickweed wintergreen *Trientalis europaea*, and the very rare twinflower *Linnaea borealis*. These northern forests are fresh with cowberry *Vaccinium vitis-idaea* and bilberry *V. myrtillus* while the pines are full in summer of the songs of willow warblers, coal tits, goldcrests, chaffinches and redstarts. The more open parts of the forest are favoured by meadow pipits *Anthus pratensis* and whinchats *Saxicola rubetra*. The eastern woods are the home of red and roe deer, red squirrels and wild cats while the western forests hold dens of the now increasing and very attractive pine marten, with otters *Lutra lutra* on the burns and lochs.

The eastern forests which lie in the valley of the Spey are the haunts of the crested tit *Parus cristatus* which favours the pine forest but also tolerates birch and alder. Special birds of the pine forests are crossbills *Loxia* which extract seeds from pine cones with their asymmetrical bills and thick leathery tongues. Other characteristic birds are siskin and capercaillie *Tetrao urogallus*, Britain's largest gamebird which was re-introduced into Scotland after the original population became extinct in about 1770. Ospreys have returned naturally to some of these forests to breed but other raptors such as the kite have disappeared. Golden eagles *Aquila chrysaetos* may, and buzzards, sparrowhawks and kestrels regularly, breed in Scots pines. The two commonest owls are the tawny and the long-eared *Asio otus*. In the spring, blackcock *Tetrao tetrix* sneeze and 'rookoo' on their favourite assembly grounds or leks; woodcock go 'roding' above the pines, and where there are burns, grey wagtails *Motacilla cinerea*, dippers *Cinclus cinclus* and, sometimes, otters occupy boulders in the running water.

A great deal still remains to be discovered about the communities of animals in the ancient pine woods and especially about the invertebrate fauna. However, there are many kinds of spiders and ants. Indeed, there are more species of ant in the old woods of Rothiemurchus and Glenmore in Speyside than anywhere else in the Highlands. Wood ants *Formica rufa* construct great domes of pine needles from which foraging paths radiate up to 30 metres or more from the nest. Various weevils and beetles are common in the old woods of mixed age but since natural forests are comparatively stable in their ecosystems they generally do not reach plague proportions. The pine beauty moth *Panolis flammea* can be seen resting on the bark and its caterpillars closely resemble the needles of the Scots pine.

To walk among these Scots pines, some of which are several hundred years old, is to appreciate something of the character of the old Boreal forests that once covered much of the British Isles and stretched from Glen Lyon and Rannoch across to Strathspey and Strath Glass and from Glen Coe to the Braes of Mar. In Ireland, there is evidence that Scots pines survived in the Irish forests only into the sixteenth century and then became extinct as a native species.

On some of the sandy and gravelly plains of southern England, Scots pines are the dominant tree species. These pines, which have been widely introduced since the eighteenth century, have colonized the heathlands with birch and perhaps small amounts of oak and beech, together with sweet chestnut in the shrub layer below. There are good examples in Surrey, around Esher, Oxshott and Leith Hill. Heather and purple moor-grass *Molinia caerulea* form the ground zone and here adders and common lizards can be seen basking in the sun.

Over the last 60 years, commercial afforestation with coniferous trees has profoundly changed many of the remote and wild parts of the countryside. Bare hillsides have been deep ploughed to break up the ground, drain the peaty land, improve the soil and reduce competition from heather and other moorland plants. Many such plantations are on grass moorland and have had to be fenced against deer and domestic stock and wired against rabbits. But they often provide havens for short-tailed voles *Microtus agrestis* which flourish and breed in large numbers, sometimes causing great damage to the trees; these small rodents are missing from Ireland. And at first, some of the heathland birds such as meadow pipits, skylarks *Alauda arvensis*, lapwings *Vanellus vanellus*, curlews *Numenius arquata* and red grouse *Lagopus lagopus* go on breeding among the tiny developing trees. Gradually the young trees begin to grow into what is called the thicket stage, when their branches overlap those of their neighbours and eventually shut out the light

When the conifer plantations are still young, and before their lower branches have been lopped off by brashing, the dense thickets provide a sanctuary for many kinds of wildlife. Bracken, hazel and the red-berried guelder rose can be seen among the conifers.

essential for the field layer below. These almost impenetrable jungles provide sanctuaries for many kinds of small mammal such as voles and shrews, stoats and weasels, foxes and perhaps polecats and pine martens in Wales. Some plantations have been provided with special gates which swing back and forth to allow badgers to leave and enter the plantations. Muntjac deer now live in a number of Midland plantations and, in other regions, there may be the larger roe deer as well. In this thicket stage, there is also a special community of birds formed largely from willow and grasshopper warblers, whitethroats, robins, wrens, dunnocks and yellowhammers – species encountered in association with natural scrub and woodland and perhaps hedgerows as well. When the plantation is about 10 years old, blackbirds, song thrushes, chaffinches, bullfinches and sometimes turtle doves *Streptopelia turtur* establish themselves and replace the earlier colonists.

When the conifers are about 15 years old the foresters cut off their dead lower branches. 'Brashing' makes it easier to reach the individual trees and also reduces the likelihood of destruction by fire. The debris from the brashings is normally left on the ground, but in Northern Ireland bundles of it are often tied to the boles of the trees and these are regularly used by blackbirds and wrens which would otherwise be deprived of nesting sites. The effect of brashing is immediate and the scrub and shrub layer birds are forced to leave. Only the species that can survive and nest in the canopies of the trees will now be seen – magpies, jays, crows, coal tits (in mouse holes), goldcrests, chaffinches, sparrowhawks, owls, ravens *Corvus corax*, buzzards and perhaps even herons. The birds that have colonized the new coniferous plantations have, with a few exceptions, come in from the broadleaved or perhaps conifer woods in the vicinity. Since there are no over-mature trees for hole-breeding birds, many plantations contain nest boxes which have enabled certain insect-eating birds like great and blue tits to establish themselves there.

Scots pine plantations tend to be in the drier and warmer regions of eastern and southern Britain and not a great deal have been planted in Ireland. Scottish plantations bear some resemblance to the old Caledonian Forest. Corsican pine *Pinus nigra* var. *maritima* has been widely planted in East Anglia, Anglesey and on the Moray Firth but it is far less easy to establish in Ireland. There are, however, stands in Co. Wexford and Co. Wicklow. The lodgepole pine *Pinus contorta*, which originates from western North America, is often planted on poorer soils in windy districts and it occurs widely throughout Ireland as well as in Wales, northwest England and

western Scotland. The maritime pine *P. pinaster* from the region of the Mediterranean has been planted at Mullaghmore in Ireland, in Devon and on the borders of Dorset and Hampshire.

Two kinds of spruce grow commonly in the British Isles. The Norway spruce, or Christmas tree *Picea abies*, grows well on most woodland soils while the Sitka spruce *P. sitchensis* from British Columbia is planted on peaty ground in regions of high rainfall. On the whole, these plantations have a limited wildlife.

Larches differ from other conifers in that they lose their leaves and then in spring assume a delightful fresh green foliage. The European larch *Larix decidua* has not been very successful in the British Isles while the Japanese *L. kaempferi* has proved more adaptable and grows faster. The hybrid between them *L.* x *eurolepis* develops even more quickly and in much less favourable environments. In Ireland, larches may appear in pure stands or often mixed with Scots pine and beech.

Other coniferous trees have been established in plantations but on a smaller scale. Douglas fir *Pseudotsuga menziesii* can be seen in the New Forest and the Forest of Dean, western hemlock *Tsuga heterophylla* in Kent in

England and at Killarney, Castle Caldwell and Rostrevor in Ireland, and western red cedar *Thuja plicata* at Friston in Sussex, in several parts of Ireland and often in hedges. Grand firs *Abies grandis* and silver firs *A. alba* have been planted as well but largely as ornamental trees.

Natural forests contain a shrub and field layer, and a variety of trees all of differing age which tend to remain comparatively stable when mature. By contrast, the uniform plantations of conifers are usually of one or only a few tree species, and all are normally of the same age. An ecosystem which is so simple is often rather unstable. Monocultures are, therefore, often prone to insect plagues and conifers may suffer from the attacks of larvae of the bordered white moth *Bupalis piniaria* and the pine beauty as well as the large pine weevil *Hylobius abietis*, the black pine beetles *Hylastes* and the ambrosia beetles *Trypodendron*. These are sometimes controlled by aerial spraying with insecticides, but although this may check a particular pest, no one can be quite sure of the indirect results on the small plants and invertebrates which form vital strands in the web of relationships in a wood. Predation by birds may help to control the numbers of harmful insects in a plantation – capercaillies feed on pine weevils and tits take many caterpillars – but it seems unlikely that birds can prevent or make much impression on an insect plague when it breaks out.

The past use of chemicals in Britain together with a number of other trends in land use and management have brought about changes in and destruction of many habitats for wildlife. The loss of woodland to housing, roads, airfields and industrial sites has also caused a diminution in the wildlife although modern suburbia with its mature trees and shrubs, well-cut lawns and carefully tended flower beds may show a higher density of breeding birds of woodland origin than the woodlands from which the birds first came. In Britain, the breeding density in a lowland oak wood of blackbirds may be only one tenth that to be found in suburban gardens. Song thrushes, robins, wrens, dunnocks, great and blue tits, woodpigeons, jays, tawny owls and chaffinches, for example, have all successfully left the woodlands and scrub to establish themselves in towns and suburbs. Other forest-dwelling species such as the woodpeckers, treecreeper, nuthatch, redstart, bullfinch, marsh tit and garden warbler and hedgerow birds such as the yellowhammer, corn bunting and linnet have failed to make the transition to full urban ways of life.

Foresters are now aware of the intensive nature of their operations and the effects on the wildlife. Some birds and other animal species may find favourable environments in the various stages of growth in coniferous plantations but the first great rise in numbers gradually dies down as the trees mature. The new State Forests in lowland Britain have largely superseded the richly varied native woodlands with their extensive wildlife while in highland Britain they have displaced the moorland habitat. Single conifer cultures cannot support the same range of wildlife as broadleaved and mixed woods. It is, therefore, vital that protection should be given to native and semi-natural woodlands where these still remain, while new broadleaved woods of native trees should be more widely established to balance the tendency to plant 'commercial' crops of conifers.

Fungi

Most flowering plants contain a green pigment called chlorophyll which enables them to manufacture food. This pigment, however, is lacking in fungi so they have to depend on other organisms for a supply of food. Some are saprophytes, living on the decaying remains of other plants or even animals, while others are parasites, invading and feeding upon living tissue. Woodlands are therefore ideal habitats for fungi since there is an abundance of decaying leaves and wood, plus large quantities of living matter.

The structure of a fungus varies very little. Each is composed of a tangle of minute branched threads or 'roots' called hyphae which together form the body, or mycelium, of the fungus. The hyphae secrete enzymes which break down the food material to a usable form. Some fungi can form a mycorrhizal relationship with the roots of a tree. This is a highly satisfactory give-and-take relationship whereby each benefits from the presence of the other.

Fungi can range in size from the microscopically small to the huge bracket fungi found growing on tree trunks. They include moulds such as penicillin, mildews, rusts, smuts, mushrooms and toadstools.

Like mosses, liverworts and ferns, fungi reproduce from spores instead of seeds and it is the reproductive organs or fruiting bodies with which we are most familiar. The fruiting bodies only appear during favourable conditions and at specific times of the year, autumn being the most common, though a few appear in the spring. The actual lifespan of the fruiting body is fairly brief though, since they cannot withstand extreme cold and are severely damaged by frost.

1

1 Although the Jew's ear fungus *Hirneola auricula* grows on oaks it is more common on elders. The name Jew's ear is said to be a corruption of Judas's ear; it was widely believed that he hanged himself on an elder.

2

2 The honey fungus *Armillaria mellea* is growing on an old tree stump in the New Forest. One of the commonest fungi of tree stumps, it is said to be responsible for the death of more trees than any other species. It tends to attack trees that have already been weakened by the poor nature of the soil in which they grow.

3

3 The stinkhorn *Phallus impudicus* is one of the best known fungi due to its characteristic shape and its unpleasant smell of rotting carrion. The slimy, spore-bearing mass in the cap is eaten by slugs and flies, which help disperse the spores.

4 *Pholiota mutabilis* is a fungus of broadleaved woodland. Here it is growing on a rotting tree trunk in autumn, surrounded by bracken.

4

5 The beech tuft fungus *Oudemansiella mucida* is an attractive, shiny, white fungus which often grows on the trunks and upper branches of beech trees.

6 The spiny, pear-shaped puff ball *Lycoperdon molle* can be found growing in both coniferous and broadleaved woodlands. The microscopic spores are dispersed in small 'puffs' or clouds when water droplets fall on the sac.

5

6

Insects

Insects are believed to outnumber all other animals by four to one. One of the main reasons for this is their ability to occupy such a vast range of habitats. In Britain alone, there are at least 20,000 different insect species representing 25 different orders. Insects belong to a group of animals called arthropods which also embraces crustaceans, spiders, centipedes and millipedes. Since the definition of an insect is based on the fact that they all have three pairs of legs, three divisions to the body (head, thorax and abdomen), and usually, but not always, wings, they are fairly straightforward to classify.

Woodlands are home to a large number of insects some of which show preferences for specific foods or plants, while others are more catholic in their taste. Insects themselves, both adults and larvae, provide a food source for many kinds of animal. Badgers will eat beetles and wasp grubs, rooks, starlings and tits eat moth caterpillars, and warblers, redstarts and spotted flycatchers feed on flying insects throughout the summer months.

In a woodland, numerous complicated inter-relations exist between the different organisms. Some woodland insects are parasites, laying their eggs on or in other insects, while others are hyper-parasites, making the parasites their victims. Butterflies and moths abound, wasps and bumble bees forage through the glades, ground beetles wander over the leaf litter, and countless flies hum and dart through the sunlit clearings. Shield bugs, aphids and capsid bugs attack plants with their piercing mouth parts, while ants scurry over the woodland floor dragging insects towards their nest. In summer, the stridulations of bush-crickets and grasshoppers add to the chorus of sounds which abounds in woodlands.

1

1 The small blood-vein moth *Scopula imitaria,* with its conspicuous reddish stripe across the wings, is fond of bushy places and hedgerows. The caterpillars can be found feeding on privet, dandelion and docks.

2

2 Among the 41 species of British ant the wood ant *Formica rufa,* which constructs great, domed nests of twigs and leaves, is one of the most familiar. Here, worker wood ants drag a dead wasp over the woodland floor.

3

3 One of the most magnificent and rare of British butterflies, the purple emperor *Apatura iris* is now confined to a few broadleaved woodlands in central and southern England. The caterpillar feeds on willow and sallows. Here a female is seen resting on oak leaves.

4 Locally common in woods and hedgerows in much of southern England and Wales the white-letter hairstreak *Strymonidia w-album* is on the wing in July and August. The larvae can be found on lime, elm and other trees while the butterflies regularly visit bramble flowers.

4

5 This carabid or ground beetle *Carabus arvensis* spends most of its life on the ground where it hunts at night for slugs and insects.

6 Stag beetles *Lucanus cervus* are the giants among British beetles. They breed in rotting tree stumps and the large larva seen here may spend several years in such a site.

5

6

Mammals

During a walk through woodland, whether broadleaved or coniferous, or a stroll along a hedgerow, both insect and bird life are readily apparent but wild mammals are very elusive. Occasionally we might catch a glimpse of a rabbit disappearing into a bank or, very rarely, see a stoat or weasel dragging an inordinantly large prey between its front legs. We might even hear the shrill chattering of shrews in the grass verge beside a hedge, the scold of a grey squirrel high in an oak tree or the warning bark of a roe deer or a tiny muntjac. We may even find a spot in a wood where, downwind of our subjects, we can watch fallow deer unobserved, see fox cubs playing round their earth, and observe badgers digging up bluebell roots. But a considerable amount of time and patience is required since many woodland mammals are nocturnal and extremely secretive in their habits.

Yet many live in a rather stereotyped way, showing the utmost regularity in their habits. Many use certain tracks and runways so frequently and at such constant times, that it is often possible to predict their movements. Many also reveal specific feeding rhythms, while others can be induced to come to bait so that they can be seen easily by the observer and watched for longer periods of time.

Although mammals may not show themselves in such an obvious way as some other inhabitants of woodlands, they all play significant roles. Hedgehogs and shrews eat many invertebrates, bats hunt for flying insects, and squirrels, small rodents and deer are herbivorous. Then there are the predators such as foxes, badgers, stoats, weasels, polecats and pine martens which all affect the populations of other animals and are at the top of the food chain that is found in woodland and hedgerow communities.

1

1 This wood mouse *Apodemus sylvaticus* took its own picture by triggering off a pair of photo-electric beams at night. It is the characteristic small rodent of woodland and is almost entirely nocturnal.

2

2 One of the denizens of the dense shrub layer in woodland and scrub in Wales and southern England is the common dormouse *Muscardinus avellanarius*. It lives on fruits such as blackberries and haws, as well as nuts, bark, shoots and seeds of trees.

3

3 The noctule bat *Nyctalus noctula* often has its roosts in buildings and trees. It emerges quite early in the evening, fluttering and diving for insects above the top of the wood.

4 The weasel *Mustela nivalis* is a carnivore, feeding on small rodents which it hunts mainly at night. Wherever mice and voles are to be found, weasels tend to be present; the weasel population appears to fluctuate with the abundance of these small mammals.

5 A hedgehog *Erinaceus europaeus* is picked out by the rays of the rising sun as it returns from a nocturnal foray in search of worms, snails and insects.

6 A kestrel's eye view of a bank vole *Clethrionomys glareolus* as it runs over a woodland bank covered with white fork moss *Leucobryum glaucum*.

4

5

6

Towns and suburbs

Towns and suburbs

population density:

	per sq. mile	per sq. kilometre
	>1200	>500
	120-1200	50-500
	12-120	5-50
	<12	<5

0   20   40   60   80 miles
0 20 40 60 80 100 120 kilometres

Poor prospects for wildlife?

The rapid growth of our towns began at a time when nature was regarded as something to be subdued and exploited: there was no place for it in the city. Even now, at first sight, our built-up areas may appear too barren to be of interest to the naturalist.

Streets and buildings cover most of the soil and where the earth is exposed, in parks, gardens and waste plots, it supports a flora which bears no resemblance to that which flourished before the town came into existence. Natural drainage systems are disrupted. Much of the rainwater is carried away underground, streams are culverted or buried, and most urban rivers and estuaries are still polluted, although locally there have been remarkable improvements. The establishment of smokeless zones has resulted in a cleaner atmosphere to the extent that it no longer carries a heavy load of particulate matter, but the air is still contaminated with sulphur dioxide and petrol fumes. The final handicap would seem to be the presence of vast numbers of people, human beings whose daily activities are no longer intimately concerned with seasonal rhythms, the elements, or the inter-relationships of living organisms and their environment. With a few exceptions, town-dwellers spend most of their time under a roof.

City buildings

Since time immemorial, however, man's dwellings, workshops, clothes and person have harboured living organisms. Man's parasites must be omitted from this discussion, but the animal inhabitants of his buildings certainly warrant inclusion, even though only a few can be specifically mentioned in a book of this size.

Most of these indoor animals are from overseas. The house mouse *Mus musculus*, which probably arrived 5000 years ago with the Neolithic farmers, may originally have lived on the Asian steppes. Although capable of outdoor independence, it is best known as a raider of food stores. It can even feast and nest inside refrigerated carcases. The rats also came from Asia. The ship rat *Rattus rattus* was introduced in either the eleventh or twelfth century, and the larger, more successful common rat *R. norvegicus* in the eighteenth. In Britain and Ireland, the ship-rat population is declining, for the species is less hardy than the common rat and its preference for an indoor life makes it an easier target for the exterminator. As a town animal it is now restricted to major sea ports, where improved control methods and the close inspection of shipping, lighterage and warehousing are lessening its chances of survival.

Stored products harbour many invertebrate pests, and beetles figure prominently on the list. Cereals and cereal products are particularly prone to infestation, and one very common species is the grain weevil *Sitophilus granarius*, the larvae of which develop in caked flour as well as in unmilled grain. Two beetle pests, *Tenebrio molitor* and *T. obscurus*, are familiar to aviculturalists and zookeepers in a different role. Their grubs are the 'mealworms' commercially bred for insectivorous birds, mammals and reptiles. That some beetles are of foreign origin is apparent from their scientific names: *Tenebroides mauretanicus* (the cadelle beetle) and *Oryzae-philus surinamensis* (the saw-toothed grain beetle). The popular names of some of the moths with destructive larvae are equally illuminating; the Indian meal-moth *Plodia interpunctella* and the Mediterranean flour-moth *Anagasta kühniella* arrived in the nineteenth century. Like many of the beetles that eat grain and flour, they have spread world wide.

Many indoor animals need warmth. Two insects, the house cricket *Acheta domestica* and the firebrat *Thermobia domestica*, have long been scavenging

Industrial pollution and urban growth have transformed much of our countryside. This desolate scene on the fringe of Port Talbot, with its stark skeletons of trees, gives the impression that man and nature are in conflict, and nature is the loser. Yet even here the bracken has survived.

in bakeries and kitchens, where they do not usually cause alarm. But the confusingly named cockroaches of heated premises provoke stronger feelings. The common cockroach *Blatta orientalis*, which acquired the misnomer of 'blackbeetle', probably arrived in the sixteenth century and is of unknown origin. Another successful immigrant, the so-called German cockroach *Blattella germanica*, probably came from Africa, which may also be the original home of the American cockroach *Periplaneta americana* and the Australian cockroach *P. australasiae*. Another tropical insect found in heated buildings is Pharaoh's ant *Monomorium pharaonis*, which needs a temperature of 27° to 30°C to breed successfully. It nests under floors, behind ovens, in cavity walls, foundations and fuse boxes, and even in cakes. Hospitals are particularly difficult to disinfest since the use of pesticides could endanger the patients, but new control methods have been tried in Liverpool; these involve using bait impregnated with the synthesis of a hormone which governs the insects' development. Worker ants take the preparation to the nests, and its consumption disrupts the breeding cycle by sterilizing the queens and arresting larval growth.

Like other ecosystems, the indoor world of Nature has its predators. Both rats and mice will take insects, and are themselves eaten by cats. There are surprising numbers of ownerless cats in urban areas, many of them finding shelter and rearing kittens in the hot air ducts of factories and hospitals. In the Birmingham area, colonies of between 30 and 40 feral cats are common, and contractors once removed 349 cats in the course of six weeks from a single building and its grounds. Amongst the invertebrates,

The house mouse, man's associate for several millennia, is likely to remain with him. It is well adapted to urban conditions and has even found a niche in such extreme environments as cold stores and coal mines.

the most obvious predators are the spiders, but these probably attract more attention in suburban buildings, and are therefore discussed at greater length in that context.

Externally, city buildings have less to offer wildlife. Unless in a state of disrepair, they are usually devoid of vegetation; even lichen growth is inhibited because of the sulphur dioxide in the air. Several bird species, however, accept town buildings as man-made cliffs, and for centuries they have provided nesting and roosting sites for feral pigeons. These ubiquitous birds are usually ignored by birdwatchers because of their ancestry; they are the free-living descendants of domesticated dovecote pigeons once kept for the table and then for trap-shooting and racing. Feral pigeons are of motley appearance but some still resemble their remote ancestors, the wild rock doves *Columba livia* which nest in coastal caves and cliff crevices.

The presence of pigeons is taken for granted, but kestrels *Falco tinnunculus* rarely fail to attract publicity when they select a town building for a nest site, especially when it is a well-known landmark like London's Law Courts, Salisbury Cathedral or the Chamberlain Tower of Birmingham University. Churches, factories, power stations, hospitals, town halls and tower blocks have all been used, and one can now expect to see this falcon over every urban roofscape. Gulls which have become roof-top residents of many coastal towns are just as newsworthy. The herring gull *Larus argentatus* is the main opportunist, and is particularly numerous in Cardiff where 425 pairs were reported in 1975. Here, as well as in Newport (Gwent), Bristol and Gloucester there is also a breeding population of lesser black-backed gulls *L. fuscus*. Both gulls have nested in towns well inland: the two species on the same factory roof at Merthyr Tydfil, the lesser black-backed at Bath, and the herring gull in London. London's gulls have occupied buildings in and around the Zoo, and, in 1973, were found on the old War Office building in Whitehall. Kittiwakes *Rissa tridactyla* have also nested on buildings at a few places, showing a marked preference for

Herring gull chicks on a multi-storey building in Aberdeen, July 1980. Aberdeen is just one of many towns where herring gulls have accepted buildings as man-made cliffs on which they can nest. The habit has only developed since man became more tolerant of wildlife. Gulls, like many other birds, were heavily persecuted in the last century.

windowsills, which closely resemble the narrow ledges they choose on natural cliffs. A well-studied Tyneside colony at North Shields, dating from 1949, held 141 pairs in 1970. Kittiwakes have also colonized buildings in Newcastle and Gateshead, over 11 miles from the river mouth. This is surprising behaviour for what has always been considered a strictly oceanic species, but the kittiwake's new habits, like its greatly increased population, reflect changes in human attitudes; these birds, which were once slaughtered for food, sport and the feather trade, now enjoy protection. The raven *Corvus corax*, also recovering from persecution, could now find nest sites in towns. In 1973 and 1974, a pair nested on Swansea Guildhall. It was perhaps the first pair to use a British town building since the late nineteenth century, when nesting took place on what is now Newcastle cathedral.

Swifts *Apus apus* and house martins *Delichon urbica* have long used buildings for nesting in preference to natural cliffs. The swift is the more urban bird. Although it breeds mainly in the inner suburbs, it can be seen feeding over city centres, as in Westminster or the heart of Birmingham. The house martin is perhaps more a bird of outer suburbia since it needs mud for nest construction, but it has nested in Edinburgh's Georgian New Town and, in recent years, as near the centre of London as Knightsbridge.

Whereas house martins need a projecting architectural member or an arch soffit to provide a nest site, swifts need a hole in the fabric. Holes are also readily exploited by house sparrows *Passer domesticus*, starlings *Sturnus vulgaris* (when there are nearby parks, lawns or grassy roundabouts to provide feeding grounds), and by the occasional pied wagtail *Motacilla alba yarrellii* or black redstart *Phoenicurus ochruros*. In Salisbury and Cambridge, sand martins *Riparia riparia* build their nests in drainpipes in the river walls.

For some birds, nesting on a building may be aberrant behaviour, man-made structures bearing little resemblance to their normal breeding sites. The habit may now be too common to be considered eccentric in the case of the blackbird *Turdus merula*, but when, as has happened, a mistle thrush *T. viscivorus* nests on the Stoke City grandstand or on a Coronation stand in Park Lane, the event causes surprise. In London, a shortage of undisturbed retreats in the heavily used parks may have prompted mallard *Anas platy-rhynchos* to lay their eggs on the roof of the Admiralty Citadel or in a window-box near the Iranian Embassy in Kensington, where, in 1980, a sitting duck found herself in the midst of a gun battle. It is hard to explain the behaviour of woodpigeons *Columba palumbus* that have taken to rainwater heads, girders and fire escapes, and reared their squabs on Buckingham Palace, the Imperial War Museum or Charing Cross Station. There is no shortage of trees in central London. Even jays *Garrulus glandarius* have broken with convention by trying to nest on Lancaster House and the Foreign Office, and have twice succeeded on houses in Kensington.

An evening visit in winter to Birmingham's New Street, Glasgow's Sauchiehall Street, or London's Trafalgar Square reveals the fact that buildings are also commandeered by roosting starlings. Roosts on masonry were first noted late last century and have now become widespread. Between 1962 and 1964 they were reported from 15 conurbations in the British Isles. The birds often frequent the busiest, best-lit streets, with a predilection for classical and sham-Gothic façades. Modern buildings with less ornament are usually shunned, and city centres in such places as Plymouth, which have been extensively refashioned since the Second World War, are spared the expense and frustration of trying to expel the birds. The seasonal pattern of roosting is not uniform. In Newcastle upon Tyne, the numbers are highest in winter, but in London the peak (about 90,000 in 1950) is

A black ribbon of starlings over the roof tops of Stoke on Trent, August 1980. Starling fly-lines provide an enjoyable evening spectacle over many of our built-up areas. Local authorities, however, do not appreciate the mess these birds make when they adopt town buildings for their roost.

reached in July, when juvenile birds join the flocks. At that time of year, however, most of the starlings roost in trees in St James's Park. The move to the buildings take place at leaf fall. These facts became known during the London Natural History Society's study of the roost between 1949 and 1952, which also settled whether the wintering birds were of local or Continental origin. The majority came from within a 22-kilometre radius, and, of the 3275 ringed at the roost, only three were recovered abroad, all in the Netherlands.

Pied wagtails will also roost on buildings, and roof-top assemblies have often excited attention, as they have in London, Liverpool, Bristol and Leicester. Hundreds of birds may flock together, as many as 1500 on one factory roof at Sparkhill, Birmingham. Just why starlings and wagtails resort to town buildings is not clear, but a scarcity of winged predators at urban roosts may be a partial explanation. More important, however, may be the fact that climatic conditions in town are markedly different from those in the countryside. 'Heat islands' develop, a result of the warmth released by fossil-fuel combustion and the reflection of solar energy absorbed by buildings and metalled surfaces. Generally speaking, the buildings also reduce wind speed, and their projecting features give roosting birds additional protection from the elements.

Street trees

Trees also influence the urban climate: they intercept solar radiation, act as windbreaks, filter pollutants, release oxygen and regulate atmospheric humidity. But even where they line the streets in city centres and Victorian inner suburbs, their more obvious role is that of habitat provision. There are many thousands of street trees; 9000 were planted in the Inner London borough of Bermondsey in the 1920s, and present-day Birmingham has over 10 times that number. Before the mid-1950s, the smoke-laden atmosphere inhibited the growth of several species by checking transpiration, and conifers were particularly difficult to establish in town parks because the sooty deposits made them shed their needles prematurely.

The grimy, lichen-free bark of town trees favoured industrial melanism, the phenomenon first recognized in 1848 when a black variety of the peppered moth *Biston betularia* was collected in Manchester. The 'normal' pale form of this moth can rest inconspicuously on lichen-covered trunks, but on blackened surfaces it is easily spotted by predators. In towns, the black variety had the advantage and lepidopterists became aware that darker specimens of this and other variable species, like the grey arches *Polia nebulosa*, scalloped hazel *Odontopera bidentata* and mottled beauty *Cleora repandata*, were more frequent in urban than in rural areas.

Two hybrid trees, the London plane *Platanus × hybrida* and the common lime *Tilia × europaea*, were planted because they tolerated smoke. The

The soot-tolerant London plane *(left)* was extensively planted when towns were more polluted than they are now. Even when bare of leaves it is easily recognized, for the flaking bark gives the trunk its characteristic, mottled appearance. The tree supports few insects, but the caterpillars of the vapourer moth *(above)* will feed on its foliage.

The ornamental cherries, beloved of nurserymen, add a fine splash of colour to the suburban road, but are of less value to wildlife than native trees and shrubs.

former, mainly found in the south, is of alien parentage and supports few insects other than the vapourer moth *Orgyia antiqua* whose caterpillars will eat its leaves. Lime foliage provides food for caterpillars of the lime hawk-moth *Mimas tiliae*, buff-tip *Phalera bucephala* and brindled beauty *Lycia hirtaria*, and becomes infested with aphids *Eucallipterus tiliae* which shower the pavement and any cars beneath with their sticky excrement called honeydew.

Silver birch *Betula pendula* and rowan *Sorbus aucuparia* are two decorative natives more usually found in outer suburbs, although both were included in the Bermondsey planting programme. Birches have numerous insect associates and produce edible seeds. The rowan, like its popular relative the Swedish whitebeam *S. intermedia*, yields berries eaten by blackbirds and mistle thrushes. Other common suburban street trees, like the ornamental cultivars of Japanese cherry *Prunus serrulata*, have a negligible ecological value.

Birds willing to tolerate street lighting and traffic noise will nest in the trees. Woodpigeons do so readily in the south, magpies *Pica pica* use them in Dublin, Belfast and Manchester, and jays have done so in South Kensington, one pair choosing a site outside the Natural History Museum. At dusk, the trees may be occupied by roosting house sparrows, starlings or pied wagtails. Dublin's O'Connell Street, long recognized as the classic urban wagtail roost, can attract over 1000 birds in winter. In the 1950s, there were complaints from motorists about the droppings. Open sports cars suffered particularly badly when parked under the trees. Meanwhile citizens of Cheltenham have suffered the presence of rooks *Corvus frugilegus* roosting and nesting in the magnificent trees of The Promenade.

Tree-lined streets have one other quality which deserves mention – quite apart from their obvious aesthetic value. They can serve as green corridors by which many types of wildlife can penetrate the urban mass from the surrounding countryside.

Houses and gardens

In the autumn, the evening influx of roost-bound starlings coincides with the exodus of human beings from the city centre. The development of transport systems that made these human movements possible gave birth to suburbia, a place where dwellings outnumber all other buildings and where private gardens make a highly significant contribution to the total area of open space.

Private gardens are the essence of suburbia. They make up a vast area which approximates to the woodland edge habitat in a wilder situation, with a wide variety of plants of various heights. But tall trees may be rather scarce except in the older, and more affluent, suburbs like Dulwich in London or Edgbaston in Birmingham. Trees are often unpopular in small gardens and on many new housing estates, and if they exist at all they rarely exceed six metres. In gardens deliberately planned to attract wildlife, care is, of course, taken to ensure the succession of vegetation of different heights, to cater for the inhabitants of all woodland layers from the high canopy to the ground zone.

The garden plants are mostly aliens or native species which have been 'improved' by the horticulturists; the 'unimproved' natives which make their appearance are regarded as intruding weeds. When trees are planted the chances are that the gardener will select an exotic species or cultivar, such as a conifer, a cherry or a foreign maple, rather than a native which may, over the centuries, have acquired a wide range of animal dependants and associates. Indeed, he may have little choice; relatively few nurseries stock native trees. Similarly, amongst the garden shrubs, one is more likely to find an alien dogwood than our own *Swida sanguinea*, and double-flowering varieties of hawthorn *Crataegus* are more in evidence than the typical bushes of the countryside, unless, as has happened in parts of Birmingham, the garden boundary has assimilated the remnants of a rural hedge.

Garden vegetation is usually subject to strict control, and chemicals may be used, not only against unwanted plant invaders, but also against the invertebrate population, most members of which are classified as pests. Fortunately, some gardeners' enthusiasm for tidiness and chemical warfare is counterbalanced by other people's negligence or their concern for conservation. The result is a remarkable diversity of vegetation and a wide spectrum of animal life.

Several woodland birds are well settled garden residents. The robin *Erithacus rubecula*, which shadows the gardener's spade, has in Britain and Ireland an affinity with man unparalleled in most other parts of its European range. Blackbirds occur at a population density of nearly three times that recorded in English woodland, and so greatly outnumber the song thrush *Turdus philomelos*, which was once the commoner urban species. These two, together with the starling and mistle thrush, have benefited from our peculiar love-hate relationship with the ubiquitous lawn. Much of their invertebrate food lives under the mown grass which is an inescapable feature of our parks, gardens and suburban road verges.

The comparatively modern habit of putting out bread, peanuts, suet and seed enables many birds to survive the rigours of winter. In 1970, the British Trust for Ornithology launched a pilot survey to discover which species were exploiting this food supply and which items were most readily taken. The enquiry proved popular, was continued in subsequent years, and yielded much information on the movements of birds and their population fluctuation.

Two of the winter visitors most frequently noted at bird tables, the blue tit *Parus caeruleus* and great tit *P. major*, are less common in town gardens in summer. Those that do stay to breed are only moderately successful; although there are suitable nest sites in walls, pipes, nest boxes, street lamps and bus-stop standards, there is a relative shortage of the woodland moth larvae the adults need for the nestlings.

Bird tables have probably contributed to the recent success of the greenfinch *Carduelis chloris*, now the commonest town finch. Its passion for peanuts is shared by the siskin *C. spinus*, which has been appearing at bird tables since 1962. Other comparative newcomers accepting the bird-feeders' hospitality are the reed bunting *Emberiza schoeniclus* and the occasional wintering blackcap *Sylvia atricapilla*. Mammals also get their share. Hedgehogs *Erinaceus europaeus* venture forth for saucered milk, grey squirrels *Sciurus carolinensis* plunder the bird table, and the red fox *Vulpes vulpes*, a very successful suburban opportunist, not only takes offered scraps, but forages in the dustbin. Raiders of another kind are the doorstep thieves – tits that drink from milk bottles and magpies which have discovered that cartons can contain eggs.

Birds can arouse mixed feelings when they turn to garden plants for nourishment. Berry-bearing shrubs may be deliberately planted for the avian residents, or in the hope that waxwings *Bombycilla garrulus* may visit during one of their invasions from the Continent. The blackbirds invited to gorge themselves on *Pyracantha* berries are less welcome, however, in the strawberry season; the amusing acrobatics of the greenfinch on the nut basket are forgotten when it devours the unripe fruits of *Daphne mezereum*; and the handsome bullfinch *Pyrrhula pyrrhula* ceases to be

The caterpillars of the large white butterfly *(top left)* and those of the other cabbage whites, cause havoc in the vegetable garden and are therefore treated as garden 'pests'. Ladybirds *(top right)*, however, are universally recognized as beneficial because they feed on aphids. They have also enjoyed protection due to their religious association with the Virgin Mary which is reflected in their name. The handsome peacock butterfly *(above)* is just one of many butterflies that are attracted to buddleia, a garden plant which has now become established on urban waste ground.

admired when it strips *Forsythia* of its flowers or deprives the fruit trees of their flower buds.

Most garden birds, however, are now regarded with affection which is more than can be said of garden invertebrates. Butterflies, with the exception of the large white *Pieris brassicae* and the small white *P. rapae*, are amongst the few invertebrates that are welcome, and they may be attracted by planting buddleia *Buddleia davidii* and the pink-flowered succulent *Sedum spectabile*. Honey-bees *Apis mellifera* and bumble-bees *Bombus* are appreciated for their work as pollinators, and the familiar two-spot and seven-spot ladybirds (*Adalia bipunctata* and *Coccinella septempunctata* respectively) are valued for the control they and their larvae exert on the aphid population. The rest have few human friends, and those described in gardening manuals as 'beneficial' are likely to suffer the same harsh fate as those classed as 'harmful'.

More aquatic insects can now establish themselves in suburbia, thanks to the popularity of fibreglass and butyl-sheeted ponds. Those to be expected include water-beetles, backswimmers *Notonecta*, lesser water-boatmen *Corixa* and *Sigara* and, mainly in England, dragonflies and damselflies. The common sympetrum *Sympetrum striolatum* is the dragonfly most likely to occur. It has even bred in Central London, in the parks and in emergency water tanks provided for fire-fighting in the last war. The southern aeshna *Aeshna cyanea* is often attracted to garden ponds. It is a strong flyer and may be seen some distance from water. Like the handsome brown aeshna *A. grandis*, which is common in the Birmingham conurbation, it is occasionally spotted flying over a busy street.

Most dragonfly and damselfly nymphs climb plant stems to escape from the water when they reach the end of the aquatic stage in the life cycle, and dragonflies will perch on emergent plants between their hunting forays and territorial skirmishes. Ponds lacking such vegetation are therefore inhospitable. Ideally, a pond should have emergent and marginal plants, and plants with floating leaves. As examples of the ecological value of the last group, water-lilies *Nymphaea* and *Nuphar* shade out algae, afford safe bathing-places for sparrows, are sites for pond snails' eggs, and provide food for the aquatic larvae of the china mark moths *Nymphula*.

Garden pools are usually intended to hold goldfish *Carassius auratus*, but they have become an important refuge for common frogs *Rana temporaria*, smooth newts *Triturus vulgaris* and – except in Ireland, where they do not occur – common toads *Bufo bufo*. Gardens are now the frog's main stronghold in Britain, for it has suffered a serious decline in the countryside. Goldfish may attract grey herons *Ardea cinerea* and, in the suburbs of Birmingham, kingfishers *Alcedo atthis*. Herons have even raided a fish pond on the roof of a Kensington department store.

Very few town gardens are large enough to enclose a lake, but this is the central feature of London's most celebrated private demesne, the 16-hectare garden of Buckingham Palace. Distinguished ornithologists attending royal garden parties were able to record little grebes *Tachybaptus ruficollis* breeding there until at least 1949, but relatively few other natural history observations were made in this secluded place until 1960. Between 1960 and 1964, Her Majesty graciously permitted a team of scientists and amateur naturalists of the highest calibre to study the garden. About 2000 different kinds of animals and wild and naturalized plants were listed, a few of them new to Britain and many of them unknown or rare elsewhere in Central London.

Lawns take up much of the area and include an almost two-hectare expanse of chamomile *Chamaemelum nobile*, which is carefully cherished. The grass by the lake is left uncut until the end of the ducks' nesting season. The tall herbage not only hides the unfledged ducklings from the predatory carrion crows *Corvus corone corone*, but also provides for moths and other insects which would otherwise have little chance of survival in this very intensively managed estate.

Gardens provide other habitats besides those already described. There are compost heaps, where microfungi and hosts of invertebrates can speed the disintegration of non-woody vegetable waste, and there are sheds, greenhouses, summerhouses, henhouses, pigeon lofts and other buildings which shelter many uninvited guests. Vixens have reared their cubs under garden sheds, and blackbirds, song thrushes, robins and wrens *Troglodytes troglodytes* often nest in them. They are the abode of spiders, particularly *Zygiella x-notata*, which makes an orb web with one section missing, the mouse-coloured *Herpyllus blackwalli* and the house spiders *Tegenaria* which make frightening appearances in the bathroom. Another indoor spider, the long-legged, ceiling-haunting *Pholcus phalangiodes*, is less disturbing, and may be accepted in both outhouse and dining-room as an unobtrusive semi-domesticated flycatcher.

The tropical ants, spiders, woodlice and other exotic invertebrates found living in hothouses at Kew and elsewhere are unlikely to colonize ordinary suburban greenhouses. Garden black ants *Lasius niger* are amongst the more usual invaders. In southern England, *L. niger* is the commonest urban ant. London pavements are sometimes swarming with these insects, and their massive nuptial flights occasionally hold up the traffic.

Artificial lighting lures a great variety of night-flying insects from the garden to the windows of the house. Some of the commonest moths to be attracted are the garden carpet *Xanthorhoë fluctuata*, the small magpie *Eurrhypara hortulata*, the square-spot rustic *Xestia xanthographa*, the heart and dart *Agrotis exclamationis* (mainly in England and Wales), and the large yellow underwing *Noctua pronuba*. Other insects drawn to the light include a yellowish ichneumon wasp, *Ophion luteus*, which parasitizes certain moth larvae; lacewings, the voracious aphid-eaters found mainly in southern England; and the occasional beetle. Londoners are quite likely to encounter the fiercesome-looking stag beetle *Lucanus cervus*.

Invertebrates are not usually popular guests. Householders may grant sanctuary to the hibernating peacock butterfly *Inachis io* and ignore the relatively harmless silverfish *Lepisma saccharina*, but they are well advised to

The collared dove, seen here on one of its favourite song posts, is found in largest numbers where there are easy pickings: in town zoos and waterfowl collections, in back-garden hen runs and at grain wharves.

deal effectively with carpet beetles *Attagenus pellio*, furniture beetles *Anobium punctatum*, powder-post beetles *Lyctus*, larder beetles *Dermestes lardarius* and the several small moths with larvae that attack textiles. One of these, the case-bearing clothes moth *Tinea pellionella*, also breeds in birds' nests, of which there may be several around, on, and even in, the house.

The house martins' nests under the eaves are often commandeered by house sparrows, and both sparrows and blackbirds make extensive use of external piping and creepers on the walls. Creepers are also favoured by the occasional spotted flycatcher *Muscicapa striata*. Starlings and other hole-nesters will take advantage of structural defects, the swift using them to gain access to a roof cavity. The Victorian houses of the inner suburbs seem to suit swifts best, whereas jackdaws *Corvus monedula*, which can make a nuisance of themselves by nesting in chimneys, are more likely to frequent the outer areas.

Jackdaws and starlings are amongst the species which sometimes 'bathe' in chimney smoke. The purpose of this curious behaviour is obscure, but it is accompanied by preening and other movements associated with feather maintenance. The birds may be reacting to the warmth of the smoke, or the effect its weak acid content may have on the skin. Chimney pots and other high points are also used by suburban birds as song posts, the very familiar collared dove *Streptopelia decaocto* often choosing a television aerial. Collared doves began their spectacular conquest of Britain as recently as 1955. Until about 1930 their range in Europe was confined to Turkey and the Balkans, and their spread across the continent since then is one of the most remarkable events in ornithological history. Their colonization of Britain was rapid and that of Ireland dates from 1959. The monotonous voices of these birds are sometimes inadvertently taped by television sound-recordists, and can introduce into costume drama an anachronism worthy of comparison with the clock striking three in Shakespeare's *Julius Caesar*.

Public open spaces
There are some open spaces which have more than a suggestion of wildness in spite of their urban surroundings. They range from the vast stretches of Sutton Park in the West Midlands, with their rich wetland habitats, woodland and heath, to small areas like the wooded half of London's Holland

Longmoor is one of the biologically important wetland habitats in Sutton Park. Together with the surrounding heathland it shows what much of the West Midlands must have looked like before urbanization. Canada geese *Branta canadensis* are now a feature of most of the open spaces in this part of Britain.

Park. They include fine commons like those of Wimbledon and Southampton, and places where steep slopes or rocky outcrops have proved too difficult to subject to the usual park management techniques: the craggier parts of Holyrood Park in Edinburgh, the Avon Gorge side of Clifton Downs in Bristol, and ravine parks like Snuff Mills Park in Bristol or Jesmond Dene in Newcastle upon Tyne. There are also the few parks where enlightened authorities have deliberately encouraged wild vegetation, as in the Linn Park, Glasgow, and part of Wandsworth Common, London. Such open spaces are exceptional. A town park is often nothing more than a green desert, a dull expanse of mown grass with a few standard trees. Some may have formal shrubberies, flower gardens, ponds and lakes, but even with these additional features they can rarely satisfy the naturalist.

Many of our parks are legacies from the last century, created in the belief that townspeople would benefit physically, and even morally, from a closer contact with Nature. They were also intended to make towns more attractive and property more valuable. Joseph Paxton's Birkenhead Park, laid out in the 1840s, was the first of these municipal ornamental parks, designed for gentle relaxation rather than for boisterous games. They were considered of educational value, stimulating the Victorian's growing, but regrettably destructive, interest in the natural world, and they brought together an assemblage of plants not found in any natural ecosystem, mingling trees from North America and the Mediterranean with shrubs from Chile and Japan. The management of such places dictated, and still dictates, the removal of autumnal leaves and fallen wood, regular grass mowing and the clearance of 'weeds'.

The parksmen's preference for alien broadleaved evergreens to native shrubs may actually be advantageous to some garden birds. Blackbirds, house sparrows and greenfinches roost in them. Evergreen clumps suit the communal nesting habits of greenfinches, and the dense foliage hides the early nests of blackbirds and song thrushes from predators. Hedges of garden privet *Ligustrum ovalifolium* seem ideal for nesting dunnocks *Prunella modularis*. The scarcity of native plants, leaf litter and rotting timber, however, means an impoverished invertebrate fauna. This, and the absence of suitable low cover, make these open spaces inhospitable to the warblers which enliven the rural woods and scrubland.

But civic gardens, for all their artficiality and tidiness, are rich in birds when compared with recreation grounds. These bleak grasslands, with their scattered or regimented trees, have few bird residents other than the mistle thrush. As the naturalist W. H. Hudson said of London's Blackheath, they are places where birds 'feed but do not live'. Their importance as feeding grounds should not be underrated, however. In spite of the great amount of human disturbance, especially at weekends, they are frequented by considerable numbers of gulls, pigeons, starlings, thrushes, finches and sparrows. Large clouds of house sparrows can be flushed from urban grassland, in late summer, when country sparrows and those of suburban outskirts are pillaging the cornfields. In Regent's Park, flocks of about 1000 have been noted in September. Migrating wheatears *Oenanthe oenanthe* pass through in spring and autumn, and wintry weather brings flocks of country birds such as linnets *Carduelis cannabina* and skylarks *Alauda arvensis*.

Gulls resort to recreation grounds to rest as well as feed. Black-headed gulls *Larus ridibundus* are the most numerous, but in some places, notably Edinburgh, the common gull *L. canus* is much in evidence. In London, common gulls are particularly attracted to Blackheath and, although occurring mainly between late July and mid-April, migrant birds continue

Black-headed and common gulls at Blackheath, London, early on an August morning. The appearance of these birds in London is no longer related to weather conditions. The black-headed gull is in fact only absent from London during the nesting season.

to appear well into May, and immature birds have been seen even in June. Blackheath's gulls also include the lesser black-backed, which before the 1920s was an irregular visitor to London and rarely recorded anywhere in Britain or Ireland in winter. Its status has altered dramatically; it is now a common wintering bird over much of Britain, and remarkably large flocks pass on migration through London between late July and early November.

In coastal towns, the gulls may be joined by waders. At Swansea, the oystercatchers *Haematopus ostralegus* move into Singleton Park when high water covers their feeding grounds in Swansea Bay, and this species may be seen accompanied by redshanks *Tringa totanus* on playing fields around Edinburgh and at Poole, Dorset.

Park grassland does not accommodate a wide variety of plant species, but those that do occur are undeterred by frequent mowing. The daisy *Bellis perennis* can regenerate from its severed stems and leaves, and side-shoots will grow from mutilated remnants of greater plantain *Plantago major*. Many of the persistent turf plants are colourful, and some of us rejoice to find the greensward enlivened by a violet patch of selfheal *Prunella vulgaris* or a golden spread of bird's-foot trefoil *Lotus corniculatus*. In spring, the recreational greensward may turn purplish-blue if slender speedwell *Veronica filiformis* gains a roothold, as it has on The Stray at Harrogate. This native of Asia Minor and the Caucasus now occurs as a garden escape over much of western and central Europe, and has reached North America.

Park waters
A park lake may be a scenic attraction and an important refuge for water-fowl, or an austere concrete tank, devoid of plants other than algae, and apparently hostile to all the higher forms of animal life. Most park waters fall between these two extremes, and even those providing facilities for boating, swimming, fishing and other activities can attract birds, especially in winter. In spring and summer, however, the recreational lakes can be very inhospitable to wildlife. Fortunately, a compromise is possible. Islands and creeks can be protected by barriers excluding boats, anglers confined to certain parts of the water, and suitable vegetation planted to provide much-needed cover.

Ornamental waters are not as forbidding. They are less disturbed and more likely to have shelving, grassy banks which allow ducklings and flightless duck to leave the water without difficulty, and provide the aquatic

The boating lake in Dartmouth Park, West Bromwich, has the conventional hard shore of most urban-park waters and is made even more unattractive by the accumulation of floating rubbish, including dead bream.

vegetation some animals need. In Birmingham's Cannon Hill Park, the coot *Fulica atra* can escape from the hazards of the boating lake to nest in the reedmace *Typha* in the garden ponds. The small reedbeds in Dorset's Poole Park attract reed warblers *Acrocephalus scirpaceus* and provide nest sites for coot and moorhen *Gallinula chloropus* and shelter for ducks.

Most park waters can accommodate a few mallard and moorhen, but sometimes the only waterfowl seen are farmyard birds: Chinese geese that are descended from the swan goose *Anser cygnoides*, domestic breeds of grey-lag goose *Anser anser*, the grotesque muscovy duck *Cairina moschata* from Central and South America, and Rouen ducks, Aylesbury ducks and other comical caricatures of the wild mallard. Waterfowl of any kind can decoy wild visitors, but, as will be seen later, a collection of pinioned ducks of non-domestic species is more likely to do so.

Birds are introduced to excite public admiration. Fish, on the other hand, are supplied mainly to satisfy the great public interest in angling. Roach *Rutilus rutilus* and perch *Perca fluviatilis* are the species most usually provided, but London's Serpentine has many others, including rudd *Scardinius erythropthalmus*, tench *Tinca tinca*, gudgeon *Gobio gobio*, ruffe *Gymnocephalus cernua*, carp *Cyprinus carpio* and goldfish. There must be few urban ponds and lakes which have not been colonized by the three-spined stickleback *Gasterosteus aculeatus*. It does not need water of the purest quality and may be found in the company of pollution-tolerant invertebrates, for example the wandering snail *Lymnaea peregra* and the waterlouse *Asellus aquaticus*.

The brooks and small rivers that wind their way through Birmingham's suburban parks are now clean enough for water voles *Arvicola terrestris*, breeding kingfishers and grey wagtails *Motacilla cinerea*. With further improvements in water quality even the dipper *Cinclus cinclus* may become a more frequent sight on urban streams, and perhaps return to some of its former nesting localities, like the Ouse Burn in Newcastle's Jesmond Dene. It is a familiar park bird in Inverness and Tavistock and makes appearances in Sheffield's parks, sometimes in the breeding season.

Bird life: observations and speculations

Ornithologists had noted an increase in the variety of bird life even before the effort was made to reduce pollution in towns. This was especially true of London, the urban area which has been most intensively studied. A change in human behaviour is mainly responsible. In the city, life may have become more dangerous for human beings but for birds it is much safer than it was in the last century. Barbarous acts are still committed: nesting swans are still molested by hooligans, but gulls are no longer shot from the Thames bridges, skylarks are no longer sold by the thousand in Leadenhall Market, and bird-nesting is not considered a normal schoolboy pastime.

In many parks and public gardens, birds will feed from the hand. Nuthatches *Sitta europaea* will do so in Kew Gardens, as will great tits, blue tits, coal tits *Parus ater*, robins, chaffinches *Fringilla coelebs*, greenfinches and mistle thrushes in Edinburgh's Royal Botanic Garden. In London, the black-headed gulls not only snatch scraps from people's fingers but, in St James's Park, even take food from the lips of those willing to try this method of feeding birds.

Pinioned waterfowl undoubtedly attract wild birds and encourage them to nest. Smew *Mergus albellus* and goosander *M. merganser* have appeared in Roath Park, Cardiff, where there is a modest wildfowl collection. The pinioned birds in St James's Park have been joined by wild wigeon *Anas penelope*, scaup *Aythya marila* and long-tailed duck *Clangula hyemalis*, and in severe winters the numbers of tufted duck *Aythya fuligula* have risen to 2000. Tufted duck ringed in London have been recovered as far away as Sweden, Finland and the Soviet Union.

The tufted duck has nested in Inner London since 1910. Given encouragement, it is, after the mallard, the duck most likely to become urbanized. In West Park, Wolverhampton, it is more plentiful in winter than in other public parks in the urban West Midlands, and stays to breed, because of the presence of introduced wildfowl – and the bread they receive. The Inner London population of pochard *Aythya ferina*, now scattered over several parks, may have originated with the pairing of pinioned and full-winged birds in St James's Park, and a colony of gadwall *Anas strepera*, which bred for many years at the reservoirs near Hammersmith Bridge, was certainly founded by the fugitive full-winged offspring of pinioned birds in the St James's Park collection.

By excluding boats from certain parts of its lakes, the Department of the Environment has done much to encourage breeding birds in the Royal Parks. In recent years, great crested grebes *Podiceps cristatus* have successfully nested on the Long Water in Kensington Gardens and in Regent's

Boats are excluded from the Long Water in Kensington Gardens, and its banks are fenced off from the public. This seclusion has allowed coot, moorhen, mallard and great crested grebes to nest, and the grey heron has become a frequent visitor.

Park. Herons are also nesting in Regent's Park. This is the only city-centre heronry in Britain, but there is also a small colony of herons within the city boundaries of Belfast.

The birds which are common or tame in one town may be scarce or shy in another. The common gull lives up to its name in Edinburgh, jostling for crumbs with the feral pigeons in the Princes Street Gardens, but in the urban West Midlands it is a comparative rarity. Woodpigeons have long been abundant and tame in London, but were almost unknown in Merseyside parks before the last war. Magpies are common breeding birds in Manchester, Leeds, Sheffield, Birmingham, Belfast and Dublin, but did not nest in Inner London until 1971. The tawny owl *Strix aluco* is resident in British town parks, but absent from Ireland.

It seems likely that other birds will colonize our parks in due course. The serin *Serinus serinus*, which breeds in Parisian parks, has nested in southern England in recent years and could well become established and there is no reason why the fieldfare *Turdus pilaris*, another new addition to the British breeding list, should not move into towns as it has in Norway and Sweden.

Cemeteries and churchyards

Well-tended burial grounds can resemble gardens, but are less disturbed. Their sombre evergreens offer roosting and nesting sites for birds, and their limestone memorials may support an interesting lichen flora, except in localities with high levels of sulphur dioxide pollution. City centres may, therefore, be devoid of lichens, while, in outer suburbia, a greater variety can be expected. In inner suburbs, some species may be confined to the older tombstones; these lichens would have begun life in more rural surroundings and in cleaner air.

The cemeteries and graveyards that are richest in wildlife are those where a tall herb layer encourages a diversity of insects and provides cover for low-nesting birds, hedgehogs and foxes. Black redstarts have nested in London's Brompton Cemetery, grey partridges *Perdix perdix* have been reported from Birmingham's Witton Cemetery, and Glasgow's Cathcart Cemetery sometimes has a fine show of common spotted orchids *Dactylorhiza fuchsii* and flocks of redpolls *Carduelis flammea*.

Walls

Churchyards are often worth examining for the plants growing on their walls. In fact, old town walls of any kind are of interest to the botanist, and detailed studies have been made of the mural flora of Cambridge, Durham, and the old county of Middlesex now physically and politically absorbed by Greater London.

Flowerless plants are well represented although, as has already been mentioned, lichens will only be plentiful where the air is unpolluted; only one species, *Lecanora dispersa*, can survive in Central London. Cool, north-facing wall surfaces suit mosses best, but *Tortula muralis*, *Grimmia pulvinata*, *Bryum argenteum* and *B. capillare* will form cushions along the wall top and withstand the heat of the sun. Ferns, too, fare best on cool, damp surfaces. Some of the typical mural species like wall-rue *Asplenium ruta-muraria* and maidenhair spleenwort *A. trichomanes* are not common in towns, but bracken *Pteridium aquilinum* can usually be found, and male fern *Dryopteris filix-mas* is abundant in London and the Midlands.

The flowering plants include many that are more readily associated with other urban habitats. Some are annuals of purely casual occurence and with no special qualifications for a mural existence. Others, like pellitory-of-the-wall *Parietaria judaica*, are well adapted because they are equally at home

Above In recent years some town cemeteries have become overgrown with wild plants and garden escapes, such as the everlasting pea seen here. This apparent neglect may attract some criticism but the botanical variety and profusion make these places valuable havens for wildlife.

The ubiquitous feral pigeon *(right)*, here perched on a gravestone in Brompton Cemetery, is almost certainly the commonest of urban birds, not only in Britain and Ireland, but over most of the temperate regions. Yet, in the past, it has often been completely ignored by naturalists. The lichens growing on the gravestones *(far right)* benefit from the nitrogenous matter in bird droppings.

on rocks. As might be expected, the wallflower *Cheiranthus cheiri* is one of the garden escapes which have become established. Snapdragon *Antirrhinum majus* and red valerian *Centranthus ruber* are others which are thoroughly naturalized. The plant which has perfected the art of mural living, however, is ivy-leaved toadflax *Cymbalaria muralis,* brought here from the Mediterranean some time before 1640. The fruit-bearing stems turn the fruits away from the light so that they deposit their seeds in cracks and crevices where they will germinate.

Although plants may exploit a wall's structural weaknesses and assist its disintegration, the destructive potential of vegetation is often exaggerated. Not all wall plants are deep rooted and their growth is slow. Many ancient walls have supported plant life for centuries without collapsing, and they often have the plants most worth conserving. The partly Roman walls of Colchester are graced by lesser calamint *Calamintha nepeta,* an East Anglian speciality, and the clove pink *Dianthus caryophyllus* adds botanical interest to the ruins of Rochester Castle.

The abundance of animal life of town walls is related to their condition and their vegetation. Holes provide nest sites for birds, as do the growths of ivy *Hedera helix* where these occur. Second-brood caterpillars of the holly blue butterfly *Celastrina argiolus* feed on the buds, and, on sunny autumn days, the fully developed flowers are alive with hover-flies (especially *Eristalis*), red admirals *Vanessa atalanta* and other late butterflies. In early spring, the ivy berries are ready for the blackbirds and woodpigeons.

The algae on the wall surfaces are rasped away by snails, which leave their radula marks and slime trails as evidence of their nocturnal wanderings. The wall's holes and crevices are occupied by the silken retreats of spiders, commonly those of *Amaurobius similis* and *Segestria senoculata,* and more rarely those of *S. florentina,* an accidental introduction recorded mainly

An urban waste site in southern Ireland *(top)* with hawksbeard in the foreground and the purple-flowered ivy-leaved toadflax on the wall behind.

The marks made by the toothed tongue or radula of a garden snail *(above)* which has grazed on the algae covering a discarded piece of linoleum.

from towns in southwest England, but also from Westminster. *Amaurobius* spins a tangled, lace-like web around the entrance to its tunnel, whereas the entrance to the segestrian parlour is marked by radiating trip wires. The very active and attractive zebra spider *Salticus scenicus*, often seen on sunlit wall surfaces, has no need of snares. It stalks its prey and jumps on it.

A colony of wall lizards *Podarcis muralis* is perhaps the last thing one might expect in a suburb, but these reptiles have been living in crevices in two railway bridges in Greater London for over 20 years. Their origin is not known, but they resemble the colour varieties found in northern Italy, which are regularly imported. The lizards not only frequent the bridges themselves, but the railway banks and adjoining gardens.

Railway banks
Railway cuttings and embankments can be regarded as linear nature reserves. In many towns, they are the last outposts of heathland plants and country flowers like the primrose *Primula vulgaris*. Heather *Calluna vulgaris* survives on railway banks at Sutton Coldfield and Solihull and in the Bournemouth–Poole conurbation, where sheep's-bit *Jasione montana* also flourishes. The common urban railside plants, however, are false oat-grass *Arrhenatherum elatius*, bracken, rosebay willow-herb *Epilobium angustifolium*, and numerous escapes from cultivation, such as buddleia, golden rod *Solidago canadensis* and horse radish *Armoracia rusticana*. Bladder senna *Colutea arborescens* is abundant around London, and lupins *Lupinus polyphyllus* are a feature of Birmingham.

In Britain, the unmown vegetation offers sanctuary to short-tailed voles *Microtus agrestis*, common lizards *Lacerta vivipara* and slow-worms *Anguis fragilis*, and the banks provide well-drained sites for the homes of suburban rabbits *Oryctolagus cuniculus*, badgers *Meles meles* and foxes. Foxes can follow railway tracks well into the built-up zone, and they were no doubt used by Lothian rabbits to reach Princes Street Gardens in Edinburgh. The railway also assisted the dispersal of the Oxford ragwort *Senecio squalidus*, a Sicilian plant now found in urban areas all over England and Wales, though still uncommon in Scotland and Ireland. In Sicily it grows on volcanic ash, but, in the 1790s, having escaped from the Oxford Botanic Garden, it found the city walls a suitable habitat. Later, with the coming of the railways, it colonized the ballast of the trackway, and its pappus-flighted seeds were carried ever further in the slipstream of rushing trains.

Urban waste sites
Oxford ragwort is one of the many flowers that add a touch of colour to the rubble-strewn wastes that are left behind when buildings are demolished. Disturbed ground is soon invaded by plants with wind-borne seeds, like creeping thistle *Cirsium arvense*, coltsfoot *Tussilago farfara*, and various species of willow-herb *Epilobium*. Seeds of elder *Sambucus nigra* arrive in bird droppings, and discarded plum stones and apple cores can give rise to tree seedlings. Hayfield plants became established on bombed sites in London because horse manure was thrown there by street cleaners.

The waste flora is cosmpolitan. Our native species mingle with other aliens besides the Sicilian *Senecio*: Canadian fleabane *Conyza canadensis*, Japanese knotweed *Reynoutria japonica*, Kew weed *Galinsoga parviflora* from Peru, pineapple weed *Matricaria matricarioides* possibly from Asia *via* America, buddleia from China, and many others. Their distribution is interesting. Canadian fleabane, common on bombed sites in London, was absent from those of Birmingham yet found near by at Coventry. Oxford

ragwort only reached Edinburgh in 1954 and was not recorded in Belfast until 1964. Wormwood *Artemisia absinthium*, rampant in the urban West Midlands, occurs in restricted areas in London. In Walsall, in 1946, it was found supporting caterpillars of the wormwood moth *Cucullia absinthii*, hitherto a mainly coastal insect. The wormwood moth is now quite common in the Birmingham area.

Other moth larvae find food on waste sites. Elephant hawk-moths *Deilephila elpenor* lay eggs on willow-herb, cinnabars *Callimorpha jacobaea* on Oxford ragwort and groundsel *Senecio vulgaris*, puss moths *Cerura vinula* on willows *Salix*, and broom moths *Ceramica pisi* on bracken. The flowers are an attraction for butterflies, bees, hover-flies and beetles. Common field grasshoppers *Chorthippus brunneus* inhabit the grassier patches. In London, they were found on the waste sites around St Paul's Cathedral and on the vast derelict expanse at Nine Elms before it was occupied by the New Covent Garden Market. In Birmingham, they live under the Gravelly Hill motorway interchange ('Spaghetti Junction') and on vacant plots even nearer the city centre.

The bricks and other debris that litter the sites provide retreats for other invertebrates: spiders, harvestmen, woodlice, centipedes, beetles, slugs, snails and earthworms. Spiders found in 1970 on the land now occupied by the New Covent Garden Market included *Tegenaria agrestis*, once considered a great rarity. Its close resemblance to the house spiders of the same genus probably led to its being overlooked, for there are now several records for urban waste ground. One specimen was found under Spaghetti Junction in 1975.

The abundance of invertebrates naturally encourages insectivorous birds. Migrant willow warblers *Phylloscopus trochilus*, whitethroats *Sylvia communis*, whinchats *Saxicola rubetra* and wheatears may only loiter to feed before passing on to more suitable breeding habitats, but wagtails will sometimes nest on site. The pied wagtail is the more usual breeding species, but grey wagtails sometimes rear young and, in 1970, yellow wagtails *Motacilla flava flavissima* bred on a vegetated rubbly waste by London's Vauxhall Bridge. In the 1940s and 1950s, the star attraction for ornithologists visiting the bombed areas was the black redstart. London had the largest breeding population (about 30 singing males were reported in 1948,

An urban waste site *(left)* in the West Midlands with the brown fruiting-heads of docks, the grey-green clumps of wormwood, and rosebay willow-herb. The flowers of rosebay willow-herb *(top)* are attractive to honey-bees and its leaves are eaten by the caterpillars of elephant hawk-moths *(above)*.

Right Motorways may transform the urban scene but wildlife can survive the changes. A wide variety of plants and small animals can be found in the shadow of Spaghetti Junction.

but not all of these were mated) and nesting took place in Birmingham and in several towns on the south and east coasts of England. Black redstarts also have a liking for industrial sites, such as power stations and gasworks, and in recent years these have been their principal haunts.

Autumn sees the influx of the seed-eaters. Cleared sites in London have accommodated flocks of linnets, goldfinches *Carduelis carduelis*, which have a particular liking for thistle seeds, greenfinches, chaffinches, bramblings *Fringilla montifringilla* and tree sparrows *Passer montanus*, and similar places in northern towns lying close to the moors are frequented by parties of twite *Carduelis flavirostris*.

Large derelict areas can fascinate the naturalist. The few London ornithologists who had access to the 130-hectare area of Surrey Commercial Docks after their closure to shipping in 1970, recorded a remarkable range of species. Of the nesting birds, the most surprising were reed bunting, red-legged partridge *Alectoris rufa*, lapwing *Vanellus vanellus*, ringed plover *Charadrius hiaticula* and little ringed plover *C. dubius*. Before the dock basins were filled in, their secluded waters were thronged with wintering duck; in January 1971, over 2500 birds of 10 species were observed on one dock.

Disused gravel pits, quarries, collieries and other mineral workings can have similar value as unofficial nature reserves, and they are not without aesthetic appeal once Nature has hidden the scars of industry with vegetation. In South Wales, the English Midlands and the North, these self-restored areas of wilderness, far richer in wildlife than the average municipal park, are often enclosed within the built-up zone. Some, with the minimum of 'improvement', have been accepted as public open space. Such a place in the West Midlands is Walsall's Rough Wood, once excavated for coal and Staffordshire Blue Clay. It now lies in a canal loop between a rubbish tip, a housing estate and a motorway. Its naturally regenerated woodland and scrub, rough grassland and many pools cater for a whole range of aquatic and terrestrial organisms which are less adaptable to the usual urban environment and are therefore normally excluded from it.

Rubbish dumps

Few expanses of industrial wasteland can escape being used as rubbish dumps. Not only do they receive old cars, mattresses, refrigerators and other bulky items from private individuals, but they may also be chosen by the local authority for tipping on a much grander scale. Population growth and urban expansion have resulted in a greatly increased volume of household refuse, the disposal of which demands a vast amount of land. One must accept the argument that covering a derelict colliery site or filling a disused clay pit is preferable to burying good farmland, even if it means the loss of a potentially interesting wildlife habitat or an important geological exposure, but the thoughtless obliteration of heaths, bogs, marshes, saltings and other valuable ecosystems is quite inexcusable. Many fine sites of scientific importance have been overwhelmed by a blanket of urban junk.

Refuse tips are not, of course, without biological interest. Much of the waste is edible and biodegradable, food for a host of organisms and the raw material of life-supporting humus. Even the inedible, inorganic constituents, the metal, rubble, plastic, pottery and glass, can provide shelter for invertebrates, reptiles, toads, rodents and foxes. And there is an abundance of plant life. The vegetation that colonizes the tips includes many of the typical inhabitants of disturbed ground, with a high percentage of aliens and garden escapes. Familiar urban waste-ground 'weeds' appear, roadside plants like hoary cress *Cardaria draba* can be extremely common,

Bury Hill, near Oldbury in the urban West Midlands, where dolerite quarrying has left behind a rugged landscape now colonized by vegetation including rosebay willow-herb, seen here flowering in August. It is frequented by linnets, meadow pipits, skylarks, yellow-hammers and willow warblers, all more usually considered country birds.

and luxuriant growths of fat-hen *Chenopodium album* may spring from freshly deposited loads of soil. Garden rejects may arrive: montbretia *Crocosmia × crocosmiiflora*, the various kinds of *Aster* we call Michaelmas daisies, purple toadflax *Linaria purpurea*, honesty *Lunaria annua*, Californian poppy *Eschscholzia californica* and several species of evening primrose *Oenothera*. Bird-cage sweepings can account for canary grass *Phalaris canariensis*, sunflowers *Helianthus annuus*, Mediterranean knapweed *Centaurea diluta*, and forbidden growths of hemp *Cannabis sativa*.

The range of invertebrate life is too great to receive adequate consideration in a book of this size. The living plants support or shelter many of the flies, beetles, bugs, ants, bees, moths, butterflies, molluscs and arachnids

associated with gardens and waste places, and the rotting organic matter and the soil which should be covering it are habitats for earthworms, potworms, woodlice, springtails, centipedes, mites and other occupants of the garden compost heap. In the interests of public health, putrescible rubbish should not be left uncovered for more than 24 hours, and large quantities should be buried under at least half a metre of soil. Exposed kitchen waste is soon found by flies, most of which will breed; fruit-flies *Drosophila* select the rotting fruit while bluebottles *Calliphora*, greenbottles *Lucilia* and flesh-flies *Sarcophaga carnaria* lay their eggs in carrion.

The heat generated by decaying refuse makes rubbish dumps suitable sites for house crickets, the presence of which can attract insect-hunting bats: noctules *Nyctalus noctula*, serotines *Eptesicus serotinus* and pipistrelles *Pipistrellus pipistrellus* have been recorded feeding at one rural rubbish tip. The more usual vertebrate opportunists are, however, the rats and mice that live both on and in the kitchen waste, the foxes that prey on them, and the scavenging birds. Gulls, starlings, crows *Corvus corone*, rooks, jackdaws and magpies pick over the fresh garbage, re-enacting the part played by the ravens, red kites *Milvus milvus* and domestic pigs that foraged in the gutters and middens of medieval London. Each of the two main refuse tips in Dublin Bay attracts over 5000 herring gulls, and the increased breeding population of this species over the British Isles is partly correlated with the abundance of easily exploitable edible waste at urban tips. This may also be the case with the great black-backed gull *Larus marinus*, once a coastal bird but now a regular visitor to inland rubbish dumps. The lesser black-backed gull is less of a scavenger, and there is no obvious connection between its increasing abundance and the prodigal behaviour of mankind.

Life with man

The importance of urban areas in wildlife conservation is likely to increase as the years go by. The countryside is under pressure. The widespread use of herbicides and insecticides on the farms and in the forests, the ploughing of downland and the so-called reclamation of heaths and wetlands, the extensive planting of exotic conifers, the construction of major roads and

Urban rubbish dumps attract a variety of scavengers of which the birds are perhaps the most obvious. Gulls, especially herring gulls, have become a feature of rubbish tips everywhere, inland as well as near the coast. Less noticeable are the vast numbers of insects which breed in the organic waste. Rats also breed in tips but are rarely seen by day, since they emerge at night to feed.

airfields, the insatiable demands of industry and tourism and the resultant pollution and disturbance are making changes even more sweeping than those caused by the Inclosure Acts, the Industrial Revolution and the growth of the towns in the last two centuries. Faced with the prospect of a greater number of built-up areas and less wilderness, it is perhaps reassuring to know that wildlife can find its place in this highly artificial setting, just as it became reconciled to other man-made environments in the past. We must recognize the fact that most of the surface of the British Isles has been modified considerably by human activities.

Just as man made the town, so is he largely responsible for what lives there with him. The uninvited pests and parasites that plagued our urban forebears are still with us to a greater or lesser degree, and new waves of destructive invaders have, through widening trade links, gained access to our food stores and household goods, some taking advantage of our central heating. The warmth escaping from our buildings and reflected from their surfaces may be one of the attractions for town-roosting starlings.

A cosmopolitan assortment of weeds and a host of associated animals have exploited the ground laid bare by our works of construction and demolition. Woodland and hedgerow birds have moved into our gardens, and avian cliff-dwellers have taken to our buildings. The more adaptable birds have not only colonized substitute habitats, but have also learned to accept as palatable such varied food items as bread, imported peanuts and bottled milk, having come to terms, therefore, with the rigours of the urban environment by changing their habits. Some of the invertebrates have demonstrated another kind of adaptation; industrial melanism is an evolutionary response to atmospheric pollution.

We do not yet fully understand why some species have proved more adaptable than others. Where artefacts resemble natural features it seems reasonable to expect the plants and animals of the latter to colonize their man-made equivalents, and yet some species, for which conditions would seem to be favourable, have only been moderately successful. The spread to artificial habitats probably occurs when the numbers of a species reach a peak, and individuals are forced to seek new living space. Many pioneers may perish in trying to extend their range, but some individuals will survive and found a permanent population.

The success of many living things is largely dependent on human tolerance and sympathy. Without encouragement, few of the vertebrates, other than the ineradicable rats and mice, would have become resident. An interest in nature was becoming a cult amongst the well-to-do by the beginning of the nineteenth century, and was to gather momentum as the century progressed, with the creation of botanical gardens, arboreta and collections of zoological specimens, both live and dead. The legacy of this movement is a mixed blessing. Some of the alien plants we now regard as noxious weeds, such as the large bindweed *Calystegia sylvatica*, giant hogweed *Heracleum mantegazzianum* and Japanese knotweed, were originally intended to be cherished by gardeners. The release of the North American grey squirrel was another unfortunate mistake. On the other hand, many of our existing urban open spaces were created or saved from the developers during this period, and waterfowl collections were established, with the happy result that visiting wild ducks were encouraged to settle in towns. It was only towards the end of Queen Victoria's reign, however, that even a tiny minority of the human inhabitants of these islands began to show any true respect for life on this planet or concern for its future. Even the celebrated Mrs Beeton could offer recipes for roast thrush and blackbird pie without causing offence.

Left One of the newly formed pools on the Priory Wood Nature Trail in the Sandwell Valley, West Midlands. Much of the Sandwell Valley is old colliery wasteland now being transformed into a vast, recreational area. But the needs of wildlife are being considered. The new pools have 'natural' banks, marginal vegetation and islands and are frequented by frogs, toads, little grebes, great crested grebes and tufted duck.

Tower Bridge *(below left)* as seen through a screen of reedmace in the William Curtis Ecological Park, a skilfully and inexpensively created wildlife oasis in an urban desert.

Restoration work on more formal lines is the landscaped garden by the church of St Dunstan in the East near the Tower of London *(below right)*. It won a landscape heritage award in 1975.

Our own century has seen the development of more sympathetic attitudes, especially over the past 40 years. People now feed wild birds rather than *on* wild birds. They make ponds in their gardens and put up nest boxes. If they want to go further they will join the Royal Society for the Protection of Birds, the local natural history society or their county trust for nature conservation. And there are evening lectures, conferences, radio and television programmes, and a spate of books to foster their interest.

Coupled with this movement is the growing public concern for the health and appearance of our surroundings. This is influencing the world of education and is beginning to impress its importance on the planners who shape and manage our towns. Determined efforts have been made to improve the quality of the air we breathe and the water in our streams and rivers. The reappearance of over 90 species of fish in the tidal Thames is one of the spectacular success stories of the century. Less than 25 years ago, the river between Kew and Gravesend was virtually lifeless.

The place of nature in cities is now publicly discussed by ecologists, landscape architects, parks' administrators, government officials and teachers, and great interest has been shown in developments in the Netherlands, where urban open space has been informally planted with native vegetation instead of the usual alien species. A proposal has been made to apply these methods to transform the bleaker parts of Liverpool.

This type of landscape renewal has already been carried out on a grand scale on much of our industrial wasteland, and is bound to increase the wildlife diversity of industrialized conurbations like Stoke on Trent, the Black Country, Teesside and Greater Manchester. Left to themselves, some types of devastation take decades to heal over, and the 'instant' establishment of tree and shrub cover, 'biotype planting' as it is called, can do much to speed up the process. The work is not without its problems. In some localities, like the Lower Swansea Valley, the soil is grossly polluted with mineral waste that is highly toxic to plant life. Vandalism is also a problem, but this has sometimes been defeated by mass planting or by encouraging local schools to become actively involved in the maintenance of the plantations.

In the educational field, much is being done to draw the town-dweller's attention to our living heritage with the help of nature trails, walkways (sometimes along disused railway tracks), and specially created wildlife habitats. Two events deserve particular mention. In 1975, the Birmingham Nature Centre was opened; there, visitors could see some of our native plants and animals and absorb some of the principles of ecology and conservation. The second event was the birth, in 1977, of the Ecological Parks Trust, which has skilfully converted a waste-ground lorry park into the William Curtis Ecological Park. Here, London schoolchildren can study a range of wild plant communities that includes mixed woodland, meadow, a sand dune, and a pool with dragonflies and sticklebacks – all within a few metres of Tower Bridge.

Plants

The vegetation of a built-up area is quite unlike that of the surrounding countryside. Throughout history, town-building has meant the destruction of woods, heaths, downland, farmland and wetland, each of which has its characteristic plants. Although a few rural fragments may remain encapsulated in the urban matrix – a wild common, a rocky crag, a hawthorn hedge or a few aged trees – the original flora is generally replaced by the cultivated, and mainly alien, plants of parks and gardens, and the similarly cosmopolitan, but less ordered, assemblage of what are usually regarded as 'weeds'.

Many of these so-called weeds are annuals, quick to colonize any disturbed ground, whether it be flower bed, building plot, demolition site, mineral working, rubbish tip or railway track. Some are true natives, originally confined to such natural features as landslips, shingle banks, sand dunes and glacial moraines. Others are invaders; the first waves arrived with the Neolithic tribes, who tilled the soil and created a new broken-ground habitat to be exploited. New settlers brought more species from Europe, and as the centuries passed, travellers and traders transported many others from across the world, some arriving as cargo, others as stowaways. Foreign trees, shrubs and herbaceous plants were introduced for deliberate cultivation, and thus we may now find five or six continents botanically represented in one urban park. Some plants, like the Japanese knotweed and the large bindweed, were intended for the garden, but fell from grace and found new lodgings in the less respectable parts of town.

Built-up areas also provide habitats for most of the groups of flowerless plants – ferns, horsetails, mosses, liverworts, fungi, lichens, slime-moulds and algae. Lichens are sensitive to sulphur dioxide pollution, however, and the presence or absence of the various species can be used to assess the quality of the urban atmosphere.

1

1 Pellitory-of-the-wall *Parietaria judaica*, elder *Sambucus nigra* and false oat-grass *Arrhenatherum elatius* growing round an untended tomb.

2

2 Red valerian *Centranthus ruber*, a native of Central Europe and the Mediterranean countries, was introduced into Britain before 1636. It is now widespread on town walls and railway cuttings, mainly in the south.

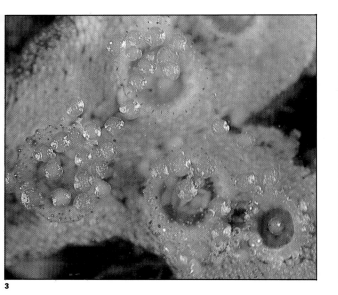

3

4

3 This large liverwort *Marchantia polymorpha* is best known as a 'weed' in greenhouses where it infests the soil of flower pots. It reproduces asexually by budding off gemmae which are dispersed by rainwater.

4 Scentless mayweed *Tripleurospermum maritimum* is a native plant of disturbed ground and arable fields, as well as urban waste sites. The silver thread moss *Bryum argenteum*, also seen here, can be found in the cracks between city paving stones.

5

5 Oxford ragwort *Senecio squalidus,* a native of Sicily, was introduced around 1690 and became established on the walls of Oxford in 1794. The coming of the railway helped it spread across Britain.

6 Wall rocket *Diplotaxis tenuifolia* is a doubt-fully native plant of walls and waste places, mainly in southern Britain. Here it is established in Barry Dock, South Wales.

7 The fruiting body of the fungus *Serpula lacrymans* infests wet timber and creates the condition paradoxically known as dry rot.

6

7

Invertebrates

Invertebrates account for 95 per cent of the animal kingdom and the built-up environment of towns and their suburbs is varied enough to accommodate a wide range of invertebrate life. Most of the major groups are represented: insects of many natural orders, arachnids (spiders, harvestmen, ticks, mites and false scorpions), centipedes, millipedes, land and freshwater molluscs, segmented worms (including earthworms and leeches), flatworms and protozoa.

To many town dwellers, the most familiar invertebrates are those living in the garden, many of which are regarded as pests by the horticulturist. Pests are an inevitable consequence of intensive management, for gardeners perpetuate a state of ecological instability, a chaotic world in which predator-prey relationships have little time to get established. Some harmful species are certain to proliferate in the absence of an effective biological control, especially when provided with an abundant well cared for food supply.

Few of the insect groups get blanket approval. Even amongst the butterflies, which are deliberately encouraged by planting buddleia, there are the unacceptable cabbage whites, and the welcome given to bees is never extended to their relatives, the wasps, ants and sawflies. Ladybirds are popular, but most other beetles are guilty of damaging garden plants, stored products, woodwork and household goods. Other kinds of invertebrates also get little sympathy: all slugs and snails are condemned, although only a few cause actual damage to cultivated plants, and lawn fanatics hate to see worm-casts scattered over their pampered turf.

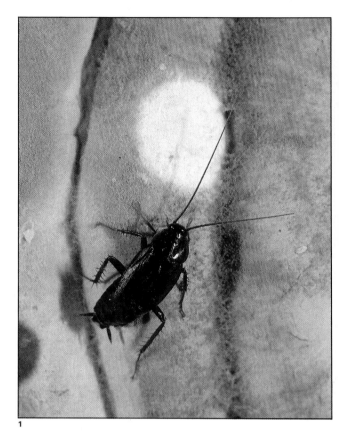

1

1 The common cockroach *Blatta orientalis* was introduced to Britain in the sixteenth century. Here it is seen feeding on mouldy bread. It is mainly a scavenger but can also cause damage to paper and fabrics, as well as to foodstuffs.

2

2 Wasps are not popular insects but they can perform a useful function as predators on harmful insects, and are also scavengers. These common wasps *Vespula vulgaris* are disposing of the corpse of a young bird which has fallen from its nest.

3

3 The garden snail *Helix aspersa* is all too common in southern gardens but is quite scarce in Scotland, in northern England and in the Midlands. Like the Roman snail *H. pomatia* it is edible, and is sometimes substituted for that species in city restaurants.

4

4 The large and rather frightening house spiders *Tegenaria* are usually found indoors. They all look fairly similar. This species *T. parietina* is one of the less common members of the genus. It has not been recorded in Wales or Scotland.

5

6

5 The death-watch beetle *Xestobium rufovillosum* may not be considered a typically urban insect, but it has caused great havoc to roof timbers in ancient city buildings, notably Westminster Hall and the cathedrals of Lincoln and Salisbury.

6 Flour beetles *Tribolium confusum* live in flour and cereals both in warehouses and in homes. A female beetle can make her way into a tightly closed packet of food and then lay several hundred eggs. But fortunately these beetles will not breed in temperatures below 18°C. Adults, pupae and larvae can be seen here.

Birds

Some birds have lived with man for centuries: house sparrows were raiding man's cereal crops before ever towns were built and the street pigeon's association with man also began in antiquity. The street pigeons are descended from rock doves, domesticated since the days of classical Greece, and perhaps from well before that in the Middle East.

Other birds have only taken to town life more recently, their successful colonization always being dependent upon whether man would allow them to co-exist with him. Medieval town dwellers accepted the presence of ravens and kites for their value as scavengers, but many of the birds we see living in our towns today were more likely to be found in the larder. Wild birds were an important food source until quite recently; in the mid-nineteenth century about 215,000 skylarks were sold annually in London's Leadenhall Market, and many species appear in Victorian cookery books. During the Victorian era there was also a great demand for caged song-birds, especially goldfinches, and birds were killed wholesale to keep the milliners supplied with plumes and severed wings. Gulls were slaughtered for 'sport', starlings and pigeons were used for trap-shooting, and all species were prey to the naturalists, who were hell-bent on filling their specimen cabinets.

Contrast this picture with that of today. Not only is there protective legislation, but a genuine change of attitude towards wildlife in general, and birds in particular. Birds are fed in parks and gardens; they may even take food from our fingers. Many species have learned to accept food items they would never meet in the wild, bread being the obvious example. Some have also modified their nesting habits. They may use a man-made site which resembles a natural feature, a building instead of a cliff for instance, or they may adopt one of a quite different type, as when a mallard nests on a rooftop or a woodpigeon builds on a fire-escape landing.

1

2

3

1 A cock house sparrow *Passer domesticus* feeding from the hand in St James's Park, London. The habit is not a general one. Town birds are not always so trusting.

2 The pied wagtail *Motacilla alba* is found nesting in most built-up areas, and large numbers from a wide radius may come into town to roost.

3 The starling *Sturnus vulgaris* is a very successful opportunist always ready to exploit any available food source whether it be a lawn infested with leather jackets, a garden bird table or offal on a rubbish tip.

5 A magpie *Pica pica* picking up a piece of bread in Greenwich Park in September, 1980. Although long established in many British and Irish towns, this bird has only advanced towards the centre of London over the past decade. It now breeds in several London parks but is still far from common.

4 Feral pigeons *Columba livia* seem more at home on buildings which resemble the cliffs inhabited by their rock dove ancestors, but they do also perch in trees. These birds are in a plane tree in Trafalgar Square, London.

6 A pair of mallard *Anas platyrhynchos* on a garden pond among the leaves of parrot's feather *Myriophyllum proserpinacoides*. Although the mallard is our commonest urban duck, it is absent from park lakes in some northern towns.

Further reading

General

Berry, R. J., and Johnston, J. L. *The Natural History of Shetland*. London 1980

Brightman, F. H., and Nicholson, B. E. *The Oxford Book of Flowerless Plants*. London 1966

Chinery, M. *A Field Guide to the Insects of Britain and Europe*, new edn. London 1974

Corbet, G. B., and Southern, H. N. (eds) *The Handbook of British Mammals*, 2nd edn. Oxford 1977

Darling, F. F., and Boyd, J. M. *The Highlands and Islands*, new edn. London 1969

Haughton, J. P., and Gillmor, D. A. *The Geography of Ireland*, Dept of Foreign Affairs, Dublin 1980

Lange, M., and Hora, F. B. *Guide to Mushrooms and Toadstools*. London 1972

Lousley, J. E. *Wild Flowers of Chalk and Limestone*. London 1950

Martin, W. Keble *The Concise British Flora in Colour*, 2nd rev. edn. London 1969 (paperback 1972, 1979)

Mitchell, A. *A Field Guide to the Trees of Britain and Northern Europe*, 2nd rev. edn. London 1978

O'Gorman, F. (ed.) *The Irish Wildlife Book*. Dublin 1979

Pennington, W. *A History of British Vegetation*, 2nd rev. edn. London 1974

Perring, F. H., and Walters, M. (eds) *Atlas of the British Flora*, new edn. Wakefield 1978

Peterson, R. T., et al. *A Field Guide to the Birds of Britain and Europe*. London 1979

Praeger, R. L. *The Botanist in Ireland*. Dublin 1934

Praeger, R. L. *Natural History of Ireland: A Sketch of its Fauna and Flora*. London 1950

Ratcliffe, D. A. (ed.) *A Nature Conservation Review*. Cambridge 1977

Sharrock, J. T. R. (ed.) *The Atlas of Breeding Birds in Britain and Ireland*. Tring 1976

Tansley, A. G. *Britain's Green Mantle*, 2nd edn, rev. M. C. F. Proctor. London 1968

Tansley, A. G. *The British Islands and Their Vegetation*, 2 vols. Cambridge 1939

Trueman, A. E. *Geology and Scenery in England and Wales*. Harmondsworth 1972

Whittow, J. B. *Geology and Scenery in Ireland*. Harmondsworth 1974

Whittow, J. B. *Geology and Scenery in Scotland*. London 1977

Coastlands and islands

Barnes, R. *Coasts and Estuaries*, ed. J. Ferguson-Lees and B. Campbell. London 1979

Barrett, J. H., and Yonge, C. M. *Pocket Guide to the Seashore*, new edn. London 1980

Cramp, S., Bourne, W. R. P., and Saunders, D. *The Sea Birds of Britain and Ireland*, 2nd rev. edn. London 1975

Dickinson, C. I. *British Seaweeds*. London 1963

Hepburn, I. *Flowers of the Coast*. London 1952

Lewis, J. R. *The Ecology of Rocky Shores*, new edn. London 1976

McMillan, N. F. *British Shells*. London 1968

Steers, J. A. *The Sea Coast*. London 1972

Wheeler, A., and Heaume, V. du *The Fishes of the British Isles and North-West Europe*. London 1969

Yonge, C. M. *The Seashore*. London 1976

Freshwater wetlands

Macan, T. T. *Freshwater Ecology*, 2nd rev. edn. London 1974

Macan, T. T., and Worthington, E. B. *Life in Lakes and Rivers*. London 1951 (paperback 1972)

Mellanby, H. *Animal Life in Fresh Water*, 6th edn. London 1963 (paperback 1975)

Whitton, B. *Rivers, Lakes and Marshes*, ed. J. Ferguson-Lees and B. Campbell. London 1979

Lowland grasslands and heaths

Duffey, E. *Grassland Life*. London 1975

Duffey, E., and Watt, A. S. (eds) *The Scientific Management of Animal and Plant Communities for Conservation*. Oxford 1972

Duffey, E., et al. *Grassland Ecology and Wild Life Management*. London 1974

Gimingham, C. H. *Ecology of Heathlands*, new edn. London 1976

Sheail, J. *Rabbits and Their History*. Newton Abbot 1971

Smith, C. J. *Ecology of the English Chalk*. London 1980

Uplands

Condry, W. M. *The Snowdonia National Park*. London 1966 (paperback 1970)

Edwards, K. C. *The Peak District*. London 1970

Harvey, L. A., and St Leger-Gordon, D. *Dartmoor*, new edn. London 1974

Pearsall, W. H. *Mountains and Moorlands*, ed. W. Pennington; rev. edn. London 1972

Pearsall, W. H., and Pennington, W. *The Lake District*, new edn. London 1974

Price, R. J. *Highland Landforms*. Inverness 1976

Walters, M., and Raven, J. *Mountain Flowers*. London 1956

Woodlands and hedgerows

Condry, W. M. *Woodlands*. London 1974

Neal, E. G. *Woodland Ecology*, 2nd edn. London 1958

Pollard, E., Hooper, M., and Moore, N. W. *Hedges*. London 1974

Simms, E. *Woodland Birds*. London 1971

Steele, R. C. *Wildlife Conservation in Woodlands* (HMSO). London 1972

Steele, R. C., and Welch, R. C. (eds) *Monks Wood: A Nature Reserve Record*. Abbots Ripton 1973

Steven, H. M., and Carlisle, A. C. *The Native Pinewoods of Scotland*. Edinburgh 1959

Yapp, W. B. *Birds and Woods*. London 1962

Towns and suburbs

Chinery, M. *The Natural History of the Garden*. London 1977 (paperback 1978)

Darlington, A. *Ecology of Refuse Tips*. London 1970

Fitter, R. S. C. *London's Natural History*. London 1946

Laurie, I. C. (ed.) *Nature in Cities: The Natural Environment in the Design and Development of Urban Green Space*. Chichester 1979

London Natural History Society *The Birds of the London Area*, rev. edn. London 1964

Mabey, R. *Street Flowers*. Harmondsworth 1976

Mourier, H., and Winding, O. *Guide to Wild Life in House and Home*. London 1977

Murton, R. K. *Man and Birds*. London 1971

Owen, D. *Towns and Gardens*, ed. J. Ferguson-Lees and B. Campbell. London 1978

Salisbury, E. *Weeds and Aliens*. London 1961

Simms, E. *Birds of Town and Suburb*. London 1975

Wheeler, A. *The Tidal Thames: History of a River and its Fishes*. London 1979

Index

252 INDEX